FYODOR DOSTOEVSKY

FYODOR DOSTOEVSKY

By

J. A. T. LLOYD

NEW YORK
COOPER SQUARE PUBLISHERS, INC.
1971

891.73
D724X
L793

135895

Originally Published and Copyright © 1947 by
Charles Scribner's Sons
Reprinted by Permission of Charles Scribner's Sons
Published 1971 by Cooper Square Publishers, Inc.
59 Fourth Avenue, New York, N. Y. 10003
International Standard Book No. 0-8154-0401-8
Library of Congress Catalog Card No. 78-164532

Printed in the United States of America, by
Noble Offset Printers, Inc. New York, N.Y. 10003

CONTENTS

Chapter		Page
I.	THE BACKGROUND	1
II.	EARLY TRIUMPH	23
III.	THE FIRING-SQUAD	45
IV.	A CURIOUS INTERLUDE	62
V.	CATASTROPHE AGAIN	81
VI.	RODION RASKOLNIKOV	99
VII.	A SIGNIFICANT INTERRUPTION	120
VIII.	THE HONEYMOON	135
IX.	ESCAPE	149
X.	BACK TO DRESDEN	170
XI.	THE DARK LEGEND	185
XII.	HOME LIFE IN RUSSIA	209
XIII.	THE INHERITANCE	227
XIV.	THE RAW YOUTH	246
XV.	GREAT SINNERS	263
XVI.	APOTHEOSIS	291
	CHRONOLOGY	313
	HIS WORKS	315
	AUTHOR'S NOTE	316
	INDEX	319

"Humble thyself, thou man of pride! Set thy hand to labour, thou man of leisure."

From the PUSHKIN SPEECH.

FYODOR DOSTOEVSKY

Chapter I

THE BACKGROUND

NAPOLEON, in 1812, was not the only Western enquirer as to the actual significance of Russia. Nor was Kutuzov without a Western ally with whom, doubtless, he was but little concerned. I refer to that determined and by no means disdained opponent of the French Emperor, Necker's illustrious daughter. Like Tacitus before her, Mme de Staël had undertaken the apparently simple task of unfolding the endlessly dissimulating Germania. Russia was, admittedly, different. But the author of *Corinne* realised that in spite of the desolation, the backwardness, the static stagnation, there was something formidably dynamic already brooding in that vast silence through which the Grande Armée itself aroused but a fugitive echo. There was neither a Goethe nor a Schiller to amplify the voice of Russia. None the less, the Frenchwoman divined that some day this dark brooding of the Russians would find expression "in what is most intimate and real in their own souls."

Gogol, who was a child of three in 1812, might have rejoiced the heart of Mme de Staël had she lived to peruse his early work. But assuredly she would have been disconcerted a little later. The bitter humorist of *Revisor,* the fashioner of that turbulent Slav Iliad *Tarass Bulba,* might have been expected to be inevitably picaresque after the manner of Lesage in such an odyssey as *Dead Souls.* Gogal was nothing of the kind. The founder of the Russian novel, in short, did not and could not fit in with any approved Western scheme of literature. Yet he believed himself to be a realist and nothing more. "Don't blame the mirror, if your mouth is crooked," is the Russian proverb attached to *Revisor*. His conscious aim in *Dead Souls* was "to drag into life all that was bad in Russia," and on the surface he succeeded only too poignantly. The poet Pushkin after reading the book exclaimed: "Heavens, what a dreary place our Russia is!"

And yet again and again in this very book that strange mysticism, incarnate in the old Byzantine dreams of the national destiny, vibrates through the bitter living satire. Its author could never have been "placed" in any well-documented catalogue by the author of *Corinne* any more than the foremost of his illustrious followers. There were several between the birth of Gogol in 1809 and the birth of Tolstoy in 1828: Turgenev, born in 1818; Nekrassov, like Dostoevsky himself, born in 1821; Grigorovitch, born in 1822; and Ostrovsky, born in 1823. Of these, however, the real heirs of Gogol are undoubtedly Turgenev, Dostoevsky and Tolstoy.

Turgenev might well have appealed to the Frenchwoman at first as a civilised being speaking to her in the language of her own civilisation. Did he not, in his love for that civilisation, accept even the croupier as its lowest symbol? But Mme de Staël would quickly have divined a certain innate antagonism in the author of *Smoke*. For Turgenev shied at the merciless crystallisation of Western judgments, at the finality of verdicts without any afterthought of appeal. Tolstoy, the pagan who wished to become more Christian than the Christians, would still more have baffled Mme de Staël by his sometimes despairing duality. For, in spite of being Necker's daughter, Mme de Staël had the undiluted French tradition in her blood, the tradition that was to pass unchanged in its dominance of will-power from the "Ou laissez-moi péris, ou laissez-moi régner" of Corneille to the joyous challenge of Balzac—"A nous deux maintenant."

But the Russian novelist who would have perturbed the French investigator is beyond question Fyodor Dostoevsky. The author of *Corinne,* mindful of her own proud hero, would have viewed that extraordinary gallery of will-less flotsam, from Raskolnikov to Dmitri Karamazov, with something akin to horror. And how would she, who had lived herself into *Corinne,* have accepted that perhaps even more extraordinary gallery of women that extends from Sonya to Nastasya? What had Corinne in common with those young women, half strangled by passion and half consumed by self-sacrifice? How can the colours of such heroes and heroines ever be adjusted to the Western spectroscope? The duality which is so evident in all the great Russian writers of the nineteenth century was intensified in Dostoevsky to a point that was maladive. The author of *The Double* was all his life, almost literally, two separate and even antagonistic people to whom *odi et amo* was the merest commonplace of human thought.

Yet the outer simplicity of Dostoevsky was no mask. He was perfectly sincere when he said in a letter to his second wife that his small son, unlike his daughter, resembled himself in his simple-heartedness. The glaring contradictions that run through his long correspondence are the result of changes of mood but not of mendacity. Though many have judged him harshly, he seems to have been, from the very beginning to the very end, his own harshest judge.

In the days that pass no stigma is attached to lowness of birth. It is, indeed, a distinction rather than the reverse. Incidentally, it is almost the only distinction that many writers bestow liberally on the novelist's family. Even that just and sympathetic biographer, E. Soloviev, stresses too heavily the plebeianism of the great novelist who, in reality, did not belong in any actual sense to the proletariat. He was, on the authority of his daughter, Mlle Aimée Dostoevsky, a descendant of Lithuanian nobles, and shortly after the birth of his elder sons his father had himself registered together with them in the book of the hereditary nobility of Moscow: "As a Moscovite noble my grandfather remained morally a Lithuanian *Schliahtitch*—proud, ambitious, and very European in many of his ideas." The following note by Anna Grigorievna, Dostoevsky's second wife, endorses this information: "F. M. was deprived of the status of the nobility in 1849 as a State criminal and was condemned to penal servitude for the Petrachevsky affair. After his exile he was reinstated to the right to hereditary nobility in 1858. In the archives of the Moscow Deputies' Council there is a separate ledger of documents relating to the question of Dostoevsky's exclusion from the register of the Moscow nobility."

Poverty, on the other hand, is, admittedly, a real stigma, and of this the novelist's family has never been acquitted. His father, the Army surgeon Mikhail Andreivitch Dostoevsky, had a post on the staff of the hospital of St. Mary in Moscow. Here, on October 21st, 1821, Fyodor Mikhailovitch was born, the second son of a large family. His mother was the daughter of a Moscow merchant named Netchaiev. The children worshipped this "pretty, gentle creature, devoted to her family, and absolutely submissive to her husband." Mlle Dostoevsky regards her grandmother as belonging to the Ukrainian type and thinks that her mother may have been from the Ukraine. All four boys resembled their father, who was a very strict disciplinarian.

The family occupied a small official flat in the hospital. The novelist's childhood was spent in the ruthlessly cramped conditions of the intellectual struglers of those days. It was the essentially city life that has been, too exclusively perhaps, associated with Dostoevsky's work: "our life flowed on in a narrow, regularly defined, monotonous channel. We rose at six o'clock, and at eight my father departed to his surgery, thence, at nine, to proceed upon his round of visits. While he was gone (that is to say, until noon) we children did our lessons, and then had dinner. At four o'clock came tea, and the evening was spent in the parlour, where we read either Karamzin's 'History' or Zhukovsky's poetry—on rarer occasions Pushkin's works."

There is nothing in these snatches of memory to suggest the tragedy in the background of that harsh, but seemingly tranquil jog-trot. But the doctor was a dipsomaniac, a violent man and exceedingly suspicious: "As long as his wife was there to intervene between him and the children all was well; she had considerable influence over him, and prevented him from drinking to excess. After her death my grandfather gave way to his weakness, became incapable of working, and resigned his appointment." The doctor was extraordinarily strict in family life: "My grandfather never allowed his pretty daughters to go out alone, and accompanied them himself on the rare occasions when they went to visit their country neighbours. The jealous vigilance of their father offended the delicacy of my aunts. Later they remembered with horror how their father used to visit their bedroom at night to make sure that they had not hidden some lover under the bed. My aunts at this time were pure and innocent children."

In addition to all this, the doctor was as niggardly as old Grandet. His meanness was all the more inexcusable because he was the owner of land and was well able to provide dowries for his daughters. The friction between father and children naturally became accentuated, but it did not last very long: "My grandfather had always been very severe to his serfs. His drunkenness made him so savage, that they finally murdered him. One summer day he left his estate Darovoye to visit his other property, Tchermashnia, and never returned." He was found some little time later smothered under the cushions of his own carriage. The coachman had fled with the horses, and many of the peasants had bolted. During the proceedings that followed, other serfs, when interrogated by the Court, admitted that the crime was one of revenge. It was a tradition among the family that the future novelist had his first epileptic fit on learning of his father's murder.

But, thanks to their mother, the children seem to have escaped scenes of violence. It was she who taught them their letters. Visiting tutors came to the flat, for, in spite of his parsimony, their father saw to it that his children should be well educated. He himself taught the two elder boys Latin. These lessons would last for an hour or more: "We brothers dared not sit down, nor rest our elbows upon the table, but stood like statues as, turn and turn about, we conjugated and declined. These lessons (the appointed time for which was the evening) we greatly dreaded, for the reason that, in spite of his goodness of heart, our father was extremely exacting and impatient, and, above all things, hasty of temper. Even the smallest mistake on our part would cause him to start railing at us."

This discipline was maintained until the boys reached the age of sixteen or seventeen; they were kept mercilessly without pocketmoney. But there was one phase of mitigation in the hard childhood of Dostoevsky. When he was nine years old his father acquired a small property in the district of Tula, and here the mother would establish herself with her children during the summer months. Soloviev has also stressed rather too heavily the inevitable tentacles of city life over the great writer. Yet, in his own biography, he cites several records showing how the little Fyodor revelled in the open fields.

"At our country house," records Andrei Mikhailovitch Dostoevsky, "we were almost constantly in the open air; and except when at play, we would spend the whole day in watching and superintending the labours of the field. All the peasantry liked us, but especially so our brother Fyodor, whose lively disposition would lead him to bear a hand in everything—to ask to be allowed to lead the horses when harrowing, and to drive them when ploughing. Also he loved entering into conversation with the peasants, who would speak to him freely whenever he did so. But his greatest delight of all was to be entrusted with some task which enabled him to make himself useful. For instance, one day a peasant woman, when going out to reap with her baby, happened to upset her *zhbantchik* (wooden can) of water, so that the poor infant would have nothing to drink. Upon that my brother caught up the *zhbantchik*, ran to the house, and brought thence a fresh canful of water." Although he played the inevitable "Indians" with his brothers, the child Dostoevsky preferred mixing with the peasants, hunting for mushrooms in the woods and getting as close to Nature as he could. "That little insignificant spot," he observed of his country home years afterwards, "bequeathed to me a strong and a profound impression which will abide with me to the end of my life. Everything connected with the place has for me the dearest of recollections."

In his memories of Siberia he recalls his delight in visualising those rural scenes of his boyhood and tells us how he loathed returning to Moscow from the country. He recalls, too, that curious hallucination of his childhood when he thought that he saw a wolf in an open field and scampered off to warn a peasant named Marei of the fact. "On hearing my cry, he had stopped his horse; and when, rushing up to him, I seized the shaft of his plough with one hand and the sleeve of his blouse with the other, he stared at me in alarm. 'There goes a wolf!' I repeated, panting and trembling all over as I clung (probably white in the face) to his smock; whereupon, with an uneasy smile, and a shake of his head which clearly bespoke concern and anxiety on my account, he looked at me and said: 'Go along, you, for being frightened! There, there, little one! Come, come!' And he put out his hand and stroked my cheek. 'Have done, have done,' he repeated, 'and may Christ have you in his charge!' " The little boy became strangely agitated: "My lips were trembling so violently that I could make no reply, nor even cross myself; and this seemed to make an impression upon him, for once again he extended a massive, black-nailed, earth-encrusted finger, and gently, very gently, touched my quivering lips. And as he did so he smiled, a sort of lingering, motherly smile."

Dostoevsky was never to forget that smile. Amid the desolate horrors of the convict prison it came back to him one day at Eastertide. "So I arose from my prison pallet, and gazed around me; and as I did so I remember that I felt as though once more I could bear to look upon my wretched companions, and to do so with a changed eye; for some miracle had suddenly cleansed my heart of all hatred and malice, and, as I walked through the prison and glanced into the faces which I encountered, it struck me that possibly any one of them—even the face of that close-cropped, ruffianly, tipsy-looking, branded peasant who was engaged in bawling out a hoarse, drunken song—might be the face of Marei himself."

The doctor, in spite of all his faults, was careful in the selection of schools for his sons. The two elder boys were dispatched to a French school the head of which was a M. Suchard. Then in 1834 they were sent to a boarding-school under M. Tchermak. Here Fyodor showed considerable progress in French, and here, after having been already introduced by his father to the national Russian writers, he showed interest in foreign authors, including Walter Scott. From childhood on, he read avidly, and it may be urged that Soloviev is unduly harsh in his claim that the novelist was wholly without culture, in spite of the fact that he cites Dostoevsky himself in proof of this assertion. Soloviev goes so far as to deny to Dostoevsky any interest in science: "Even psychopathy and psychiatry, as sciences, failed to attract his attention; and if I have called him a prince of psychopathologists, my reason has lain in his genius rather than in his cultural attainments."

Admittedly, Dostoevsky's tendency was in the direction of philosophy rather than in that of the exact sciences. Here is one appeal, of so many, dated February 22nd, 1854: "Send me the Koran, and Kant's *Critique of Pure Reason,* and if you have the chance of sending me anything not officially, then be sure to send Hegel, but particularly Hegel's *History of Philosophy.* Upon that depends my whole future." Then in another letter to his brother Michael, dated March 27th, 1854: "Send me—not newspapers, but European histories. Economists—Church Fathers—as many of the classics as possible. Herodotus, Thucydides, Tacitus, Pliny, Flavius, Plutarch, Diodorus, etc., in French translations. And the Koran and a German Dictionary. Not all at once, of course, but as much as you can. Send me Pissaren's *Physics* too, and a manual of physiology, any one, in French if better than in Russian, all in the cheapest editions. Not in one consignment, but slowly, one book after another. I shall be grateful for every little thing you can do for me. Do realise how urgently I need this intellectual food."

Those who lightly brand this strange psychopathist as a desultory reader, almost an ignoramus, should remember that his life was not that of the cloisters. They should remember, too, that in his dark homesetting the whole world of "dangerous" ideas was strictly taboo. It is no wonder that, at the age of sixteen, he welcomed eagerly the emancipating challenge of George Sand. Even thirty years afterwards he was to endorse his gratitude: "Ever she held stoutly and gloriously and consistently to her ideals; and the reason for this lay in the fact that she possessed a soul capable of *formulating* ideals. . . . She cherished an unconditional belief in the human personality, to the point of its being immortal, and ever upheld and diffused her theory of personal freedom."

Early in 1837 Dostoevsky's mother died, and in the same year the two elder boys presented themselves for examination at the School of Engineering. Here Fyodor the weakling was passed by the doctors, but his, seemingly, more robust elder brother was rejected. This was a heavy blow to the future writer, who had great dreams of life together at the School as they jogged along with their father to Petersburg: "It was the month of May, when we set out, almost at a foot's pace, and with halts of two or three hours at every post-house on the road. Never shall I forget the tedium of that journey, which lasted for nearly a week. . . . We ourselves cherished passionate belief, and, though we knew all that was awaiting us in the coming mathematical examination, our heads were filled, rather, with poets and poetry."

Robbed of the companionship of his brother, Fyodor Dostoevsky felt himself isolated in the School, though he established friendly relations with D. V. Grigorovitch. Here is a glimpse of him at this period, given by M. Saveliev: "From the authorities and the elder pupils he held aloof; and even during his term in the senior class he was generally to be seen alone—whether working at his desk or pacing the classrooms with head bent and his hands clasped behind his back." But he worked with diligence and seems to have had an absolute loathing of dissipation. "I wonder," he once wrote to his elder brother, "whether my boding thoughts will have become more restful. . . . I am beginning to think that soon I shall lose my senses. To live without hope is a terrible thing."

For the first time in his life, probably, this analyser turns his analysis on to his father. "How I pity our poor father!" he exclaims in a letter to Michael in 1838. "What a strange character! What troubles he has borne! How very sorry I am not to have been able to help him! Do you know? Our father knows nothing at all of the world! He has lived in it for fifty years and he retains the same opinion of people as he had at thirty. Happy ignorance!" This note is striking in view of Freud's specifically branding the novelist with the Oedipus complex.

But in the spring of the following year, with infinite caution and endless apologies, the boy applies to the doctor for forty roubles. Like the sad hero of *Poor Folk,* he harps pitiably on such things as tea and boots: "When, owing to bad weather and rain, one is soaked through under the canvas of one's tent, or when, in the same kind of weather, one returns from drill frozen and tired out, if one does not take tea, one will fall ill, as was the case with me last winter. In spite of all, however, I understand your position, and I will not take tea. Only sixteen roubles are necessary for me to buy two pairs of ordinary boots, then I must arrange my things somewhere: books, boots, pens, paper, etc., etc., must be placed somewhere. For this I must have a chest, for in camp there are no arrangements other than the tents."

Such poverty in early youth does not tend to produce optimism, but it is a deplorable error, in spite of all the novelist's railings against life, to assume that he took in any sense a rancorous view of humanity. It is true that, like many a smaller man, he has expressed the conviction that our poor planet is in reality a sort of purgatory. But, even in the hell of a convict prison, he was to detect undying gleams as from the veritable indestructability of the human soul. His childhood was certainly harsh, but he has described it, though he would never refer to it in the family circle of later days, as a happy period. And even if in those boyhood years one can catch a hint of suicide, it must be remembered that only two months before his death the novelist vibrated with the will to live and exclaimed in a letter to the associate editor of the "Russky Viestnik": "Let me not say good-bye to you! Indeed, I intend to live another twenty years and to go on writing."

As for that pitiful letter to his father, it was one of the very last that he was to write to this strange being. That very year the doctor died under the painful circumstances already narrated. The death was certainly tragic, but a far deeper tragedy lay in the inheritance of alcoholism. Dostoevsky's daughter always thought that the novelist had his father in mind when he drew the character of old Karamazov. She admits, though, that the portrait is not exact, that Fyodor Karamazov is a buffoon while the doctor was always dignified. Old Karamazov was a profligate, but the doctor was a faithful husband. The father of the brothers Karamazov washed his hands of them, but the doctor gave his children a carefully supervised education. But certain common traits are only too obvious, including the physical effect of disgust produced upon the doctor's children. The world-famed writer, however, does not permit Alyosha to share this disgust: "The great psychologist in embryo must have divined at times that his father was, after all, but a diseased and unhappy being. It must be understood that this likeness between my grandfather and the old Karamazov is merely a supposition on my part, for which there is no documentary evidence. Yet it may not simply be a coincidence that Dostoevsky has given the name of Tchermashnia to the village where old Karamazov sent his son Ivan just before his death." This was the name of the village where the doctor was murdered; Mlle Dostoevsky's supposition is also supported by the fact that there was a tradition in the family that the novelist had drawn himself in the figure of Ivan Karamazov.

Be that as it may, the doctor's alcoholism played havoc in many lives: "His eldest son Mihaïl and his youngest son Nicolaï inherited his disease. My uncle Mihaïl, though he drank, was at least able to work; but the unhappy Nicolaï, after a brilliant course of study, was never able to do anything, and remained a burden on his family all his life. My father's epilepsy, which caused him so much suffering, was probably due to the same cause. But the most miserable of the family was certainly my Aunt Barbara." This particular relation developed into a fantastic figure who might have taken her place in the most fantastic productions of the novelist. Married to a relatively rich man, her children comfortably settled in the world, and with everything to assure the comfort of her old age, Aunt Barbara became more sordid than any creation of Balzac. Spending money became a torture to her. She dismissed her servants. She lived without a fire in winter, wrapped up in a cloak. She dispensed with cooking and would go twice a week to purchase a little bread and milk to sustain life. In the end, like Dostoevsky's father, she was murdered, robbery, though, being the motive in her case. This crime took place long after the death of the novelist. But the inheritance of misfortune does not end here. The doctor's shadow hovered over the younger generations: "The disease persisted in my uncle Mihaïl's family; the second and third generations were victims to it. My Aunt Barbara's son was so stupid that his folly verged on idiocy. My uncle Audrey's son, a young and brilliant savant, died of creeping paralysis. The whole Dostoevsky family suffered from neurasthenia."

Constantin Pobedonoszev became the guardian of the doctor's family. They seem never to have referred to the murder, and the elder generation regarded it as a disgraceful family secret. The novelist's life remained stark and difficult, but in 1841, while still at the School of Engineering, Dostoevsky appears to have caught a glint of freedom in the long tunnel of his adolescence: "Brother, brother, let us hasten to the port, let us hasten to liberty! Liberty and a vocation are the great things. I begin to dream of them again as I did before. The soul grows large enough to comprehend the grandeur of life." But in the same year, in another letter to Michael, he alludes to those long white nights which, like the whitened walls of hospitals, were to find such sinister reflection in his future work. And in the letter asking for the precise date of his brother's forthcoming marriage there is another allusion to insomnia: "As for me, I find it impossible, at least at present, to write to you fittingly. Would you believe it, I am writing at three o'clock in the morning; last night I did not go to bed at all." The excuse for this was examinations, but years afterwards it was always in the small hours of the morning that the novelist evoked those formidable creations that must well have appeared to him familiar spirits in life rather than characters in fiction.

Dostoevsky has been so often represented as inhumanly rancorous to the outside world that the following fragment to Michael is not without significance: "I am exceedingly culpable towards your dear fiancée—my little sister, as precious and as dear as you, but of a disposition—forgive me, my good friend that I do not understand. Can she have so little confidence in her relative, or has she already formed a monstrous opinion of me—of my impoliteness, of my lack of consideration, of my ill-feelings, in fact of all the vices—as to be so prejudiced against me as not to believe in my assurances, and have a grudge against me for my silence, when I speak of lack of time?"

In another fragment to his brother he defends himself more specifically against the appearance of a *mauvais caractère*. But this was some years after he had retired from the Service: "I was ill, brother. I remember that you once said to me that my relations with you excluded mutual equality. My dear brother, that was wholly unjust. But I have such a villainous and repulsive character. I have always regarded you as being better than I and superior to me. I am ready to give my life for you and yours, but sometimes, when my heart is swimming in affection, a good word cannot be wrung from me. My nerves do not obey me at these moments. I am vile and ridiculous, and because of this I must always suffer unjust judgments. They say that I am harsh and without heart." And with the same painful self-condemnation he goes on to apologise for some real or imaginary rudeness to his brother's wife: "I cannot show that I have heart and affection, except when external circumstances or opportunity tear me by force from my ordinary baseness. Until then, I remain vile. I attribute this unevenness of temperament to my malady."

In 1841, while he was still at the School of Engineering, his friend Riesenkampf gave a picture of him which shows clearly enough that long before he went to Siberia he was threatened with the malady of which he became definitely the victim in the convict prison: "The face was rounded and full; the nose slightly retroussé; the hair light brown, worn short. A broad forehead, and beneath thin eyebrows little grey eyes, set deep in the head, pale cheeks, covered with freckles. A sickly, almost livid complexion, and very thick lips."

In 1843 he finished the full course at the School of Engineering. He then entered the Army with a commission as a Designer in the Department of Engineering. At this stage, according to all accounts, including his own, he led a wholly rudderless existence: "On leaving college, Dostoevsky embarked upon a Bohemian, bachelor life which was full of privations, seeing that (it need hardly be said) his pecuniary embarrassments continued as numerous as before. True, if we include in our estimate of his income his official salary and sundry remittances from his guardian, he received the sum of about five thousand roubles a year; but he was eminently unpractical, and money slipped through his fingers with incredible rapidity." There was no roulette in those days, but he seems to have had a passion for billiards; at that game, too, he was nearly always a loser. His extravagance pursued him all through life. Without ballast in his youth, he certainly never acquired it in maturity. But the young officer had in him something far deeper than billiards, the waywardness of youth, and even ballast itself!

He was becoming preoccupied by literature and he embarked on a translation of *Eugénie Grandet,* apparently without realising how he was already, in actual fact, the very antithesis of Balzac. Inevitably, at the back of his head, a quite different inspiration was stirring. In any case. he soon wearied of the Army. "The Service disgusts me like potatoes." In this year he met Turgenev for the first time, and the following year he left the Army, determined to gamble, neither at billiards nor roulette but on a manuscript of his own composition. "I have no regrets," he informed his brother Michael. "I have a hope. I am in the act of finishing a novel of about the length of *Eugénie Grandet.* The novel is rather original. I am re-copying it; towards the 14th I shall certainly have a reply. I shall place it in the "Otechestvennia Zapiski" (I am pleased with my work). I shall get perhaps four hundred roubles; that is all that I can hope for. I would have given you details about my novel, only time is pressing."

In the spring of 1845, there are other allusions to the writing of this novel. The distressed young author had made up his mind to print at his own risk. "I have made a desperate decision," he told Michael. "I am going to wait, run once more into debt, and towards the first of September, when everybody is coming back to St. Petersburg, and people are scenting novelties as a sporting dog scents game, I am going to have my novel printed with my last resources, and they perhaps will not be sufficient. When one places something in a Review, one puts oneself under the yoke, not only of the principal hotel-keeper but also of all the underlings, and of all the scullions in the places where civilisation is propagated. There is not only one dictator—there are twenty of them. Printing oneself, that means digging one's own hole, and, if the work is good, not only will it not be lost, but it will also deliver me from my troubles and my debts, and will give me bread. . . . If the affair does not succeed, I may have to hang myself." But from the beginning he had sworn to himself not to write to order, though, after a fashion, he was to write to order, with very few interludes, all his life. Already this boy has grasped the danger of his chosen calling: "In the *Invalide* I have read the feuilleton in which they speak of the German poets who have died from hunger, from cold, or else in lunatic asylums. There are at least twenty of them, and what names! I shiver at it at the present instant. One must be a charlatan. . . ."

He was never a charlatan, though again and again a cynic might exclaim: "This is the voice of Zosima, yet one seems to catch the half-strangled grin of Fyodor Karamazov." But one need not be a cynic in demanding great caution as to the over-simplification of this apparently open but exceedingly tortuous mentality. Above all, one must beware of explaining the contradictions in the novelist by the facile word "hypocrisy." And though the newer psychologists might well have hailed him as their legitimate quarry, he is neither to be explained by Freud nor Jung, nor, in spite of his union of self-depreciation with exasperation against mankind, by Adler. It has been claimed that all his heroines, like those of Tolstoy, are devoid of culture, and it cannot be said that this Russian of genius was at any time permeated by the age-old culture of Europe any more than he was devoured by the tireless devotion to erudition of the genuine scholar. But his genius responded unerringly to something that was deep in his own nature. He had loved well the open country, but it had not been given to him to tell the story of Nature's tranquillising secrets. Like Gustave Flaubert, born in the same year in a hospital, the son of a doctor, and also a prey to epilepsy, this Russian had been steeped in romanticism during his adolescence. But he did not begin the *via dolorosa* of letters as a pupil of Chateaubriand only to become afterwards the formidable castigator of M. Homais. Life had already closed in on Dostoevsky with its own form of reality which is so distinct from literary realism. His were to be neither those tranquillising secrets of Nature, nor yet those solacing secrets of art. His were to be primarily the secrets of houses and pavements, of long fog-laden streets, of closed windows in stifling brooding rooms, of sudden cries of anguish, of despair, the secrets of the full terror of life which are beyond the range of the terror of death. For Dostoevsky the city was to assume an enigmatic personality choked with evil and yet embracing the sinless, the simple and the kind. Even at twenty-three, because he was so close to its very core, the novelist had divined the city's meaning, which was so different from the glitter and the glamour of palaces. And because he understood the cellar in its miasmic hopelessness he was to understand the underground self-condemnation of the human spirit. Dostoevsky from the very beginning rejected only the proud, whose doom it was never to learn from the humiliated and wounded. Repeatedly, he is to return to this untaught thesis which is so utterly different from the preaching of any gospel of suffering merely *qua* suffering. And though his instinct led him to the acceptance of an hereditary faith, no one was to understand more easily the Mephistophelean punishment of endless enquiry. For, as I have already indicated, this novelist, constantly preoccupied by the existence or non-existence of the deity, has accepted—in an only too literal sense—the atmosphere of the police-court as one of literary routine. If the admirable Sainte-Beuve really wished to wash his hands after reading Balzac, how would he have felt after reading Dostoevsky?

The Russian novelist had to go his own way, had to accomplish what there was in him to accomplish, had to accept the lessons of reality and to reject the lessons of imitation. But at twenty-three he could not foresee the magnitude of *Crime and Punishment, The Idiot, The Possessed, The Brothers Karamazov*. Not so very long ago, he had been standing to attention while his doomed father ladled out what was left to him of Latinity. Almost recently, he had been forced to plead for tea and books and boots and pens. He had been forced to think in kopeks while his thoughts wandered naturally to Schiller, Pushkin, Homer, Byron, Victor Hugo, Corneille, Racine. Only the other day, he had been plunging wildly into the riot of youth in the hope of finding that happiness which was perhaps to elude him to the grave. He had remained a gambler and he was about to gamble, by no means for the last time, with a masterpiece. Above all, this boy of twenty-three, again like Flaubert, had sworn to himself never to be the slave of dictated thought. To this, however persecuted by publishers, he was to remain no less faithful than the French master. But whereas Flaubert was to toil ceaselessly for the *mot juste* in literature, the Russian was to content himself, at all events at the beginning, with a wholly unequivocal reading of the equivocal human soul.

Chapter II

EARLY TRIUMPH

DOSTOEVSKY, who loathed being hurried in his work and who was to be hurried over every other production with one exception, wrote *Poor Folk* almost at his leisure. But he was quite in despair over his story when his old schoolfellow, D. V. Grigorovitch, exclaimed one day: "Give me that manuscript of yours. Next year Nekrassov is intending to start a review, and I will show him your story." The young author handed his friend the manuscript, and a little later on was introduced to Nekrassov, in whose presence he could only utter a few almost incoherent words. He believed that his *Poor Folk* would meet with nothing but ridicule, and yet—"This story of mine—I have written it with zest, and almost with tears in my eyes. Surely, then, the many hours which I have spent with a pen in my hand have not been all a lie, all a mirage, all a period of insincere feeling?"

Thus he pondered on the old seesaw between hope and despair. He reached home at about four in the morning, and was soon startled by a ring at the door: "It was Grigorovitch and Nekrassov! Rushing into the room in transports, and almost in tears, they embraced me again and yet again. It seemed that, on the previous evening, they had returned home early, and started to read my manuscript, thinking to themselves, 'The first ten pages will show us what it is good for,' and that, when those pages had been read, they had decided to read yet another ten, and that, in the end, they had sat up all night over the book, taking turns to read the manuscript aloud, according as one or the other of the pair had grown weary."

The manuscript was at once submitted to the Petronius Arbiter of Petersburg. After reading it, Bielinsky said to Nekrassov: "Bring me this Dostoevsky. Bring him to me at once." This true critic, true penetrator into the real meaning of literature, read the young novelist's intention as something utterly distinct from Anglo-Saxon pathos: "For in this unfortunate *tchinovnik* of yours we see a man so inured to servitude, a man reduced to such a pass, that in his abasement he does not dare to think himself unhappy—he considers the very least shadow of repining to savour of 'free thought.' Oh, terrible, terrible! What a tragedy! Yet you have delved to the very essence of things, and at a stroke have revealed a great truth. Value your gift, I beg of you, and remain ever true to it. Thus will you become a great writer."

Is it surprising that on leaving the critic the novelist stopped at the corner of the street and asked himself: "Am I really so great as they say?" Is it any wonder that in that moment he dedicated himself afresh to his chosen calling? "But I must strive to show that I am worthy of their praises; I must strive, through humble labour, to become as glorious as they; I must remain ever true to my gift, even though I comprise in myself much triviality, and am compounded (did Bielinsky but know it) of trashy, sordid elements. *Littérateurs*, they say, are proud and vain; and so, very possibly, they are; but in all Russia they alone hold fast to that truth which, with justice and virtue, will ever prevail over vice and wrong-doing. Yes, *we* shall prevail.

Oh, to become one with, to become one of, those men!"

Is it any wonder that in Dostoevsky, too, flashes of vanity were revealed? The change had been too abrupt; the transition from the hard isolation of adolescence to what seemed to him the life of "roses, roses all the way" was obviously not without peril. In the November of that year he exclaims to his brother Michael: "I think that my fame will never reach greater heights than those to which it has soared today. I meet everywhere with the greatest respect; curiosity about me is immense. I have made the acquaintance of a great many people in good society. Prince Odoevsky begs me to honour him with a visit, and Count S— is tearing his hair in despair; Panaiev has assured him that a talent has made its appearance which will surpass them all. S— has been all over the place, and, when at Kraevsky's, asked him suddenly: 'Who is this Dostoevsky? Where shall I get hold of this Dostoevsky?' Kraevsky, who does not mince matters with anybody and always says things straight out, answers that Dostoevsky would not care to honour him with a visit. That is quite true: the aristocrats perch on stilts, and imagine that they will annihilate me beneath the weight of their favours. I am received everywhere as a marvel. I cannot open my mouth without people repeating in every corner, 'Dostoevsky has said this, Dostoevsky wishes to do that.' "

There is a Sophoclean irony about all this, and it is rather pitiful to watch the novelist, who had such a truly terrible life in front of him, condemning himself by his own lips in his youth. Not until the very end of his life was there to be any real echo of such exultation. I refer to his exclamation after the unveiling of the Pushkin statue: "My name is worth a million roubles to them." In the meantime, it is only just to note that his enthusiasm was by no means confined to himself. In this very letter there is an allusion to the future author of *Smoke,* from whose age Dostoevsky deducts several years: "Ah, my brother, what a man! He has a real talent, he is a poet, an aristocrat, good-looking, rich, intelligent, well-read. He is twenty years old—I do not know what Nature has been able to refuse him! Finally, he possesses a character that is absolutely honourable, formed in a good school, and a perfect disposition."

What is the secret of the extraordinary appeal of *Poor Folk?* It consists merely of a series of letters between a half-crazed drunkard, Makar Djevuschkin, and a half-starved seamstress, Varvara. The girl confides to the old clerk that she is going to marry a rich man. Makar has always helped her in the miserable past, and naturally he will be delighted to help her in the radiant present. It is the sort of situation which our own Dickens would have given with all the humour of pathos and the pathos of humour. Incidentally, M. Gide is unjust to Dostoevsky when he practically denies him the saving grace of humour in any shape or kind. But the creator of Tom Pinch has a tendency always to defend his dearest creations from the pressure of life, unless he is endowing them with the halo of martyrdom. It may be said that none of the Russian novelists of the nineteenth century takes sides against life. Certainly, it never occurs to Dostoevsky to drag the poor old clerk into the zone of poetic justice. But in one moment the unhappy drunkard, realising that all he loved in life has been torn away from him, cries out as age may cry for youth in its bewildered regret. In that moment he understands his loneliness, and yet, as that great critic Bielinsky noted at once, "in his abasement he does not dare to think himself unhappy." That is indubitably the Russian touch, emerging from life and never losing contact with it. Dostoevsky, perhaps more deeply than either of his two great rivals, was to be permeated by it to the very last.

But inevitably the young novelist was to meet with criticism infinitely less penetrating, and less merciful, than that of Bielinsky. M. Soloviev has given us this typical fragment from the *Memoirs* of Mme Panaiev-Golovachev: "The first time that Dostoevsky came to see us he came with Nekrassov and Grigorovitch—the latter of whom had just entered the literary field. At the first glance he could perceive that the newcomer was a young man of an extremely nervous and impressionable temperament. Short and thin, he had fair hair, an unhealthy complexion, small grey eyes which wandered uneasily from object to object, and pale lips which maintained a restless twitching. Almost every one present was known to him, yet he seemed bashful, and took no part in the general conversation, even though successive members of the company tried to draw him out, to banish his reserve, and to make him feel that he was a member of our circle."

Dostoevsky's visits, unfortunately, became only too frequent, and still more unfortunately his reserve vanished. His tone became one of arrogance, as though he were, indeed, the possessor of that infinitely exploited inferiority complex of the later psychology. The result might easily have been foreseen, and indeed was foreseen. They began to bait the author of *Poor Folk*. Inevitably the ironical Turgenev could not refrain from this cruel sport, the cruelty of which could not then be detected: "With back (so to speak) planted against the wall, Dostoevsky would strike out at random in defence of views which, voiced in the heat of the moment, were mostly so uncouth that it afforded Turgenev the highest pleasure to attack them." Inevitably, too, the maladive Dostoevsky became a prey to a mild form of the persecution mania. He suspected these people one and all of mocking his talent. His suspicion went so far as to fasten upon Bielinsky. He even allowed himself to speak scornfully of his patron: "To think of a man of sense spending even ten minutes over an idiotic pursuit like cards! Yet Bielinsky spends two or three hours at a time in that way! Truly the society of *littérateurs* is in no way distinguishable from that of *tchinovniks,* seeing that each of those categories passes its leisure in the same pursuit."

This, admittedly, is an absurd pronouncement, particularly from the future author of *The Gambler*. But it is by no means difficult for people of the most modest mentality to lure a man of genius into absurdity. It was particularly easy in the case of the maladive and exasperated author of *Poor Folk*. Besides, the mild persecution was by no means confined to people of modest mentality. All his life Turgenev seems to have been swayed between irony and genuine kindness of heart. Irony, unfortunately, triumphed almost from the very beginning in his relations with Dostoevsky; the great artist who was to write *Smoke* became the leader in baiting the future author of *The Brothers Karamazov*.

Bielinsky showed himself very much more merciful. When some of Dostoevsky's outbursts were reported to him he merely shrugged his shoulders and remarked sadly: "What a pity! Undoubtedly he has talent. But if, instead of developing that talent, he should make up his mind that he is already a genius, he will never get any further." This point of view is obviously debatable, but what follows was at the time only too true: "What he needs is medical treatment: this sort of thing comes of over-excitement of the nerves. Evidenty life is beginning to jar upon him, poor fellow! Yet grievous times are ahead of us, and it will need the nerves of a bullock to support the conditions of present-day existence. Should the dawn not speedily break, *all* of us will become psychic invalids." Within a few short years, Dostoevsky was sentenced to Siberia, and Bielinsky himself escaped the same fate only by death. On one occasion in the same drawing-room, Turgenev drew a mocking picture of a young provincial who regarded himself as the possessor of astounding talent. Without waiting for the end of the story, Dostoevsky turned away pale and trembling with rage; he left the room and the house. He never entered the house again and avoided the whole circle, even crossing a street so as to avoid one of its members.

In a letter to Strakhov long afterwards, he was to explain this rupture with old ties from quite a different point of view: "It was with Bielinsky as a phenomenon of Russian life rather than with Bielinsky as an individual, that I quarrelled. In those days he represented one of the grossest, the meanest, the most pestiferous manifestations of that life; and were he alive now, he would still be foaming at the mouth, and inditing those pagan articles which used to disgrace our country, and to deny it its greatest son (Pushkin). . . . But look you here. You never knew the man; whereas I knew him, and saw much of him, and have since been able to apprise him at his value. *He* fell foul of *me,* although he and all his fellow agitators put together were not fit to hold a candle to Our Saviour Christ. The truth is that he was incapable of detecting to what an extent he and his world were charged with malice and intolerance and mockery and baseness and conceit." This clearly is yet another regrettable outburst of exasperation which, as Soloviev notes, was contradicted by other expressions of opinion towards the man who, in the whole world of men, had most befriended him in his youth. In a letter written in 1846, Dostoevsky applies the epithet "noble" to the Russian critic.

There is another version, too, of what may be accepted as the final estrangement between Dostoevsky and Turgenev. One day there was a card-party at the elder writer's house, among the guests being Bielinsky, Ogarev and Herzen. Dostoevsky was a little late, and just as he entered the room there chanced to be a general outburst of laughter at a silly mistake of one of the card-players. Turning pale, Dostoevsky left the room without uttering a word. No notice was taken of this, as they expected him back. Then, as time passed, Turgenev went out to see what had become of his missing guest. His servant informed him that for the last hour Dostoevsky had been walking up and down outside the house without his hat. Turgenev rushed out to ask his guest for an explanation of this odd conduct. "By God!" the other exclaimed. "It is intolerable! Wherever I go, everybody mocks me. I had scarcely put foot in your house when you and your guests overwhelmed me with your ridicule. Are you not ashamed of it?" Turgenev tried to convince him that no one had intended to make fun of him, but it was all quite useless. Dostoevsky refused to listen to reason and returned to the hall for his hat and overcoat, after which he left without another word.

It is no wonder that the author of *Poor Folk* was becoming once more isolated. What was still more serious was the fact that he was thoroughly in the grip of the publisher Kraevsky. He had to work day and night over that curiously alive *Netotchka Nezvanova* which, like *The Brothers Karamazov* itself, was never completed. The passion to get clear of debt which was to cling to the novelist all through life was already oppressive: "With Kraevsky's aid I hope to pay off the whole of my obligations. Indeed, my one aim is to work for him all the winter, and then, by the summer, to have not a kopek of debt. But *shall* I ever get rid of my indebtedness? Terrible indeed to have to work as a journeyman, for it means the ruin of everything—of one's talent, of one's youth, of one's hopes. Yes, work of that kind merely spoils one, and makes of one a scribbler rather than a writer."

The triumph of *Poor Folk* was, seemingly, never to be repeated. A novel entitled *The Twins* was labelled "so dull as to be unreadable." The story entitled *The Landlady,* in which the author appears to have had considerable faith, was dismissed by Bielinsky himself as "hysterical rubbish." The young writer was blamed on all sides for *The Double*. But this book is a work of genuine significance, not so much on its own account as because it foreshadows what is to come. Goliadkin is, as it were, a burlesque of some of the most formidable figures in the later novels. Mr. Janko Lavrin, in his acute study of the Russian novelist, is abundantly right when he claims that Dostoevsky anticipated Freud in the examination of the real nature of dreams as projected from the conscious into the unconscious Ego. Then, the strange heroes of Dostoevsky again and again demonstrate that theory of split personality which, despite so many cases from real life, is losing weight in popular opinion. Versilov, the principal character in *A Raw Youth*, has claimed himself to be an example of this in almost exactly the same sense as in the case of Dr. Jekyll himself: "I am really split in two mentally, and I am horribly afraid of it. It is just as though one's *second self* were standing beside one; one is sensible and rational oneself, but the other self is impelled to do something perfectly senseless, and sometimes very funny; and suddenly you notice, you are longing to do that amusing thing, goodness knows why. I once knew a doctor who suddenly began whistling in church, at his father's funeral."

In a modern French novel the hero, Salavin, is seized at the beginning by exactly the same impulse towards buffoonery. But, needless to say, the orderly French mind rejects any attempt to sustain any such buffoonery for many pages; neither the antics of Goliadkin nor the infinitely more profound duality of Raskolnikov, Stavroguin and the brothers Karamazov, appear in French fiction.

But long before the coming of Dostoevsky, or any other nineteenth-century exponent of psychological processes, the theory of duality began to haunt mankind. Asked whether Helen had actually gone to Troy, the shade of Achilles is said to have replied in the negative. Helen had remained in Egypt, and the Greeks knew that she was there but had fought for

EARLY TRIUMPH

glory and the spoils of Ilium. The Trojan war had seemingly been waged for a phantom. But, when it was claimed for Helen that not she herself but Aphrodite was answerable for the waywardness of her beauty, Euripides claimed that what was called Aphrodite by Helen of Troy was in reality the lust of her own heart.

Doubles, physical in appearance, are quite familiar to the annals of occultism; they have even been elaborately documented. It is the mental and spiritual duality, revealed in the novels of Dostoevsky, that light up the darkest recesses of the human mind. It is no wonder that this novelist was perhaps the only writer of fiction to be taken seriously by criminologists. It was not for nothing that Nietzsche himself, who disparaged Flaubert and for whom our own Thomas Carlyle, with or without reference to Jean Paul Richter, was little better than a comic figure, bowed before the author of *Crime and Punishment*. No one, not even Luther, not even Frederick the Great, not even Goethe, not even Schopenhauer, not even Heine, ranked the Herrenfolk lower than did the trumpeter of the blond beast to come. Yet this arrogant advocate of brutality is humble before the man who all his life rejected the theory of force: "The criminal type is the type of the strong man made sick. . . . Concerning the problem before us, Dostoevsky's testimony is of importance. Dostoevsky, who, incidentally, was the only psychologist from whom I had anything to learn: he belongs to the happiest windfalls of my life, happier even than the discovery of Stendhal. This profound man, who was right ten times over in esteeming the superficial Germans low, found the Siberian convicts among whom he lived for many years—those thoroughly hopeless criminals for whom no road back to society stood open—very different from what even he had expected—that is to say, carved from about the best, hardest and most valuable material that grows on Russian soil." That this is an exaggeration of the author's real verdict on his fellow-prisoners goes without saying, but, curiously enough, he was in actual fact to assimilate the hardness of the Siberian convicts to no small extent in spite of his frail physique.

But during this period of failure, following the success of his first novel, Dostoevsky became deeply depressed. Buoyed up at one moment by immense pride in his sense of power, he would be a prey to the sense of utter nothingness the next. He became apprehensive of all sorts of calamities, including that of insanity. In short, even at this period of his youth he experienced, at all events partially and, mercifully, in passing spasms, precisely that *frayeur mystique* which was to cloud the later years of his tormented life. It must be noted, though, that the actual break with the *Sovremennik* (an association of which Bielinsky and Nekrassov were the accepted leaders) was due to political as distinct from purely personal reasons. The religious belief of Dostoevsky was essentially antipathetic to the association, and in it the novelist was regarded as a conservative, almost the most contemptuous label that could be fastened on him. What was the reality of this man as he neared the ebb-tide of his grudged youth? Life in 1846 had seemed almost benevolent to him. It was the year of the publication of *Poor Folk* in Nekrassov's "Petersburg Almanac"; it was the year of Dostoevsky's being received by his fellow-writers on terms of equality. Besides this, he was in this year on good terms with his family, including his two sisters, Varya and Vera, who had made commendable marriages. Then came this break with a world that he had, in spite of all his exasperation, regarded with almost naïve respect. It had turned finally against him, as he believed.

In one sense he was essentially born for isolation, but in another sense he was undoubtedly gregarious. Acquaintances swarm all through his life, even in Siberia, exactly as subordinate characters swarm in his novels. He is indeed very like this and that central figure of his greatest works. Each one of them is swayed by instinct rather than by logic and, though they reason with a dialectic worthy of a criminal court, one feels always that at the back of their heads they give no credence to Euclidean demonstrations. Above all, they must never be asked to explain their real thought. Did not Dostoevsky say, through the lips of one of his characters, that when he endeavoured to explain an idea he at once began to lose faith in it? But with an extraordinary tenacity, almost resembling the cat-like wiriness with which this frail man was to cling to life, he clung to the tenets of the New Testament. If they were untrue, if what is called natural law has never been violated by anyone on earth, what is there left? For Dostoevsky, as indeed for the utterly different Leo Tolstoy, what is left is precisely the equation $0-0$. But of "conversion" in Tolstoy's sense Dostoevsky was wholly innocent. Indeed, he regarded that conversion, when news of it reached him, as nothing less than madness.

Dostoevsky never dreamed of leaving the world of actuality. He never shrank from any phase of its full hideousness. It never occurred to him that by any possibility he could be excluded from the ranks of sinners. He knew that he was of those who, like the Karamazovs, are swayed by their passions. But he also knew that there was a way of life beyond their tumult. On reaching that, one had only to listen to one's own heart to get, here and there, fugitive glimpses of the truth. But never, on any excuse, must one turn aside from the great mass of one's fellows. Raskolnikov, by no means the will-less worm that Gide has labelled him, committed that sin. His redemption came to him only when, through the despairing appeal of Sonya, he is brought back to the herd. For Dostoevsky, who was obsessed by the now almost forgotten motif of sin, every type of sinner, perhaps with a very few exceptions, receives the hope of pardon in the pages of this Russian realist. Well, did not Gilles de Retz himself exclaim, "I am redeemable"? An exception in Dostoevsky's analysis is not Ivan Karamazov but Stavroguin; another is not Raskolnikov but Svidrigailov. Ivan Karamazov distrusted the pride of his own doubt; Raskolnikov yielded at long last to the magnetism of the herd. But Stavroguin can never pierce the ultimate void and dies from its horror, whilst Svidrigailov is doomed to persist until he, too, dies by his own hand on the long road from which Raskolnikov has been dragged away by Sonya. For without humility it seemed to Dostoevsky, as to the Founder of Christianity, there can be neither wisdom nor pardon. Clinging to these tenets, absolute in their simplicity, the young writer was swayed, with all his horror of paganism, by the grip of the Orthodox Church with its semi-pagan appeal. Curious, far-off dreams floated from his unconscious to consciousness. And from them all, as a resultant of conflicting urges, there came the old instinctive national dream to place the cross above the crescent in Byzantium. No more fantastic, inexplicable mass of contradictions could have contended in a single brain. Is it any wonder that the advance guard of Russian freedom, the people who demanded close attention to economics instead of to philosophy, regarded him as confused, backward, a denier of human progress?

But Dostoevsky never became a pan-Slav in the real sense. He pleaded for Russia to remain Russian, and for the destruction of that passionate imitation of Europe which was merely a cloak for backwardness. At the same time, he had that intense, unreasoned faith in his country which no Russian writer—not even Turgenev—is without. It has become the fashion now to mock at *l'âme russe,* but to Dostoevsky it was something absolutely real. He believed that it would find expression even in atheism itself, by reason of the national thirst for what seemed to be the truth. In this, as in many other respects, Dostoevsky, so often dismissed as a *détraqué* utterly devoid of balanced judgment, has proved a true prophet. But at this period he had no sort of right to speak for Russia. His brief triumph had been swamped in the miasma of repeated failure. He had given no hint, not even in *Poor Folk,* of the power that was to reveal itself in the later novels. Sometimes he might still feel arrogant, but the mood would pass only too quickly and despair would seize him. But as yet he was saved from the malady of introspection, from that permanent *peur de la vie* which Flaubert long afterwards was to confess to

George Sand, who, for her part, seems to have been wholly ignorant of its meaning.

It was under these conditions that the sombre young novelist, ostracised from one circle, turned instinctively to another. It was the Circle of Petrachevsky, and the sub-section to which he attached himself was that of Sergey Fyodorovitch Durov. At the time of his joining the group, the Censorship was one of the great objects of attack. The emancipation of the peasantry was also a question eagerly discussed. Naturally, Dostoevsky was an eager listener to such comparatively academic debates. He was not then, or at any time of his life, a revolutionary. He was in fact the exact opposite, warning Russians against following the footsteps of the bloodstained bandits of old Europe. But he was deeply compassionate, and because of this he was regarded hopefully by his new associates. "To this day," notes Debut, "I seem to see Theodor Mikhailovitch speaking at our evening gatherings at Petrachevsky's, and to hear him relating how a sergeant-major had been made to run the gauntlet of a Finnish regiment, and how landowners were accustomed to treat their serfs. And no less vividly do I remember him reciting his *Netotchka Nezvanova*—though in an ampler form than that of the printed version; while, lastly, I have a clear remembrance of the real, the very human, sentiment with which he had begun to treat the social product which subsequently he personified in the character of Sonetchka Marmeladov."

In reality, Dostoevsky was a disciple of Fourier, who stood so simply for the oppressed against the oppressor. But it was the novelist's sincere belief that the bloodthirsty French Revolution had not accomplished its mission of liberty, equality and fraternity. "Our people," he exclaimed, "will not follow the tracks of European revolutionaries." To this there was a swift riposte: "And if there are no other means than Revolution to free the peasants, what must be done then?" In the excitement of the moment the young writer fell headlong into the trap of compassion: "In that case, Revolution." That was enough. In the early morning of April 23rd, 1849, the novelist divined in his sleep curious-looking figures beside his bed. "I heard the clank of swords," he related to the future Mme Kovalevsky years afterwards, "which were hacking at something. What did it all mean? I opened my eyes with an effort, and heard a gentle sympathetic voice say, 'Get up.' I looked up and saw a police officer with a magnificent beard. But it was not he who had spoken, but an officer in a light-blue uniform, with a lieutenant-colonel's epaulettes. The light blue uniform is worn exclusively by gendarmes, a regiment which is always placed at the service of the secret police. 'What on earth is the matter?' I asked as I raised myself in bed. 'In the Emperor's name.' I looked round. It was evidently in the Emperor's name.

There followed a thorough search for incriminating evidence. The Commissary of Police went so far as to rummage among the ashes of the stove with his pipe-stem. The novelist was then escorted to a miserable cell, lit by a single small lamp. The cell was so wet that even the Commander exclaimed when on his rounds the next morning: "This is really not proper." Dostoevsky asked him the reason for his arrest; the reply was: "That you will know altogether at the trial." The first examination, however, hung fire for ten days, during which Dostoevsky was without any sort of occupation: "I had neither paper, nor books. The only interruption to the monotony was when the cell door opened five times a day: at seven o'clock when they came to bring me water for washing and to dust the room; ten o'clock for the inspector's round; twelve o'clock to bring in dinner (two portions of cabbage or some other soup and a bit of veal torn in shreds, as neither knives nor forks accompanied it); seven o'clock for supper; and lastly, when it got dark, they brought the lamp, which after all was superfluous as they gave me nothing to do." This sort of life in a cell within the casemates of the Petroparlovsky Fortress continued for eight months on the puerile charges of having attacked the Censorship; of having read, at a meeting in March 1849, Bielinsky's letter to Gogol, of having read it afterwards in Durov's house, and of having given it to Marbelli to copy; of having listened at Durov's house while various articles were read aloud; of having knowledge of the project for the installation of a clandestine printing press, and so on.

The intention of the authorities had been to arrest his elder brother Michael at the same time, but, through a blunder, his younger brother André had been arrested in his place. Long afterwards the novelist wrote to André in appreciation of his younger brother's attitude at this crisis: "I remember, my dear, I remember when we saw each other (for the last time, I believe) in the famous White Hall. You had only a word to speak in the right quarter and you would immediately be set at liberty, for you had been mistakenly arrested instead of your elder brother. But you listened to my arguments and my

EARLY TRIUMPH 41

prayers; you understood with generosity that your brother was in a pitiable financial position; that his wife had just become a mother and was not yet restored to health—you understood all that, and you remained in prison in order to give your brother time to prepare his wife and procure for her the necessary means of existence during an absence which might have been long; in spite of the fact that he knew then that he was in the right, and that in the end he would be set at liberty, he could not tell how and when the affair would end."

For the novelist the affair was very much more dangerous. But after the first two months the prisoners were allowed books, though very few in number. They were kept in complete ignorance, however, of the evidence against them and of how the examination of their case was progressing. But the great writer had become conscious that there is in man "a great reserve of endurance and vitality," and the tone of his letters to Michael at this time expresses resignation and regret rather than apprehension and despair: "Already three months have gone by since we have been in prison; what is going to happen to us? It may be that all this summer we shall not see the green leaves. Do you remember how they took us for a walk in the garden in the month of May? The verdure was commencing to appear then, down there, and I thought of Revel and of the time when I went to pay you a visit about the same time of the year, and of the garden which was attached to the house of the Engineers." In another letter he speaks of his delight at being allowed to walk in the prison garden, which contained "almost seventeen trees."

He uttered neither protest nor complaint. His

health remained fairly good. He was able to work, and in this first period of captivity he produced that charming and subtle study of childhood entitled *The Little Hero*. By his own admission, he had never worked more eagerly than in the Fortress. But at night the old nervous terror would close on him remorselessly. The very floor of his cell would seem to him to shake as though he were on board a steamer. His dreams became hideous, adding to the torment of already nearly exhausted nerves. But he would make use even of this misery. "When a nervous state like this," he informed Michael in a letter from the Fortress, "used to take possession of me, I would make use of it by writing—in that condition one writes always better and more—but now I curb myself so as not to finish myself altogether." But after a rest of three weeks the novelist was able to continue that sympathetic study of childhood's awakening, one of so many pictures of the kind to follow in the future, both in the famous novels and in the less known short stories.

He could not receive many books, but a copy of the Bible reached him; the two Testaments were in both the Slavonic and the French text. The study of the Bible was to be a great solace to him in the bitter years to come. But it must not be imagined that during this imprisonment Dostoevsky was "converted" suddenly, in the popular sense. Nor was he, like Count Tolstoy, as it were, dragged slowly and unwillingly to the sanctuary of belief. Dostoevsky was by temperament, as Merejkovsky has noted, a novelist of Christianity. But he was also a peculiarly alert transmitter of the significance and the wonder of the life around him. This so-called conservative was at all times contemptuous of the perfunctory, and even in his letter of thanks for this bundle of books that included a copy of Shakespeare he found time to criticise a comedy by Turgenev in a Russian periodical: "There is no originality: it is the old beaten track. All that has been said before him, and very much better." This characteristic letter stresses his gratitude for Shakespeare, even more than for the Bible, and ends with a request for another parcel of books.

The strange lull was now drawing to its close, and as yet there was nothing to suggest that Dostoevsky was indeed what Soloviev has rightly called him —the prince of psychopathists. No one at that time, in spite of the tumultuous welcome of *Poor Folk,* could have foreseen how he would be hailed in after years. No one could have foreseen that this frail figure, so soon to be stripped to his shirt in the depths of the Russian winter as he waited second by second for death, would live to become the accepted teacher of Russian youth. Still less could it have been foreseen that this victim of a Tsar's whim, "to teach those young people a lesson," would be eagerly sought out as an honoured guest by the Imperial rulers of Holy Russia.

Although he introduced propaganda into almost all his works, he was never to be a propagandist in the Western sense. He knew nothing of that long series of artifices which lead up from mere presence to the full glory of publicity. It certainly never occurred to him to claim omniscience in any direction. He was the last person in the world to deal out ersatz instruction on topics ranging from politics and religion to education and art. He made no sort of claim to leadership, in the quest of any new plan for a better and more adroitly manipulated life. He was deeply conscious of an all-pervading mystery and, always with that duality which made naïveté impossible, he accepted religion as its one available interpretation. He accepted, too, the Tsars of Russia as the natural product of history as he understood it. He accepted equally, with the same mysticism, the Byzantine rôle of Imperial Russia, just as Gogol accepted it. No human being could very well be less a rebel from the standpoint of the Orthodox Greek Church or, indeed, from the standpoint of Tsardom itself, than this unhappy writer who, in the December of 1849, was abruptly condemned to death.

Chapter III

THE FIRING-SQUAD

THERE were twenty-one prisoners in all. They were blindfolded and fastened to posts. The first batch of three was already waiting for execution. Dostoevsky was in the second batch and expected only a few more minutes of life. "I remembered you, brother," he wrote to Michael some three months later, "immediately after the terrible ordeal, and all your family; at the last instant, it was you, you alone, who were in my thoughts; then I understood how much I loved you, my own dear brother!"

The detailed description of the Ordeal in Dostoevsky's own words has been recorded in the *Memoirs* of Mme Kovalevsky: "I was condemned to be shot! Nothing was said about the time, but scarcely an hour had passed when the gaoler appeared and told me to put on my clothes. Under strong escort I was led out into the yard, where nineteen of my companions were waiting. It was seven o'clock in the morning. We were put into carriages, four in each, accompanied by a soldier."

The prisoners asked where they were being taken, but the soldier refused to tell them. The carriage windows were covered with ice and they could see nothing outside. In this manner they reached Semyonovski Square. Then they could see a scaffold erected in the middle. Up to this scaffold they were led and arranged in two lines. They were carefully watched so that it was impossible to mutter more than a few words even to those who stood nearest. The sheriff made his appearance on the scaffold and read out the sentence of death which was to be executed then and there. "Twenty times the fatal words were repeated: 'Sentenced to be shot!'" And so indelibly were the words graven into my memory that for years afterwards I would wake in the middle of the night fancying I heard them being read. But at the same time I distinctly remember another circumstance: the officer, after having finished the reading, folded the paper and put it into his pocket, after which he descended from the scaffold. At this moment the sun broke through the clouds, and I thought: 'It is impossible, they can't mean to kill us!' and I whispered these words to my nearest companion, but instead of answering he only pointed to a line of coffins that stood near the scaffold, covered with a large cloth."

Dostoevsky's last hope vanished. Death now seemed certain. "It gave me a great fright, but I determined not to show any fear, and I kept talking to my companion about different things. He told me afterwards that I had not even been very pale." Then suddenly a priest mounted the scaffold and asked if any of the condemned men wished to make confession. "Only one accepted the invitation, but when the priest held out the crucifix we all touched it with our lips."

Those regarded as most culpable, Petrachevsky and two others who were considered revolutionary leaders, were already tied to poles. Each head was hidden in a sort of bag; the soldiers stood ready awaiting the command to fire: "I thought I might perhaps have five minutes more to live, and awful those moments were. I kept staring at a church with a gilt dome, which reflected the sunbeams, and I suddenly felt as if these beams came from the region where I was to be myself in a few moments!"

Dostoevsky was short-sighted and so could not realise exactly what was taking place. But as he peered at the scene he became aware of an officer who galloped across the square, waving a white handkerchief. He was an emissary of the Tsar, announcing the prisoner's delivery from death. The sentence, the condemned men learned, had been intended as "a lesson not to be forgotten." The lesson was not without dire consequences for several of the prisoners: "When Grigoriev was released from the pole, he had become mad through the terror he had undergone whilst waiting for the fatal shot, and he never recovered his reason. Nor do I think that any of us escaped without life-long injury to his nervous system. Besides, when we were taken up to the scaffold, they took off our clothes, so that we had spent more than twenty minutes standing in our bare shirts in a cold of 22 deg., Réaumur, below freezing point! When we came back to our prisons, some of us had their ears and toes frozen; one got inflammation of the lungs, which ended in consumption. As for myself, I don't remember to have had the slightest sensation of the cold."

The sentence of death had been changed to four years' penal servitude, to be followed by military service in the ranks. The black cloth had not concealed coffins, though the mistake had been natural enough. Of all the twenty-one prisoners, only one, Palm, had received a full pardon. Dostoevsky had been standing beside Durow, the President of his little group of Fourierists, and had said good-bye to him and to Plestcheev while he was preparing to take his place in the second batch.

The novelist was never to forget that twenty minutes during which he had waited in the depths of a Russian winter, clad only in his shirt, for death. In *The Idiot* the hero, who is so very nearly an incarnation of Dostoevsky himself, exclaims: "Now with the rack and tortures and so on, you suffer terrible pain of course; but then your torture is bodily pain only (although no doubt you have plenty of that) until you die. But *here* I should imagine the most terrible part of the whole punishment is not the bodily pain at all—but the certain knowledge that in an hour—then in ten minutes, then in half a minute, then now—this very *instant*—your soul must quit your body and that you will no longer be a man—and that is certain, certain! that's the point —the certainty of it. Just that instant when you place your head on the block and hear the iron grate over your head—then—that quarter of a second is the most awful of all!" And Prince Mishkin goes on to argue that by reason of this certitude of terror the sentence on a criminal, without hope of reprieve, is far more awful than what he has inflicted upon his victim.

On the very day that he was to be sent to Siberia, two visitors came to the Fortress. They were Michael Dostoevsky and A. P. Milyukov, a former member of the Durov circle. The visitors were conducted to a room in the Commandant's quarters where they waited until two prisoners were brought into the room in charge of an officer who, all through the interview, kept in the background as much as possible. Milyukov found both Dostoevsky and Durov but little changed. Fyodor expressed delight that his elder brother was not sharing his fate and asked eagerly for details about Michael's family. Both prisoners praised the humanity of the Commandant, who had treated them as well as he possibly could. Neither of them complained of the harshness of the sentence; neither appeared to realise the ordeal that was so soon to make the youthful and debonair Durov a shattered old man. As for the novelist, in Milyukov's opinion he was infinitely less agitated than his brother. While Michael wept and trembled, Fyodor remained impassive: "Don't do that, brother, why, you know me. . . . We shall see one another again, I am sure of it; I confidently hope for that, I have no doubt at all that we shall meet again."

That strange inner calm of Dostoevsky, so deep a contrast to those spasms of terror which would sweep over him at long intervals, did not desert him on the very eve of his desperate journey. Eight months before, at the time of his arrest, he had shown greater anxiety about his brother Michael than about himself, and now he actually remembered a book that he had borrowed from a lady: "When I was arrested," he wrote long afterwards to his old friend the poet Maïkov, "this book was taken from me, but afterwards it was returned to me: but, being in prison, I could not have it sent back to her, and I knew what value she attached to it. All that caused me a great deal of pain. Two hours before my departure for Siberia, I asked Commandant Nabokov to return this book to its owner." It seems never to have occurred to Dostoevsky that he should be treated as a political prisoner and as such should be saved, so far as possible, from those degrading contacts which in the after years were to be thrown in his teeth by the woman who bore his name. "The convicts," he reminded Michael, "are not wild beasts, but men probably better, and perhaps much worthier, than myself. During these last months I have gone through a great deal, but I shall be able to write about what I shall see and experience in the future."

In spite of all his cruel experiences of actuality, he was never afterwards to depart from a point of view so typically compassionate. The pity of Dostoevsky was at no time merely verbal: "I never could understand the reason why one-tenth part of our people should be cultured, and the other nine-tenths must serve as the material support of the minority and themselves remain in ignorance. I do not want to think or to live with any other belief than that our ninety millions of people (and those who shall be born after us) will be some day cultured, humanised, and happy. I know and I firmly believe that universal enlightenment will harm none of us. I also believe that the kingdom of thought and light may be realised in our Russia even sooner than elsewhere, because with us, even now, no one defends the idea of one part of the population being enlisted against the other, as is found everywhere in the civilised countries of Europe."

Perhaps the whole gist of Dostoevsky's gospel, which is so utterly non-revolutionary, can be found in those few lines. It was to be repeated again and again throughout the great novels for which his merciless experiences in Siberia undoubtedly prepared the way. Gustave Flaubert might well have echoed the arrogant outburst of Théophile Gautier: "Tiberius, Caligula, Nero, mighty Imperial Romans! O you whom the world so little comprehends, at whose heels the rabble-rout of rhetoricians is ever barking! I am your fellow-sufferer, and all the pity that is left in me is compassionate towards you!"

The pity of Dostoevsky was far otherwise and, it cannot be emphasised too heavily, the man who so often complains in his letters of losses, difficulties and so forth, was almost incapable of actual self-pity.

One recalls the long journey to the School of Engineering, undertaken by the two brothers when they set out at a foot's pace, with halts of two or three hours at almost every post-house. That journey had lasted for nearly a whole week, but it had been undertaken in the genial month of May. Now the novelist was being prepared for this other journey at midnight on Christmas Eve: "Precisely at midnight on that Christmas Eve," he wrote from Omsk some five years later to Michael, "did chains touch me for the first time. They weigh about ten pounds, and make walking extraordinarily difficult. Then we were put into open sledges, each alone with a gendarme, and so, in four sledges—the orderly opening the procession—we left Petersburg. I was heavy-hearted, and the many different impressions filled me with confused and uncertain sensations. My heart beat with a peculiar flutter, and that numbed its pain."

But the fresh air revived his spirits and he examined the lit-up windows of the festive houses. He remembered that Michael was taking his children with his wife to a Christmas party at the publisher Kraevsky's: "I did feel dreadfully sad as we passed that house. I took leave, as it were, of the little ones. I felt so lonely for them, and even years afterwards I often thought of them with tears in my eyes." After three or four stations there was a halt at an inn: "There we drank tea with as much avidity as if we had not touched anything for a week.

After the eight months' captivity, sixty versts in a sledge gave us appetites of which, even to-day, I think with pleasure." The orderly proved unexpectedly kindly, and Dostoevsky and his companions were allowed a covered sledge, which, naturally, was considered a great privilege.

The next day was a holiday, and consequently it was easy enough to get food at the halts, every five or six stations. But it was so cold that the prisoners could hardly thaw themselves in the station waiting-rooms. For all that, Dostoevsky's health seemed to improve though the cold increased: "Mournful was the moment when we crossed the Ural. The horses and sledges sank deep in the snow. A snow-storm was raging. We got out of the sledges—it was night —and waited, standing, till they were extricated. All about us whirled the snow-storm. We were standing in the confines of Europe and Asia; before us lay Siberia and the mysterious future—behind us, our whole past; it was very melancholy. Tears came to my eyes." As they passed through the different villages the peasants would line up to get a view of them and, untouched by their fetters, the people at the different stations would treble the prices of provisions. But at Tobolsk, where they arrived on January 12th and where they met many of the "Decembrists" and their wives, the reception was very different: "Those noble souls, tested by five-and-twenty years of suffering and self-sacrifice! We saw them but seldom, for we were very strictly guarded; still, they sent us clothes and provisions, they comforted and encouraged us. I had brought far too few clothes, and had bitterly repented it, but *they* sent me clothes."

At Tobolsk the novelist made enquiries as to the

THE FIRING-SQUAD 53

kind of people who would so soon have him at their mercy: "They told me that the Commandant was a very decent fellow, but that the Major, Krivzov, was an uncommon brute, a petty tyrant, a drunkard, a trickster—in short, the greatest horror that can be imagined." In *The House of the Dead* Dostoevsky has paid attention to these "majors by the mercy of God." He was attached to the Second Division, in which the discipline was far more severe than in the other two Divisions which belonged to the factories and the mines: "Not only for us *dvoriané* was it more severe, but also for all the prisoners, in that its directorate and its organisation were of a military character, and caused the Division closely to resemble one of the disciplinary battalions which obtain in Russia proper."

Members of the Second Division were always in fetters, always under escort on marches, always living under lock and key, while these terrible restrictions did not obtain in the other two Divisions to anything like the same extent. The extraordinary thing was that the life did not strike the novelist as astounding or, at all events, unexpected: "Indeed, I even formed the impression that prison life was easier than I had anticipated while on the journey, as well as that the labour was less hard and penal. Only long afterwards did I realise that the severity and the punishment of that labour lay less in its arduousness and its constant repetition than in the condition that it was *forced* labour, labour performed under penalty of chastisement." At the beginning, as indeed at the very end, Dostoevsky never regarded himself as a victim of injustice. He accepted his tasks almost with a positive eagerness. He actually liked the quarrying of alabaster and the clearing away of snow. But the barrack ward was from first to last an inferno: "smoke and grime, curses of an unspeakable cynicism, an atmosphere mephitical in its nature, a constant clashing of fetters, and an eternal babble of imprecations and lewd laughter."

The Major, Krivzov, was too horrible even for this milieu; he was court-martialled two years after Dostoevsky's arrival: "He used to come to us mad drunk (I never once saw him sober), and would seek out some inoffensive prisoner and flog him on the pretext that *he*—the prisoner—was drunk. Often he came at night and punished at random—say, because such and such an one was sleeping on his left side instead of his right, or because he talked or moaned in his sleep—in fact, anything that occurred to his drunken mind. I should have had to break out in the long run against such a man as that, and it was he who wrote the monthly reports of us to Petersburg." As for the convicts their loathing for the nobles was almost pathological: "They would have devoured us," Dostoevsky assures Michael in the longest of his letters, "if they only could. Judge then for yourself in what danger we stood, having to live with these people for some years, eat with them, sleep by them, and with no possibility of complaining of the affronts which were constantly put upon us."

After a long spell behind dungeon walls, the novelist was to enjoy the luxury of hard labour. In winter his strength would fail him in spite of his curious, cat-like wiriness. While he was working in a temperature at which quicksilver froze, one of his feet was frost-bitten. But it was the living together in a single barrack-room that tortured him: "Imag-

THE FIRING-SQUAD

ine an old, crazy wooden building, that should long ago have been broken up as useless. In the summer it is unbearably hot, in the winter unbearably cold. All the boards are rotten. On the ground filth lies an inch thick; every instant one is in danger of slipping and coming down. The small windows are so frozen over that even by day one can hardly read. The ice on the panes is three inches thick. The ceilings drip, there are draughts everywhere. We are packed like herrings in a barrel. The stove is heated with six logs of wood, but the room is so cold that the ice never once thaws; the atmosphere is unbearable—and so through all the winter long."

The prisoners washed their linen in this same room so that the whole place was dripping. They were forbidden to leave the room from twilight till morning: "The doors are barricaded; in the anteroom a great wooden trough for the calls of nature is placed; this makes one almost unable to breathe. All the prisoners stink like pigs; they say they can't help it, for they must live, and are but men. We slept upon bare boards; each man was allowed one pillow only. We covered ourselves with short sheepskins, and our feet were outside the covering all the time. It was thus that we froze night after night. Fleas, lice, and other vermin by the bushel. In the winter we got thin sheepskins to wear, which didn't keep us warm at all, and boots with short legs; thus equipped, we had to go out in the frost."

Their food consisted of bread and cabbage soup. The soup ought to have contained a quarter of a pound of meat for each prisoner, but, as sausage meat was substituted, the novelist never received any genuine flesh. Porridge was served on feast days, but with scarcely any butter. On fast days there was only cabbage. The unhappy writer was soon a prey to all the torments of indigestion. In spite of all these horrible conditions, the convicts managed to do work of some kind and to sell the products of their labour. Dostoevsky was able to secure tea and an occasional piece of meat from outside. He provided himself, too, with tobacco, without which he would have been suffocated in such an atmosphere. But all these small compensations were without the knowledge of the officials.

Dostoevsky, naturally, found himself frequently in hospital. The doctor, indeed, appears to have been almost the only human being who regarded the convict as a human being. Malingering was by no means infrequent. "Well, brother!" the doctor would exclaim on such occasions, "I suppose you have been here long enough, and got fairly rested. It is time for you to go." But there was no malingering in the novelist's case. His nerves were wrecked and he had become a prey to those epileptic fits which were to torture him all through his life. In addition to this, he had rheumatism in the legs. "But except for that," he assures his brother, "I feel right well." Starved in body, he was also to be starved in mind: "Add to all these discomforts the fact that it was almost impossible to get oneself a book, and that when I did get one, I had to read it on the sly; that all around was incessant malignity, turbulence and quarreling; then perpetual espionage, and the impossibility of ever being alone for even an instant—and so without variation for four long years: You'll believe me when I tell you that I was not happy. And imagine, in addition, the ever-present dread of drawing down some punishment on myself, the irons, and the utter oppression of spirits—and you have the picture of my life."

But the novelist, merciful in his analysis of the monstrous, frequently noted in *The House of the Dead* the childish side of his fellow-prisoners. The man of genius realised the alleviation of manual labour, but this idea was derided by his companions. He would hammer alabaster gladly into white powder; he would willingly turn the fly-wheel in the turner's workshop. At other times he would be glad to find himself a member of a party sent to shovel snow away from the Government buildings. The convicts themselves revelled in this particular work: "A tremendous task was appointed us; we each had a shovel given us, and we all set to work unanimously, thrusting our shovels deep into the soft fresh snow, which had hardly time to freeze on its surface, and throwing it over our shoulders in huge white lumps, which turned into a silvery dust as they fell. The fresh wintry air and the exercise always had an exhilarating effect on the men. They laughed and shouted, threw snowballs at each other till the air grew thick with flying masses of snow, and the more sensible members of the party put a stop to the proceedings, and the whole thing ended in a violent quarrel."

The convicts showed their delight, too, in private theatricals, which were permitted them occasionally. They delighted in strutting backwards and forwards in front of an audience, forgetting for the moment the actualities of their lives. "Poor fellows!" the novelist comments. "They had nothing to look forward to except long years of a life as monotonous as the dripping of the rain on a gloomy, chilly autumn day, and to-night they had been allowed to forget their misery for a moment." The convicts would also show their human side in their love of pets, and on Christmas Day something like peace reigned among them. Even the sergeant-at-arms would wish the convicts a "merry Christmas" as he came in to count them. The scene that followed was almost like any other Christmas festivity: "Akim Akimytch did not spend much time over his prayers that morning, but hurried off to the kitchen, together with several others, to see how their geese and pigs were getting on, and to superintend the important operation of roasting them. We could see from our snow- and ice-covered windows the blaze of the kitchen fire as it shone out against the dark winter morning. The convicts were running about the yard and rushing in and out of the kitchens. A very few had already paid the tapster a visit, but these were the most impatient ones. On the whole, they all conducted themselves with great propriety, and neither quarrelled nor swore." But it could not last; the day closed in the old atmosphere of rage and insult.

Dostoevsky studied the officers just as carefully as he did his fellow-prisoners. There was a certain Lieutenant Jerebajtnikov who seems to have been a worthy rival of the monster Krivzov. This lieutenant would pretend to forgive a prisoner on the ground of his being an orphan, after which he would roar at the top of his voice: "Beat him! Flog him; strike him harder, harder, harder! Faster, faster! Flog the orphan; flog the scoundrel! Go at it; go at it! More, more, more! Faster, faster!" Then there was another official named Smekalov who was accepted, for some reason or other, by the convicts as a humorist. He would ask a prisoner if he knew a particular prayer, and when he replied that he did would order him, quite pleasantly, to repeat it. When the convict arrived at the words "in Heaven," the officer would order the flogging to commence. "What a good fellow he is! and so jolly, too!" was the general verdict. They had another comedian in the person of a Jew named Issai Fomitch who succeeds in becoming the central figure of that terrible scene which seems to stand out as the very essence of convict life. Of this Turgenev observed significantly: "Le tableau du bain, c'est vraiment du Dante." Here perhaps the grotesque converges with the horrible in a picture of distorted manhood that Dostoevsky himself was never to repeat in art, having snatched it, once and for all, so terribly from life:

"The shelves were covered with convicts who tried to screw themselves into the smallest possible space. Few, however, of the convicts really washed themselves, as the common people care but little for soap and hot water, their idea of a bath consisting in getting up to the highest shelf, whipping themselves violently with a bundle of birch twigs and then pouring cold water down their backs. About fifty birch rods were in constant movement on the shelves, water was being continually thrown at the hot oven to make more steam, till the heat was almost unbearable. And all this mass of human beings was swaying backwards and forwards, shouting and yelling, and clanking their chains on the floor. Some, in trying to cross the floor, were caught in the chains of those who were sitting down, and, falling on their heads, knocked them down, cursing and swearing. The dirt and filth actually flowed in streams everywhere. The men were perfectly wild with excitement and yelled and shrieked like demons. A dense crowd had collected round the window where the cans of hot water were handed in, and carried by the buyers to their respective places, not, however, without spilling half of it over the heads of the bathers who squatted on the floor. From time to time the moustached face of a soldier would look in at the door or window to see if there were no disorders going on. The closely cropped pates and red-hot bodies of the convicts appeared to me more hideous than ever. Their backs were covered with scars from the lash or the stick, which stood out more vividly on the red surface, and looked like so many fresh stripes. I could not help shuddering with horror at the sight of them. More water is being thrown over the hot stones, and a thick cloud of vapour rises from them and fills the whole bathroom, which resounds with maddening shrieks and howls."

It would seem difficult for any particular monster to emerge from such monsters as these. But Issai Fomitch, the Jew, has climbed on to the highest shelf of the bath. From this vantage-ground his howls rise in a crescendo of horrible enjoyment. In Fomitch we have, as it were, the very grin of outrage, the grin of Siberia: "He is nearly beside himself with the heat and whipping, but it seems as if no earthly heat could ever satisfy him. He hires a man for a kopek to whip him, but the latter soon finds the heat too much for him, throws down the rod and runs away to refresh himself with a cold shower-bath. Issai Fomitch, nothing loth, hires another, then a third—he can be generous at times, and has as many as five men to whip him to-day. 'Hurrah for Issai Fomitch!' shout the convicts from below. Issai Fomitch feels that at this moment he is high above everybody else and can look down upon us, and triumphantly shrieks out his pæan, 'la, la, la,' in a shrill voice like a madman's." The impression produced on the novelist was that he had been looking into the very heart of hell.

And yet human beings were to be found even in this collection of outcasts. Among them was a Caucasian named Aleï whom Dostoevsky taught to read Russian in the New Testament. Like Sonya in *Crime and Punishment,* the Caucasian found inspiration in the Sermon on the Mount. He discovered in the New Testament both the beauty and the compassion of Issa, the prophet of his own race. Turning to his brothers, he addressed them in his own language: "They talked long and gravely together, nodding their heads as if in approval of what was said. Then they turned to me, with the quiet dignified smile I liked so well, and informed me that Issa was a prophet of God, and had done great miracles, that he had formed a bird of clay, breathed on it, and that it had flown away—all of which was written in their sacred books."

Just a week before the long letter to Michael which, together with *The House of the Dead,* forms such an intimate record of what the novelist endured in Siberia, his sentence in the prison at Omsk was completed. Before going to Siberia he had been stripped of his military rank and had lost his title of nobility. The following month he entered the 7th Siberian Regiment of the Line. At the end of the month he arrived at Semipalatinsk with his regiment. Two months later the private soldier composed a poem on the European happenings of 1854.

Chapter IV

A CURIOUS INTERLUDE

IN NOVEMBER 1854 a person of considerable significance in Dostoevsky's seemingly insignificant life arrived at Semipalatinsk. Baron Alexander Vrangel had been present at the ceremony in Semyonovski Square on December 22nd, 1849. In 1854 he was appointed District-Attorney to Siberia. He had known Michael Dostoevsky in Petersburg and he brought the novelist a letter from him, linen, books and the sum of fifty roubles. He also brought a letter from Apollon Maïkov. In the course of his duty Vrangel was obliged to spend quite a long time at Semipalatinsk, and on his way there he had visited Omsk. When there he had made the acquaintance of the humane Mme Ivanova, a Frenchwoman by birth, whose husband was an officer of the Gendarmerie. She, like so many of the Decembrists' wives, had done all she could for the political offenders, and particularly for Dostoevsky. "He told me himself," Vrangel notes, "that neither in the prison nor later during his military service was ever a hair of his head hurt by his superiors or by the other prisoners or soldiers; all the newspaper reports that declare otherwise are pure invention. For it has frequently been maintained that Dostoevsky's fits were brought on by the corporal chastisement he received: and many appear to believe this legend."

Vrangel found Dostoevsky no longer in barracks, but living in his own quarters, having obtained permission to do so under the supervision of his cap-

A CURIOUS INTERLUDE 63

tain, Stepanov. A sergeant had been selected to keep him under surveillance but had been bought off for a trifle and gave the novelist no trouble at all. Vrangel's first impressions of the private soldier were rather disconcerting, as his host did not realise who he was or why he had come: "He wore a grey military cloak with a high red collar and red epaulettes; his pale, freckled face had a morose expression. His fair hair was closely shorn. He scrutinised me keenly with his intelligent blue-grey eyes, as if seeking to divine what sort of person I was. As he confessed to me later on, he had been almost frightened when my messenger told him that the District-Attorney wished to see him."

The novelist read his letters at once and tears came into his eyes. His guest began to experience exactly the same sense of despair and desolation which had been Dostoevsky's for so long. While they were talking together, a bundle of letters from Petersburg was brought to this District-Attorney, who almost seems to have stepped bodily out of one or other of Dostoevsky's novels: "I ran through the letters and suddenly began to sob; I was at that time unusually emotional and greatly attached to my family. My separation from all who were dear to me seemed insupportable, and I was quite terrified of my future life. So there we were together, both in a desolate and lonely condition. . . . I felt so heavy-hearted that I forgot my exalted position as District-Attorney, and fell on the neck of Fyodor Mikhailovitch, who stood looking at me with mournful eyes. He comforted me, pressed my hand like an old friend, and we promised one another to meet as often as possible."

During the months that followed, the two men

became friends. Dostoevsky lunched frequently with the District-Attorney, who visited the hovel in which the novelist lived in the dreariest part of the dreary town: "It was of rough timber, crazy, warped, without any foundations, and with not one window looking on the street. Dostoevsky had a quite large, but very low and badly lit room. The mud-walls had once been white; on both sides stood broad benches. On the walls hung fly-spotted picture-sheets. To the left of the doorway was a large stove. Behind the stove stood a bed, a little table, and a chest of drawers, which served as a dressing-table. All this corner was divided from the rest of the room by a calico curtain. In the windows were geraniums, and curtains hung there which had once been red. Walls and ceiling were blackened by smoke, and it was so dark in the room that in the evenings one could scarcely read by the tallow candle (wax candles were then a great luxury, and petroleum lamps not known at all)!" To add to the misery of this unfortunate man beetles swarmed in the room which in summer was infested with more voracious vermin. The District-Attorney could not imagine how the novelist could write all through the night by a tallow candle, but he was even then at work on *The House of the Dead,* which he had commenced, or rather tried to commence, in prison.

P. K. Martyanov obtained much information on the novelist's imprisonment from several naval cadets who had been degraded and transferred as privates to the line regiment at Omsk. He has noted with much surprise the antagonism, during imprisonment, that existed between the novelist and Durov: "The cadets observed with amazement that Dostoevsky and Durov hated one another with all the force of their beings; they were never seen together, and during their whole time in the prison at Omsk they never exchangd a word with one another." It will be recalled that in *The House of the Dead* there is no actual mention of Durov by name though there are oblique references to "the other prisoner of noble birth." Dostoevsky, according to the cadets, had the attitude of a wolf in a trap and regarded everyone with suspicion. In his prison clothes with the yellow badges on his back, with the white brimless cap in summer and a cap with ear flaps in winter, the chains on his arms and legs clanking with every movement, the great writer had not lost all the insignia of his birth and training.

But, curiously enough, he did not convey then the impression of weakness and ill-health: "Dostoevsky looked like a strong, somewhat thick-set, well-disciplined working-man. His hard fate had, as it were, turned him to stone. He seemed dull, awkward, and was always taciturn. On his pale, worn, ashen face which was freckled with dark-red spots, one never saw a smile; he opened his lips only to utter curt, disconnected remarks about his work. He always wore his cap dragged down on his forehead to his eyebrows; his glance was sullen, unpropitiating, fierce, and mostly directed on the ground." According to this evidence, he was unpopular among his fellow-prisoners, who all liked his one-time companion, Durov. This political prisoner, on the cadets' testimony, "looked like a fine gentleman even in prison clothes." Martyanov's record, incidentally, endorses the District-Attorney's statement to the effect that the novelist was never subjected to actual physical violence during his imprisonment.

But the notorious Major Krivzov once discovered him in the prison where he had been detained for "house-work" after the other prisoners had gone out to perform their allotted tasks. He was ill and lying on his plank bed. The Major made pointed enquiries about him and was told that the novelist had just had an epileptic fit. "Nonsense! I am aware that you indulge him too much," Krivzov roared to the cadet who was trying to shield the novelist. "Out to the guard-room with him this instant; bring the rods!" While the unfortunate man was being hustled along to the guard-room the cadet dispatched a report of the occurrence to General de Grave, who came at once to the guard-room and prevented the whipping. He gave orders that under no circumstances were sick prisoners to be subjected to corporal punishment and administered a public reprimand to this notoriously brutal major.

Dostoevsky, after his imprisonment, seems to have harboured no ill-feeling whatever towards Durov and referred pleasantly to him in his correspondence as well as in conversation. But there were real enemies both of the writer and of the District-Attorney in the desolate town of Semipalatinsk. The officials, who were thoroughly venal, would question Vrangel ironically about this private soldier with whom he spent so much time. The Governor himself warned him to beware of the revolutionary who might influence his inexperienced youth. But Vrangel stood by his friend and interested the Military Governor, Spiridonov, in the unfortunate writer. He even obtained an invitation for Dostoevsky to the Governor's house, and after this all doors seem to have been opened to the private soldier. One of these houses belonged to a certain Captain

Alexander Ivanovitch Issayev, a fellow-exile of the novelist, a victim of consumption, a drunkard and the husband of Maria Dmitrievna, "about thirty, an extremely pretty blonde of middle height, very thin, passionate, and *exaltée*." This lady took a compassionate interest in the novelist, but, in the District-Attorney's opinion, she was not in the least in love with him: "She knew that he had epileptic attacks, and that he suffered dire poverty; she often said he was 'a man without a future.'" But, such as she was, she appealed intensely to the novelist, who could deal with her "fantastically" as with one or other of his future creations in fiction.

In the days of peace, before Munich was associated with international mendacity, the phrase "du Munich" was sometimes applied to objects of derision. In exactly this sense the phrase "C'est du Dostoevsky" was used in after years by Ivan Turgenev. Now, in a quite different sense and without the impertinence of scorn, some of us are inclined to echo that "C'est du Dostoevsky" in the hope of explaining much that seems otherwise inexplicable. But why should the future Mme Dostoevsky reject the author of *Poor Folk* as "a man without a future"? That work, at all events, could not be idly dismissed as formless—the old charge against the future creator of the Karamazovs. M. Gide, whose own mind is a superb example of the perfection of orderly French logic, was very quick to perceive a deadly cohesion in the apparent turmoil of a Dostoevsky novel. Not for a second would this famous French writer permit himself to say of Dostoevsky what a well-known English writer remarked of him years ago: "He is a better writer than Hall Caine."

In reality, the Russian author, in spite of the

harassed speed at which he wrote, always preserved a sense of words. One remembers how Anatole France, having condescended to the cliché "le Vésuve fumait," exchanged the last word for "riait" in disgust at what he called his lapse into *pâtisserie*. Now Dostoevsky, even in his early youth, showed an almost equal disgust for such *pâtisserie*. His one-time fellow-student Grigorovitch, almost the only human being who had really made friends with him at the School of Engineering, once read aloud a story of his containing this harmless sentence: "When the organ stopped, an official threw a copper coin out of his window, which fell at the organ-grinder's feet." Dostoevsky protested at once: "No, that's not right, it's much too dull: 'The copper coin fell at the organ-grinder's feet.' You should say, 'The copper coin fell *clinking* and *hopping* at the man's feet.'" The emendation is certainly far less striking than, for instance, Edgar Allan Poe's emendations of Mrs. Browning's poetry. But, quite rightly, it impressed Grigorovitch during that brief period when the two shared rooms in Petersburg, living as best they could, half the time on rolls and coffee. It was the period when Dostoevsky was translating *Eugénie Grandet* while at the same time beginning to be haunted by the creations of *Poor Folk*. In those days, his old friend notes, his health was becoming worse and the troubles which had shown themselves even in his boyhood had now become frequent: "Sometimes he would even have a fit on one of our few walks together. Once we chanced to come on a funeral. Dostoevsky insisted on turning back at once; but he had scarcely gone a few steps when he had such a violent fit that I was

A CURIOUS INTERLUDE 69

obliged to carry him, with the help of some passers-by, into the nearest shop; it was with great difficulty that we restored him to consciousness. Such attacks were usually followed by a state of great depression which lasted two or three days."

Baron Vrangel tells us that during his appointment at Semipalatinsk he never witnessed any such attack, but the future Mme Dostoevsky was only too right in viewing the novelist as a victim of actual epilepsy as distinct from *le petit mal*. The District-Attorney did not like the Issayevs, and it was in vain that Dostoevsky tried to get him to their house. But his friendship with Dostoevsky never slackened, and the novelist's landlady would usually send for him whenever her lodger had one of his terrible seizures. After each one of these the victim's brain refused to work for some two or three days. He told Vrangel specifically that the first fits had overtaken him in Petersburg but that the malady had developed in the convict prison. At Semipalatinsk, he would have one on an average of once in three months. But in spite of this calamity Dostoevsky seems, at this period, to have been unusually kindly and free from those outbursts of exasperation which were to be such a trial to his second wife during the first months of their marriage. Vrangel wrote on April 2nd, 1856, a particularly revealing sketch of his friend: "Destiny has brought me into contact with a man of rare intellect and disposition—the gifted young author Dostoevsky. I owe him much; his words, counsels, and ideas will be a source of strength to me throughout all my life. I work daily with him; at the moment we think of translating Hegel's *Philosophy* and the *Psyche* of

Carus. He is deeply religious; frail of body, but endowed with iron will. Do try, my dear Papa, to find out if there is any idea of an amnesty."

The novelist at this time showed his characteristic sympathy for the poor and the distressed. "Everyone who knew him well," Vrangel notes, "knows of his extraordinary goodness of heart. How pathetic is his solicitude, for instance, about his brother Michael's family, about little Pasha Issayev, and many others besides!" While the Crimean War continued the two friends naturally abused Western Europe, and Dostoevsky's prejudice against any imitation of Western progress considerably deepened. He dismissed the idea of any sort of Russian Constitution on Western lines as wholly ridiculous, and he expressed personal dislike of Petrachevsky and disapproval of that leader's political plans. But all the time he was preoccupied by something quite different from Russian politics. He was in love with Mme Issayev, and when she and her husband were transferred to Kusnezk, a town some five hundred versts away, the novelist was in a state of utter despair.

The good-natured baron determined to help his friend without paying much attention to the discretion demanded by his official position: "Dostoevsky and I decided to go part of the way with the Issayevs. I took him in my carriage, the Issayevs sat in an open diligence. Before the departure, they all turned in to drink a glass of wine at my house. So as to enable Dostoevsky to have one last talk undisturbed with Maria Dmitrievna before she went, I made her husband properly drunk. On the way I gave him some more champagne, thus getting him wholly into my power—then took him into my car-

A CURIOUS INTERLUDE 71

riage, where he forthwith fell asleep." Dostoevsky then joined Mme Issayev in the open diligence. The youthful baron, in spite of the grotesqueness of the situation even under the glamour of moonlight, seems to have been sincerely touched by the final parting: "Those two embraced for the last time, and wiped the tears from their eyes, while I dragged the drunken and drowsy Issayev over to the carriage; he at once went off again, and never knew in the least what had been done with him. Little Pasha was fast asleep too. The diligence set off, a cloud of dust arose, already we could see it no more and the sound of the little bells was dying away in the distance; but Dostoevsky stood stark and dumb, and the tears were streaming down his cheeks."

The novelist was in despair; he even stopped working on *The House of the Dead*. The letters of Mme Issayev added nothing to his peace of mind. She complained of poverty, ill-health, the sufferings of her drunken husband, the hopeless future. On June 4th, 1855, four months after the accession to the throne of Alexander II, Dostoevsky writes to his future wife in terms of the deepest respect towards her and her husband: "You two treated me like a brother. I remember that from the very first I felt at home in your house. Alexander Ivanovitch could not have been kinder to his own brother than he was to me. With my unendurable character, I must have caused you much vexation, and yet you both loved me. I recognise it and feel it, for indeed I am not quite heartless. You are a wonderful woman; you have a heart of rare childlike kindliness, and you were like a sister to me."

It is so very difficult to reconcile the deep sincerity of this fragment with the jocund description by the baron of the novelist's parting with Mme Issayev that not a few of us will feel inclined to echo the old cliché, "C'est du Dostoevsky." They will echo it even more loudly when they consider two interludes that might well have been embedded in one or other of the world-famous novels as yet unborn. The District-Attorney, wrapped up in a love-affair of his own, took some long journeys by way of diversion and was absent from Semipalatinsk for two months. Now, at the Issayevs' house Dostoevsky had been told of a certain Marina O., the daughter of a Polish exile, and, at Mme Issayev's request, had given her some lessons. She was a very pretty girl of seventeen, and she was more than willing to flirt light-heartedly with her instructor. Vrangel had hoped, indeed, that Marina would efface Dostoevsky's fatal passion for Mme Issayev, to whom he was writing all the time at great length. But on his return to Semipalatinsk the baron found a sad change in the young girl, a change that had nothing whatever to do with the novelist. At this stage, the story resembles Maupassant quite as much as Dostoevsky. The Mayor of the dreary town had a son of eighteen who seduced and then deserted poor Marina. But that was not enough. The youth's coachman, a scoundrelly old Circassian, discovered the affair and threatened to divulge it to the girl's father and stepmother unless she yielded to him. Marina in her fear consented, loathing him all the time. Blackmailed and plundered, she revealed to Dostoevsky and Vrangel her unendurable plight. The District-Attorney fell back on his official powers and had the Circassian expelled from Semipalatinsk at once.

But a year later Marina's father, in his turn, used compulsion and forced the girl to marry an old

Cossack officer. She lost no time in rousing her husband's jealousy, and when Dostoevsky was married Marina was the cause of painful scenes between him and his first wife. There is no reason to believe that she became Dostoevsky's mistress, but, on the other hand, students of the novelist have a rather absurd, and not always well-meaning, attitude towards his emotional life. Dostoevsky himself was by no means secretive on all occasions. He was not at all severe towards the Mimi Pinsons of Petersburg. The only thing that he had against them was that they cost a great deal of money. His daughter, naturally enough, is incredulous towards the frolics of her illustrious father's youth, but a defence is, only too often, worse than an attack. At all events, this particular defence has led to quite unjustified suspicions of delayed virility in regard to an excellent and much loved father of a family. But at this period the novelist was undoubtedly solely preoccupied with the lady who became his first wife.

In January 1856 he became a non-commissioned officer, and the following March he addressed a letter to be delivered by Baron Vrangel to the great Todleben. Vrangel, who had left Semipalatinsk shortly before, had been deeply grieved at having to part from the novelist: "I was young, strong, and full of roseate hopes; while he—great, God-given writer—was losing his only friend and had to stay behind as a common soldier, sick, forsaken, desolate in Siberia!" Dostoevsky refers to Vrangel in this letter as one who "has done more for me than my own brother could have done."

He goes on to give a résumé of his life since his sentence: "I was guilty, and am very conscious of it. I was convicted of the intention (but only the intention) of acting against the Government; I was lawfully and quite justly condemned; the hard and painful experiences of the ensuing years have sobered me, and altered my views in many respects. But then, while I was still blind, I believed in all the theories and Utopias. When I went to Siberia, I had at least the one comfort of having borne myself honestly before the tribunal, of not having tried to shift my guilt on others, and even of having sacrificed my own interests, if thereby I thought I could save those others. But I was at that time still convinced of the truth of my opinions; I would not confess all, and so was the more sternly punished. Previously I had suffered for two years from a strange moral disease: I had fallen into hypochondria. There was a time when I even lost my reason. I was exaggeratedly irritable, had a morbidly developed sensibility, and the power of distorting the most extraordinary events into things immeasurable. But I felt that though this disease had had a really evil influence upon my destiny, it was nevertheless a poor and even a degrading excuse for me. And I was not so entirely convinced, either, that it *had* had that influence." The letter goes on to speak of "the terrible defence of Sebastopol" with obvious sincerity, and concludes "with deepest respect and the sincere thanks of a Russian."

The result of this appeal is given in a minute by the famous general to the effect that Dostoevsky is to receive the rank of ensign in a regiment of the Second Army Corps and is to receive permission to continue his career in literature so long as his works have a lawful tendency. And now we come to the second Dostoevsky story from real life, which is at the same time, both in its simplicity and in its complexity so close to his own fiction. Mme Issayev became a widow during the year that followed her departure from Semipalatinsk, but very soon afterwards announced her engagement in a letter to Dostoevsky. He was in despair, but, exactly as though he were the poor clerk in *Poor Folk,* he did his best to help the couple to marry. It is, possibly, because of this trait in his character that his critics have acquitted him of jealousy. In actual fact this quality, more or less common to mankind, leaks out occasionally in the correspondence. It is by no means to be ignored in many a seemingly almost naïve composition of this extraordinarily complicated human being. In this particular case, however, jealousy must have been of short duration.

For the widow announced, without much preamble, that the engagement had been broken off. The novelist was promptly summoned to Kusnezk and was shortly afterwards married to this engaging blonde. But the matter was in reality, as so often in the novels, very much less simple than the bare narration seems to suggest. According to the novelist's daughter, there was in the background a certain teacher named Vergunov whose existence had probably been discovered by Mme Issayev's former suitor when he broke off his engagement so abruptly. This Vergunov had had a liaison with Maria Dmitrievna during her first marriage and was to continue it during her second. And just as Dostoevsky had esteemed Captain Issayev as his brother, so he was to esteem the man Vergunov with the same feelings of fraternity. The situation would appear to be one of fiction rather than of real life.

When Dostoevsky regained his commission he was

allowed to live in Tver, and in the November of the same year he was at last permitted to return to Petersburg. Vergunov, at one stage distance behind, followed the couple. But Dostoevsky's first wife soon became the victim of tuberculosis and, finding the climate of Petersburg too harsh for her, left her husband and went to Tver. Here, as she grew worse and worse, she was deserted by her once so singularly persistent lover.

In the meantime the novelist was working for the "Vremya," in which *The House of the Dead* appeared— to be published in book form in 1862, the year in which he visited Europe for the first time. On this occasion he was in Paris, London and Geneva, and the following year he went to Rome and thence to Germany and Denmark. In this last capital he was to become the guest of Baron Vrangel a few years later; but they saw comparatively little of each other during the period of Dostoevsky's return to Petersburg from Siberia.

During these travels in 1863 the life of Dostoevsky was peculiarly tangled. The "Vremya," which was edited and published by him and his brother Michael, was in difficulties. His wife was seriously ill and in poverty. His stepson the little Pasha, who was to be a very serious burden to him in after-life, had of course to be duly supported. Money must be provided, and Dostoevsky in a letter to Michael from Turin dated September 8th-20th, 1863, explains something of his difficulties, still further intensified by his traveling companion, A. P. (Mlle Apollinaria Suslova), the Pauline of *The Gambler*. Dostoevsky is puzzled as to why, in spite of such companionship, his adventures have been frankly boring: "Now even happiness I take with pain, because I have separated myself from all those I have hitherto loved and suffered for many a time. Throwing up everything in search of happiness, even matters in which I could be of use, is egotism, and the thought of this is now poisoning my happiness (if it indeed exists)." Then in reply to Michael, who had reproached him with gambling away his very last money while travelling with the being he loves, the novelist exclaims, not without a certain indignation that rings true in the Dostoevsky sense: "Misha my friend! At Wiesbaden I invented a system of playing, I put it into practice and won at once 10,000 francs. Next morning, in excitement, I was unfaithful to my system, and lost at once. In the evening I returned to my system again, in full vigour, and immediately and without any effort I won 3,000 francs. Tell me after that how could I help being carried away, how could I help believing that if I followed that system, luck was in my hands?"

In letter after letter through the years one can see much the same argument about the same system. Many, of course, have foolishly dismissed the great writer as a slave to roulette; many, on the other hand, have pooh-poohed the very suggestion that Dostoevsky was a gambler. In exactly the same spirit of exaggerated attack and equally exaggerated defence some have assailed Dostoevsky as the very worst of sensualists, while others have accused him of lack of ordinary physical development. These last have gone so far as to suggest that the companionship of that slender and engaging student was strictly platonic. Pauline is said to have followed the example of George Sand in *Elle et Lui,* but, after a brief interlude, to have returned to Dostoevsky. It was not until 1881 that she became Mme V. V. Rozanov, an unhappy union which terminated in 1886. Rightly or wrongly, Pauline is supposed to have cherished the memory of the Russian novelist until her death.

But now in this year 1863 at Baden A. P. had to keep out of the way because of her lover's encounter with Turgenev: "He is sulking although he has recovered his health in Baden. He is here with his daughter. He told me of all his moral sufferings and doubts, philosophic doubts converted into stark reality. He is a bit of a coxcomb. I did not hide from him the fact that I was gambling." The letter concludes with a note of deep anxiety in regard to the novelist's wife: "I am afraid that Marie Dmitrievna may write you something unpleasant. Yet I do not suppose she will. She may, of course, need no money till the middle of October. But how can I tell? Perhaps I have placed her in a false position. She needed a hundred roubles for something, but had not decided to make that expense. But after getting my letter, in which I said that I was sending her money, she may have incurred that expense. And now she is perhaps without money. I tremble at the thought of it. If only someone had sent me an account of her health!"

In the same month Dostoevsky further elaborates on his roulette system in a letter to his sister-in-law, Varvara Dmitrievna Konstantinov: "Please do not think that I am showing off, from delight at not having lost, if I say that I know the secret of how not to lose, but to win. Indeed, I know the secret; it is awfully silly and simple and it consists in restraining oneself every minute, whatever the phases of the game, and in not getting agitated. That's all, and to lose then is simply impossible, you are bound to win. But the point is, having perceived the secret, is one able or can one avail oneself of it? You may be as wise as the serpent, with the most iron character, and yet you will break loose."

Even the philosophic Strakhov, the novelist claims, would break loose, and therefore he regards as blessed those who view roulette with repugnance. Then, getting down to the business side of folly, he informs Mme Konstantinov that having won 10,400 francs he went back to his hotel and put the money in his bag, determined to leave the next day without another visit to the tables. But such abstinence was too much for him; he broke loose and found himself left with only 5,000 francs. "Anyhow I decided to keep part of the gain, and the other part I am sending to Petersburg, namely, part to my brother to hold for me till my return, and part to you to be handed over or forwarded to Marie Dmitrievna."

Obviously, all through the letter Dostoevsky sees no enormity in this effort to support his wife, while travelling with his mistress, through an original system of roulette. But the ordinary reader is only too likely to detect in the situation the atmosphere of parody. Now it is precisely this atmosphere of parody—as distinct from the more familiar "du Dostoevsky"—that pervades *The Gambler* almost from the first page to the last. Yet, in a sense, it does convey the impression of having been snatched largely from real life, as indeed it had been.

But glancing back on those fourteen years since this man of genius had waited for death in Semyonovski Square one is conscious of a deep frustration. Dostoevsky was so essentially fertile in creativeness;

the bitter years had admittedly given him *The House of the Dead*. But what else? *Uncle's Dream, Stepanchikovo Village* and that pale impression of the great novels—*Injury and Insult*. Then there had been two poems, one of which at least had reached the hands of the Tsarina. The tale entitled *A Silly Story* had followed *The House of the Dead* in the "Vremya." In short, after this break in his life from 1849 to 1860, Dostoevsky was in danger of being swamped by journalism. And journalism itself was becoming in this year 1863, when the novelist published *Winter Notes on Summer Impressions,* increasingly difficult. His old friend Strakhov had contributed an article on the Polish question which led to the suppression of the journal by the Censor. Then, to add to Dostoevsky's difficulties, his wife became seriously ill during the winter. For all that, in the December of 1863, he found time to devote a letter of appreciation to his old enemy Turgenev. In this letter he urges that the imitators of the masters in literature "have brought the realistic to such a pitch of banality, that people would just be delighted with the poetical work (a most poetical work). Many will receive it with a certain perplexity, but with a pleased perplexity." Then, in allusion to his rival's *Ghosts,* he alludes to that nostalgia which pervades almost every work of Turgenev. Assuredly it is this, and no aspect of political controversy, that not even the hostility of a Dostoevsky can kill, any more than it can kill the perfume of dead rose-leaves.

In the meantime, this menacing year closed without any permission for the continuance of the "Vremya" under another name having as yet been accorded to Michael and Fyodor Dostoevsky.

Chapter V

CATASTROPHE AGAIN

ON MARCH 24th, 1864, the "Vremya" reappeared as the "Epoch," but at a lower price and without any fresh subscribers. The "Vremya" had been a successful journal and a great deal of Michael's original indebtedness was beginning to be paid off. Now, fresh indebtedness was absolutely necessary. In the midst of these desperate difficulties, the novelist was summoned to Moscow, where his wife was dying. There had been painful relations between him and his first wife, almost from the beginning. There had been scene after scene. In one of these the wife, with incredible cynicism, described her love-affair with the young teacher. They had laughed together, these two lovers, at the unsuspicious man of genius who was so secure in his wife's love. "No self-respecting woman," she exclaimed to the novelist, "could love a man who had worked for four years in a prison as the companion of thieves and murderers." She would stand in front of Dostoevsky's portrait shaking her fist at it and shouting, "Convict, miserable convict."

On the authority of Mlle Dostoevsky, the novelist's first wife was the daughter of one of Napoleon's Mamelukes who had been made a prisoner during the retreat of the Grande Armée. He was brought to Astrakhan, where he changed both his name and his religion. He eventually married a young girl of good family and joined the Russian Army, in which he rose to the rank of colonel: "My father never knew him. By some freak of Nature, Maria Dmitrievna inherited only the Russian type of her mother. I have seen her portrait. Nothing about her betrayed her Oriental origin. On the other hand, her son Paul, whom I knew later, was almost a mulatto. He had a yellow skin, black glossy hair, rolled his eyes as negroes do, gesticulated extravagantly, and was malicious, stupid and insolent."

But, in spite of everything that he had endured through the dead woman, her husband seems to have cherished her memory as of this or that wronged character in his novels. Still, in view of the known facts of his marital life, it is difficult to grasp the magnanimity disclosed in a letter of 1865 to Baron Vrangel, a magnanimity which almost equals that of Chatov in *The Possessed*: "My wife, the being who adored me, and whom I loved beyond measure, expired at Moscow, whither she had removed a year before her death of consumption. I followed her thither, and never once throughout that winter left her bedside. Yet the end came on April 16th, and she passed away in full consciousness, unable to take leave of, and to remember, all (including yourself) to whom she wished to send her last greeting. Cherish her, I beg of you, as a fair and goodly memory. My friend, she loved me beyond measure, and I returned her affection to a degree transcending all expression; yet our joint life was not a happy one."

The novelist promises to tell the whole story to his friend at their next meeting and continues: "But for the present let me confine myself to saying that, apart from the fact that we lived unhappily together (a circumstance due to her strangely suspicious, painfully fanciful nature), we should never have lost our mutual love for one another, but have become more attached in proportion to our misery. This may seem to you strange; yet it is but the truth. She was the best, the noblest, woman that ever I have known. For a year my heart had been torn by the spectacle of her slow decline, and to the full I had come to realise the true worth of what I was about to lay within the tomb; yet I should never have conceived that, when the earth lay heaped upon her coffin, there would have entered into my life such an aching void."

It had been his intention to fill the void by marrying his mistress, Pauline Suslova. This lady, the type of the "eternal student" made familiar to us in all sorts of Russian novels, was attracted by Dostoevsky, in his daughter's opinion, not so much on account of his character, his person, or his work, as on account of his influence over her fellow-students. She would enroll herself at the University every autumn, but she avoided examinations just as she avoided any particular course of study: "However, she frequented the University assiduously, flirting with the students, visiting them in their rooms, preventing them from working, enciting them to revolt, getting them to sign protests, and taking part in all political manifestations, when she would march at the head of the students, carrying a red flag, singing the *Marseillaise,* abusing and provoking the Cossacks, and beating the horses of the police. She in her turn was beaten by the police, and would spend the night in a police cell. On her return to the University she would be borne aloft in triumph by the students and acclaimed as the glorious victim of 'Tsarism.'" For the rest, Pauline attended the balls and literary soirées given by the students and shared eagerly in all the new ideas of the day. Chief of these was Free Love, and Pauline seems to have been a great favourite with the students from that standpoint, though apparrently she did not attract the novelist at first: "She hovered about my father, making advances which he did not notice. She then wrote him a declaration of love. Her letter was preserved among my father's papers; it is simple, naïve and poetic. She might have been some timid young girl, dazzled by the genius of the great writer. . . . He took Pauline for a young provincial, intoxicated by the exaggerated ideas of feminine liberty which were then reigning in Russia."

Pauline, however, started alone on the proposed honeymoon after a promise to await the novelist in Paris. But only two weeks later he heard from her to the effect that she had formed an attachment to a Frenchman whom she had just met: "All is over between you and me! It is your fault: why did you leave me so long alone?" Dostoevsky rushed off, on that first journey to Europe, in search of Pauline. But when he found her at least it was only to learn from her own lips that she was not bound to him, that she had given herself of her own free will and could separate from him at the moment of her choice. Dostoevsky left Paris for London to visit Alexander Herzen, in whom he always took a great interest, in spite of his antagonism to revolutionary ideas. Incidentally, it was during this visit to London that he, the most prejudiced writer against both the French and the Germans, became so curiously biased in favour of the English. For him the Englishwoman presented the type of feminine beauty that he admired most, and though Mr. Astley in *The*

Gambler is rather like a caricature of the late Thomas Huxley's "calm, strong angel," the Russian novelist hardly ever has a word of derision against the English character. Even the bulldog Falstaff in *Netotchka Nezvanova*, in spite of his incredible cunning, is treated with respect. For all that, Dostoevsky made a curious prophecy about the future of our country. It was his belief that the English would eventually abandon their island: "If our sons do not witness the exodus of the English from Europe, our grandsons will."

At last Pauline's Russian lover returned to Paris, but only to arrange a tour through Italy with his trusted friend Nicolas Strakhov. In his letter to Strakhov on this occasion he says: "We will walk together in Rome, and, who knows, perhaps we may caress some young Venitian in a gondola." Such aspirations, as his daughter notes, are exceedingly rare in Dostoevsky's correspondence, but there was no romance awaiting the novelist in Italy. Yet he did not go back again to Paris, where he might have encountered Pauline once more. He returned alone to Petersburg and contributed *Winter Notes on Summer Impressions* to the "Vremya," which was so soon to disappear from circulation. But the following spring a letter arrived from Pauline, imploring him to take her away from Paris as her French lover was unfaithful to her. When he hesitated to take the journey, at this peculiarly difficult period of his affairs, she threatened suicide, and off he rushed to the French capital. The scene that followed makes nothing in *The Idiot*, for example, seem in the least extravagant: "Finding Dostoevsky too cold, Pauline had recourse to heroic measures. One morning she arrived at my father's bedside at seven o'clock, and brandishing an enormous knife she had just bought, she declared that her French lover was a scoundrel, and that she intended to punish him by plunging this knife into his breast; that she was on her way to him, but that she had wished to see my father first, to warn him of the crime she was about to commit. I do not know whether he was deceived by this vulgar melodrama. In any case, he advised her to leave her big knife in Paris, and to go to Germany with him."

Pauline agreed to this suggestion and they went to the Rhineland to establish themselves at Wiesbaden. Here the novelist developed his passion for roulette which he had experienced on his first journey to Europe. Later on, the lovers went to Rome and Naples. Dostoevsky's jealousy, a quality denied to him by so many commentators, was now frequently aroused. In real life there can be no doubt that he experienced towards Pauline exactly the duality of *odi et amo* which he expresses through the hero of *The Gambler,* who says of Pauline: "There were moments when I would have given half my life to be able to strangle her. I swear that could I have plunged a knife into her breast I would have done so exultantly. And yet I swear, too, by all that is sacred to me, if at the summit of the Schlangenberg she had said to me: 'Throw yourself over that precipice,' I would have obeyed her, and even obeyed her joyfully."

But Pauline is by no means the only figure in *The Gambler* who is taken absolutely from life. One can never forget the Grandmother, so much more alive, in the novel at least, than Pauline. She takes the centre of the stage at once and gambles away the immediate prospects of those who had been banking on her death. This lady is a certain Mme Kumanin, a rich aunt of the novelist, who, long ago in the days when he was translating *Eugénie Grandet,* had saved him from starvation by a small allowance. In this still more difficult period, Mme Kumanin had become one of the very few assets of the novelist. Incidentally, the inheritance of the Dostoevsky family long afterwards at her death was to overshadow his life, quite literally, until his last day on earth.

It was at this desperate period of an unusually luckless life, the spring of 1864, that *Letters from the Underworld* appeared in the "Epoch." No less a person than Léon Chestov claims that this extraordinary monologue has a kinship with the lofty outpourings of Zarathustra. Meier-Graefe seems to me right in his refusal to endorse this claim. Dostoevsky's "underworlding" belongs as little to Nietzsche as does Raskolnikov. But Chestov is always interesting, and not least in his other claim that all the work of Dostoevsky in reality has its source in two books: *The House of the Dead* and *Letters from the Underworld.* The first book seems to have revealed that second pair of eyes which, Chestov suggests, had been given to the novelist in the convict prison of Omsk, a pair of eyes for which Dostoevsky himself made no claim, though he laid great stress on the difference between what the poet sees and what the ordinary citizen detects with his own blurred vision. The second book undoubtedly expresses, as probably very few other records in literature, including even the confessions of the saints, the burden of introspection which seems to have been the Russian's birthright. The "underworldling" rebels from his subterranean sanctuary against the outside world, against society, against scienic thought, against all human judgments and sanctions and, above all, against the finality of twice two=four. But it is not mere railing, and though the novelist registers the deepest contempt for his extraordinary hero, he allows him by no means infrequently to speak for Fyodor Dostoevsky. The "underworldling" sees the contradictions between dictated truth and what all the world knows to be true, the difference between Claude Bernard's truth—Chestov insists on reading Aristotle into Claude Bernard—and the truth of simple experience. He is indeed an excuse for his compatriot's claim that all the characters of Dostoevsky are merely the author under so many masks, a point of view that can be very easily controverted.

We in England have been long inured to rather terrible little people laying down the law on this or that in very lofty language. But Chestov's simplicity has a disarming irony of its own of which the very loftiest of us may well beware. It is, I submit, with a smile only half hidden that he drags in the world-famed grotto of Plato as a parallel to the underground man's cellar. It is perhaps with a badly hidden smile, too, that he claims for Dostoevsky a deeper perspicuity than Kant's, though the smile would have no scorn whatsoever for the author of *The Brothers Karamazov*.

Dostoevsky, in actuality, had as little to do with the Categorical Imperative as that French poet who rightly maintained that he was *si peu philosophe*. Least of all was he burdened by the kernal thought of the Nietzsche to come, when he depicted the tormented subterranean man endeavouring to escape from the torture of his contradictions in thought to

CATASTROPHE AGAIN

the simplicity of action. The Russian novelist, no less than Chestov himself, perceived that the man of action, when he becomes a thinker, is relatively insignificant. The enemies of Nietzsche were very quick to suggest that he himself suffered from this transference of energy, in spite of the Greek dictum that the goal lies in action, not in thought. However this may be, the "underworldling" has a quite definite task before him as he pours out the poison of his soul—redeemed not infrequently by uncontaminated aspiration—to the listening prostitute Lisa. He will save Lisa. That much, underground man though he is, he will accomplish in the hideous outside world of action with its twice two=four judgments against which he rails so hopelessly. The result of his well-intentioned quest is as cruelly grotesque as anything in the Dostoevsky novels, but it has, in its own way, the same inevitable closeness to life.

The book is important undoubtedly, though in naming as the source novels of the great realist just these two—*The House of the Dead* and *Letters from the Underworld*—one would seem to be forgetting *Poor Folk,* on what one may call the simple side of Dostoevsky, and *The Double,* which, though more or less a *jeu d'esprit,* none the less foreshadows all the infinitely complicated work to come. *Letters from the Underworld* does not foreshadow Beyond Good and Evil, but before Nietzsche or any other of the accepted excavators of the human mind Dostoevsky arrived at the idea of the superman. But whereas Nietzsche glorified him, the Russian either dragged him to the sanctuary of humility or to the finality of self-destruction. In the case of the "underworldling," he left him to the poison of his solitude, which could never exude any sort of antidote of healing, though it must be remembered that the tortuous contradictory mind of the Russian novelist rejected both penitence and remorse as seen by Plato's plain man.

Dostoevsky was no more the "underworldling" than he was Stavroguin, but at this particular period he was undoubtedly becoming desperate. The "Epoch" was beginning to fail. Michael's health, undermined by alcoholism and anxiety, began to give way while his brother was absent in Moscow wtih his dying wife. A year later, while he was at work on *Crime and Punishment,* he reveals the torture that he had gone through the year before: "True, when I had buried her I hastened back to his side (he was now the only person left to me); but, three months later, after a serious illness of only a month, he went the same way that my wife had gone. All that he had had to bequeath was a sum of three hundred roubles; and these I applied to the expenses of his funeral. Yet his total indebtedness had reached twenty-five thousand roubles; and therefore his wife and family found themselves destitute and thrown upon the world without a crust. For myself, I represented the poor widow's only hope; wherefore she came to me with her children, and begged of me to save her. I had loved my brother passionately. How could I deny her her request? So I decided what to do. I went straight to Moscow, and there begged of a rich old aunt of mine ten thousand roubles. With these I returned to St. Petersburg, and started another journal. But the journal's chances stood ruined in advance."

Without hesitation, Dostoevsky made himself responsible not only for the debts of his dead brother but for the support of his wife and four children. He acted with characteristic generosity, but one cannot help thinking that the dead man had never really reciprocated the deep affection of his younger brother. One remembers that long letters from Omsk in which he describes to Michael the journey to Siberia. It is dated February 22nd, 1854: "But before I write another line I *must* ask you: Tell me, for God's sake, why you have never written me a single syllable till now? Could I have expected this from you? Believe me, in my lonely and isolated state I sometimes fell into utter despair, for I believed that you were no longer alive; through whole nights I would brood upon what was to become of your children, and I cursed my fate because I could not help them. . . . I am like a slice cut from a loaf nowadays; I long to grow back again, but can't. *Les absents ont toujours tort.* Is that saying to come true of us too? But be easy in your mind: I trust you."

It was in Dostoevsky's nature, apparently, to forgive anybody anything. Doubtless, he would have accepted Michael's alleged attitude towards his younger brother, "Let him stay in Siberia," as due to reasonable caution. Certainly, he accepted willingly the burden of debts which would never have been enforced by any court of law. Repeatedly in the record of his second wife we find comments on this burden. The young bride mentions in her diary a small day-dream in the life of poverty from which roulette has failed to rescue them: "I forgot to say how I reckoned up with Fyodor what he would do with twenty thousand roubles: four thousand would go in paying off debts, then another three thousand, then another four thousand; Pasha would get two thousand, Emilia Fyodorovna and Fedya three thousand; that would leave us four thousand, on which we could live for a whole year. How lovely that would be. I said how if I were to win some money, or come into it anyhow, I should immediately pay off all the debts, that Fyodor might have peace of mind. But these are only dreams and castles in Spain. I went to bed at twelve and lay thinking of all sorts of family affairs, of Emilia Fyodorovna and Pasha, and their intrigues against me, till I got into such a rage that my heart started thumping, and I couldn't sleep." For Dostoevsky's second wife Michael's widow became a regular *bête noire*: "I wouldn't think anything of it at all, if I knew that all this misery was unavoidable, but that we should have to suffer so that one Emilia Fyodorovna and her lot can live in clover, and that I should have to pawn my coat so that she can have one, wakes a feeling within me the reverse of nice, and hurts me to find such thoughtlessness and so little understanding and human kindness in anyone I love and prize so much. He declares it is his duty to stand by his brother's family, and they stood by him; but has he then no duty towards me, and have I not devoted my whole life and soul to him, and from the bottom of my heart am I not prepared to put up with everything only to make him happy?"

In actual fact, his brother's family stood by him only in the sense of clinging to him for support. As for the stepson, the one-time little Pasha, who had participated in that frolic journey of farewell fast asleep like his intoxicated father, the little Pasha for whom the distracted writer had pleaded to the Tsar, he was to become a veritable scourge to the young wife.

CATASTROPHE AGAIN

In regard to Michael himself, it has been often enough said that the novelist, after having extracted large sums from his elder brother, brought him quite literally to ruin. This charge is grotesquely unjust. Admittedly, Dostoevsky received a little money from Michael during his long sojourn in Siberia, but for the greater part of the time he had not communicated with him in any way, quite clearly wishing to dissociate himself from a convict whose fate he had been in serious danger of sharing. Michael had been a tobacco merchant, at one time comparatively prosperous, and it has been urged that his younger brother induced him to risk the hazards of the literary life. The facts are quite different. The tobacco business was failing, Michael had in his youth been attracted by journalism and at this later stage he had embarked on the experiment of his own free will. Journalism, with his gifted brother beside him, saved him from bankruptcy.

It was undoubtedly the suspension of the "Vremya" by the Censorship that ruined the elder of the two brothers. The novelist, in actual fact, bore the full burden of this journalistic venture: "I alone managed everything, I read the proofs, settled terms with authors, arranged with the Censor; I corrected articles, I procured money; I remained up until six in the morning, and slept only five hours altogether. At last I succeeded in establishing order in the review, but it was too late." When the "Epoch" came finally to grief, the novelist became "temporarily insolvent," in his own words. "Oh my friend!" he exclaims to Vrangel, "willingly would I return to prison for so many years, if only my debts might be paid, and I might feel myself a free man!" At the time his position seemed quite hopeless. "I saw him," says a critic, "in the thick of his troubles. After the suppression of his paper, after his brother's death, and while being hunted for debt, he never lost heart. It is impossible to imagine circumstances which would have crushed him. His terrible susceptibility made self-control difficult, and he generally gave full play to his feelings. Perhaps this made life possible."

On the surface, there was little in favour of this persecuted man. He was threatened by imprisonment and he understood, practically, not merely theoretically, what imprisonment meant. He had been cut off for years from the whole world of enlightment, but, for all that, he had learnt men and things in the hardest of all hard schools. He was no longer the sub-lieutenant of Engineers who had chanced upon fame through a pathetic novel. He had studied human nature, and perhaps its strangest manifestations, Russian human nature, in a manner denied mercifully enough to the majority of writers. He understood the mixture of naïveté and cynicism, credulity and scepticism, blasphemy and awe. It was in his power now to interpret not only the clash between two wrongs, the clash between two rights, the Sophoclean clash between the smaller and the larger right, the clash of romanticism between two loves, the balanced clash of poise between two hatreds, but he had penetrated to the very core of that dangerous *odi et amo* which was perhaps the innermost secret—deeper even, because more concrete, than the conflict between the God-man and the Man-god —of his haunting duality.

But he was strangling himself for years to come by those suspended weights of his brother's family in addition to the burden of Paul Issayev. Here is another fragment from his second wife's diary that sheds a searching light on her difficult honeymoon in Dresden: "At four we went to the post and Fyodor got two letters. One was from Pasha, sending on some letters that were sent to Fyodor's address after he left, and the other from Apollon Nikolaevitch Maïkov. He opened both of them immediately. I peeped through and read while he was reading; one of the letters I could see was from S. . . . Then there were two letters from Praskovia full of nothing but wanting to get as much money as possible out of Fyodor's pocket, although he gave her as much as he possibly could before going away." The Praskovia referred to had been the mistress of Michael Dostoevsky, and the novelist had assumed responsibility for the support of his illegitimate nephew. Just at this time there seems to be no evidence of demands for money from the heroine of *The Gambler*, though she had undoubtedly resumed her correspondence with the novelist. Certainly it was a strange honeymoon for a bride of nineteen; it was further complicated by the chances and changes of roulette. But, at the present stage, Dostoevsky did not know even of the existence of the one human being who was to establish something like order in the chaos of his life.

Long afterwards, when Paul Issayev had married, he calmly proposed that he and his wife should live indefinitely with Dostoevsky and his family. Anna Grigorievna told him that it was out of the question, whereupon his young wife protested. "He promised me," she told Dostoevsky's second wife, "that we should all live together, that you would keep house, and that I should have nothing to do. If I had known that he was deceiving me, I certainly would not have married him." Dostoevsky's daughter, with her usual sense of justice and objectivity, adds: "This selfish little creature became, under the discipline of years and sorrows, an excellent wife and mother, respected by all who knew her. Poor woman! her married life was a long martyrdom." As the years passed, one dependant after another was to fall away from the weary shoulders of the great writer, but Paul Issayev, together with the drunken Nicolaï, maintained this grip unceasingly.

Dostoevsky appears to have met with no gratitude from his relatives. Certainly he told his bride, Anna Grigorievna, that they had helped him, but one fails to discover in what way. His daughter, at all events, is under no illusion as to their real attitude towards their illustrious kinsman: "They were quite ready to live at their uncle's expense, but were by no means inclined to obey him. They laughed at Dostoevsky behind his back and deceived him." The fiancé of his favourite niece, who had a deep grudge against her uncle "because he had insulted the Russian student in the person of Raskolnikov," once spoke insolently to the novelist. Dostoevsky expressed a wish to his sister-in-law that she should refuse to allow the young man into her house. The result of this was that the young people married without inviting the novelist to the wedding. When his niece met him later as a bride she simply laughed in his face. But some years later her husband endeavoured to make friends with his wife's kinsman and induce him to take an interest in his numerous children. This is just one example, out of many, of the manner in which Dostoevsky's relations stood by him: "Indeed, the behaviour of the whole family was abnormal. Instead of being proud to have a genius for their brother, they hated him because he had made his name famous. My uncle Andrey was the only one who was proud of his brother's literary gifts; but he lived in the country and very rarely came to Petersburg."

But, in the first flush of his generosity, the novelist was far from fore-seeing so strange a response. As yet his nephews and nieces were mere children who could not be expected to penetrate his loneliness. Maria Dmitrievna was dead; Michael was dead. Before the end of the year his old friend and collaborator, Apollon Grigoryev, died. The separation from Pauline seemed at the time to be final, though later on she appears to have made a definite effort to resume her sway. A day was undoubtedly to come when the "eternal student" of Free Love was to force her way into the novelist's house. On that occasion Dostoevsky was unable to recognise the mistress who had deserted him in the long ago. That is perfectly credible; what is harder to accept is the claim put forward by some romanticists that, to the very last day of his life, the novelist remained in love with his first wife. Still, nothing is wholly incredible in regard to Dostoevsky, a point on which his calumniators have long relied.

In any case, the year 1865 found him once more without ties, "a slice cut from a loaf." It was under this sense of loss and under the burden of voluntary responsibility and indebtedness that in the summer of this year he went abroad for the third time. And now at last he was to commence that series of novels which was to establish him as one of the most profoundly interesting novelists in any language. But even at this stage, seemingly like the needle to the north, he made his way to Wiesbaden, from which alluring spot he wrote to his old friend Baron Vrangel who notes: "When in 1865 I returned to Copenhagen from my summer leave, I found a despairing letter of Dostoevsky's from Wiesbaden. He wrote that he had gambled away all his money, and was in a desperate situation—he had not a penny left, and creditors were pressing him on every side." The good baron expresses surprise about the gambling, as the novelist had never touched a card in Siberia where gambling was so universal. But he never dreamed of being censorious, sent the great writer what money he could, and invited him to stay with him at Copenhagen, where Dostoevsky duly arrived on October 1st for a visit of a week: "He extraordinarily pleased my wife, and was much devoted to the two children. I thought him thin and altered." The meeting delighted them both and they discussed their memories of Siberia. "We spoke much of his first wife, Maria Dmitrievna, and of the fair Marina, of whom she had been so terribly jealous." But Vrangel admits frankly that the real relations between Dostoevsky and his first wife had always been a mystery to him; they were to remain so to the end, and not only to the kindly Baron Vrangel.

The next month Dostoevsky returned to Russia, and, before the year was out, disposed of his author's rights to the publisher Stelovsky. The novelist spent the summer at Lublin near Moscow while his first great novel was continuing to appear in the "Russky Viestnik." It is the work of which Dr. A. Brückner so truly observed: "Not in *Faust,* but rather in *Crime and Punishment,* does 'the whole woe of mankind' take hold of us."

Chapter VI

RODION RASKOLNIKOV

SOME of us cannot help suspecting that Nietzsche's "Yes" to life was more odious than Schopenhauer's "No." But there are still more in our country who would lightly dismiss the most ferocious bellowings of Zarathustra as leading nowhere. That they did, definitely, lead somewhere would pass quite unnoticed when the time actually came. What is still more curious is the fact that many are inclined to see in Dostoevsky, the champion of the disinherited, nothing but a rival protagonist of the über-Mensch. You can no more convince such people of this profound error than you can convince them, for example, of Hamlet's sanity in spite of all the overwhelming evidence in favour of a view so emphatically substantiated by Shakespeare.

In reality, the Russian novelist examined independently the now only too familiar thesis of Nietzche, merely to refute it in one work after another. The first of these is the book that was now appearing in the "Russky Viestnik" under the title of its hero's name. Before examining this powerful novel, which was to make Dostoevsky's name known all over the world, it would be well to examine certain quite simple tenets which were to be repeated throughout the whole series of Dostoevsky's chief works. These tenets, indeed, may be said to constitute the main issues of the Idea which the ex-convict brought back with him so hopefully from Siberia to Perersburg.

Dostoevsky was emphatically Slavophil in one

sense, but not really pan-Slav in any sense whatsoever. Though he regarded his country as European, he always maintained that it was utterly distinct from the rest of Europe: "We are convinced, finally, that we are a nation apart, original in the highest degree, whose problem it is to create for itself a new manner of life, suitable to it, having its roots in our own soil, in the spirit and the principles of the people." He was opposed not only to the Westernism of Turgenev but to what seemed to him the narrow outlook of Count Tolstoy. For instance, it seemed to Dostoevsky incomprehensible that Tolstoy should reject with indifference the appeals for aid from beyond the Russian frontiers. Dostoevsky believed that any imitation of Europe would be fatal to Russians, on the ground that Europe was already committed to a road which must lead inexorably to the chaos of war and revolution.

The great Russian writer was never tired of emphasising his distrust of the Intelligentsia because of their atheism, which would lead them, not to the higher civilisation of which they dreamed, but rather downward to that other chaos of *tout est permis*.

Another tenet, to be developed at great length in *The Possessed*, is the clash between the God-man and the Man-god. Yet though Dostoevsky accepted a personal national God, a Russian God, he also accepted, no less than Turgenev himself, the implacable intention of Nature in contradistinction to the passionate waywardness of man. And, like Turgenev again, he knew well that no group of clever talkers could kindle a flame in Russian souls, and that any spiritual resurgence must come not from without but from within.

Above all, he insists, particularly in *Crime and Punishment,* on the impossibility of any human being possessing strength enough to endure being utterly separated from the common herd. He urged, indeed, that the slice cut from the loaf must at all costs return to it, as he had indicated long ago in Siberia.

Finally, he was to express the conviction, by implication as well as by direct statement, that to atheism itself Russians would bring an exaltation that would turn it into a sort of religion.

It is no wonder, then, that, in this first volume of the great series, we have no endorsement of the superman's arrogant demands on life but, on the contrary, a rebuke to the arrogance of isolation. The book is permeated, though, by the duality which had first shown itself in *The Double.* The half-famished student, Raskolnikov, is thus described by his friend Razoumikhin:

"I have known Rodion for the last eighteen months; he is gloomy, morose, proud, and haughty. Of late (though the germs may have been brooding in him previously) he has become suspicious and hypochondriacal. He is kind and generous, but cannot bear to show his feelings, and would sooner appear brutal than expansive. Sometimes he does not appear hypochondriacal in the least, but simply cold and absolutely unfeeling. One might almost say that there exist in him two natures, which alternately get the upper hand. Sometimes he is extremely taciturn; everything and everybody seem against him, and he will lie in bed and do nothing! He never indulges in raillery, not because he is not of a sarcastic turn, but rather because he disdains to waste his words. He never cares to hear what anyone has to say, and takes no interest whatever in what is occupying the attention of everyone else at the time. He has a high opinion of his own ability, not altogether without justification, I will own."

This character-sketch strikes one as applying to the novelist himself rather than to a criminal type, in the disputed sense of Lombroso. But Raskolnikov has been playing with the idea of crime; he has contributed a paper to a journal exalting the criminal as a being "beyond good and evil" in Nietzsche's contorted thesis. He has argued the point endlessly, but his thesis is tedious; it does not convince the man himself. But the *idée fixe* has a powerful urge; it cannot be denied expression. That always interesting critic, Mr. Meier-Graefe, is perhaps quite wrong, though, in dismissing Dostoevsky's statement that a "meaningless discussion in the tavern has an extraordinary influence on the further development of the matter." Dostoevsky would not have written such words idly, and it is possible to detect in them a seed similar to that sprayed upon the prepared mind of Macbeth by the witches. But this critic is eminently just in refusing to dismiss the strange amateur criminal as "a will-less worm." Yet, rather in the manner of Dostoevsky, Meier-Graefe allows himself occasional contradictions even in external description. For instance, he describes Raskolnikov as "handsome even in rags; well-built, of fine appearance, a splendid type, to whom even dirt gives a noble complexion, since nothing hinders his movement and his soaring spirit wards off every kind of ugliness." But on the same page we read of the same man: "There he struggles with the axe, this slender, delicate, fever-stricken youth whom conversation exhausts and who is too weak even to eat."

But, such as he is, he kills instantly the feeble old woman pawnbroker, and after her the poor weak-minded Lizaveta whom he never expected to meet. It is a reflex like any other, and from the moment that he steals out of his miserable lodging-house until the deed has been accomplished he has acted as an automaton. Yet in his desire to save himself after the crime he becomes at once clumsy, reckless and utterly indifferent to the surface motive of the murder—booty.

He has become a murderer, and just as he was obsessed by the test of murder, so now he has become obsessed by the idea of pitting himself against anyone who may suspect him of the crime. Zametov, the district-official, is his first opponent. Zametov has ventured to sneer at the murder as obviously the work of a mere novice. Raskolnikov regards this as a personal insult and goes on to sketch the crime with actual details known only to himself. It never occurs to the district-official, however, that any murderer in his right mind would give himself away quite like that.

At another interview Raskolnikov exclaims: "What if I myself had murdered the old woman and Lizaveta?" and this time Zametov's suspicion is sharply aroused. The murderer, realising then that he has gone too far, sets to work at once to allay suspicion. But when he matches himself against the examining lawyer, Porphyry Petrovitch, the half-starved student, begins to recognise his potential master. There is nothing, though, about Porphyry of that magisterial emptiness which booms through so much of Anglo-Saxon fiction. Still less is there anything suggestive of the Mephistophelean at the first interview: "Porphyry Petrovitch was in morning costume—dressing-gown, slippers down at heel, speckless linen. He was a man of thirty-five, below medium height, stout, and even somewhat corpulent. He had neither beard nor moustache, and his hair was cut short. His large round head was particularly fleshy in the nape of the neck. His bloated, round, and slightly flat face was not wanting in vivacity or cheerfulness, although his complexion, of a darkish yellow, was far from indicating sound health. Had it not been for the expression of his eyes—which, hidden under almost white lashes, seemed to be continually blinking, as if to make signs of some kind or other—one might have taken his face for a good one. But it was this expression which singularly belied the rest of the countenance. At first sight one could not help noticing the more or less rustic physique of his frame, but an attentive observer was soon undeceived as to that."

The unhappy student is a very attentive observer. From first to last he becomes more and more deeply swayed by this fantastic burrower into his innermost secrets. Like a moth to the candle he returns; Porphyry becomes more and more interested in him as in someone quite outside of the common run of criminals: "That man will make me a call, he will come of his own accord, and that before very long! If he is guilty he will be bound to come. Other kinds of men would not do so, but this one will." Porphyry is unerringly right. In the heart of Raskolnikov confession has become another *idée fixe*. At all costs, he must rid himself of the isolating burden that is crushing him. Yet it is not before the representative of justice but before Sonya, the prostitute, that he struggles towards humility. She is the daughter of one Marmeladov, a drunkard dragged up from depths of which the sad hero of *Poor Folk* knew nothing. Sonya herself is like no other prostitute in literature. The author of *Les Misérables* has not the touch of pity which belongs to this Russian. The author of *Resurrection* is singularly cold in the treatment of his regenerated heroine in comparison with his great rival. This coldness, approaching almost to indifference, is by not means confined to a single novel but is to be discerned all through the powerful creative work of him whose object it was to come to grips with the very core of the Russian *moujik*.

Mlle Dostoevsky has attributed this coldness, both literary and political, both national and international, to the actual origin of Count Tolstoy. Dostoevsky's daughter rightly points out that European biographers have been inclined to contrast the aristocratic Tolstoy with the plebeian Dostoevsky, while in reality both belonged to the same union of hereditary nobles. The author of *Crime and Punishment*, of the two, would appear to have been of more ancient lineage: "Not only were the Tolstoys never great Russian aristocrats, they are not even of Russian origin. The founder of the Tolstoy family was a German merchant named Dick, who came to Russia in the seventeenth century and opened a store in Moscow. His business prospered, and he decided to settle in Russia. When he became a Russian subject he changed his name of Dick, which in German means 'fat,' to the Russian equivalent, Tolstoy." Dostoevsky's daughter maintains that the descendants of German families in Russia may become Orthodox and even forget the German language, yet none the less they "retain their German souls incapable of understanding and sharing our Russian ideas." In her view, Tolstoy was a typical example of this incapacity: "Orthodox, he attacked and despised our Church. A Slav, he remained indifferent to the sufferings of other Slavs, sufferings which stirred the heart of every *moujik*. An hereditary noble, he never understood this institution, which has had such an immense importance in our culture. A writer, he did not share the admiration of all his *confrères* for Pushkin, that father of Russian literature." Then, as an example of this tranquil indifference, she cites the case of Levin, admittedly the portrait of Tolstoy himself, in *Anna Karenina*. Levin, it will be remembered, finds it impossible to understand the bubbling excitement over the triennial election of a new Marshal of the Nobility. His one anxiety is to escape to his village as quickly as possible.

However this may be, the powerful and magnetic creator of Levin was in his inner being just as much purely Russian as was the father of Mlle Dostoevsky. It is indeed improbable that she would ever have stressed that alleged German descent of the author of *War and Peace* if she could have foreseen what Germans would actually do to his loved Russian home. In his strong and admirably documented *Mother Russia,* Maurice Hindus makes it clear that people are wrong to assume that the sub-human brutishness of this planet finds complete fulfilment in the German private soldier. All such people seem to have forgotten the German officer who was at his very best in Yasnaya Polyana. Here he stole right and left with German thoroughness and attention to detail. Two German physicians are cited as dividing their share of the plunder conscientiously between them. The full filth of the German officer, now a byword all over Europe, expressed itself with extraordinary vigour in the home of Count Leo Tolstoy. The room in which *War and Peace* was written resembled, after the Germans had been driven out, "the foulest den I have ever seen," in the words of an old servant of the family. Nothing, in short, could have been more systematic than the befouling energy of these German officers and gentlemen in the destruction of this sanctuary of Russian culture on whose walls there hung the portraits of the greatest German musicians. Naturally they stole what they did not burn, but mercifully their visit was too short to permit them to ship to the beloved Fatherland every article of value in Yasnaya Polyana. Still, they were meticulous in leaving behind them the indelible "mark of the beast" which is now accepted all over the world as the German officer's conventional signature.

The regeneration of Raskolnikov and Sonya, wholly Russian as it is, is on a quite different plane from that of Nekhludov and Katusha. Raskolnikov was never to become a disciplined man of the world in the sense of Nekhludov, but he was at no time the will-less worm that M. Gide has seen fit to depict him. Still less is he what Léon Chestov insists that each of the characters of Dostoevsky is in turn—a mere mask for the author. Apart from that criminal *idée fixe,* the half-starved student lacked neither heart nor intelligence. He spent almost his last kopek on the funeral of a drunkard whom he had met by accident. In spite of his repellent manner, he was devoted to his mother and sister. At the University he almost literally starved himself to support a consumptive, and after the sick man's death he did everything in his power to help his family. On another occasion his compassion went to the length of a sincere desire to marry a young girl, not because he loved her but because she was suffering and unhappy. On yet another occasion he rescued two children from a fire at the risk of his own life. His intelligence held the attention of no less a person than the investigating lawyer Porphyry. For all that, he is a typical example, in Dostoevsky's manner, of the conflict between those two truths, that of the Man-god and that of the God-man, the conflict between the pride of the intellect and the humility of the heart, which was to reach its apotheosis in Ivan Karamazov.

But the poor student has not travelled any great distance along the path of Ivan Karamazov. He does not naturally belong to the fraternity of those who imagine themselves to be beyond good and evil. Still, the man is guarded even in his approach to humility. Attracted by pity towards Sonya, he none the less challenges the existence of the Deity in her presence. Then, suddenly, she becomes for him the symbol of lacerated humanity. Bending down, the murderer kisses the feet of the prostitute. Sonya is startled, and Raskolnikov gives the real reason of his action: "I did not bow down to you personally, but to suffering humanity in your person." To Sonya he confesses, asking what is to be done. The girl's eyes had been filled with tears, but now they brightened as she rushed up to him. " 'What must be done?' 'Rise!' (Saying which, she seized Raskolnikov by the shoulder; he rose slightly, looking at Sonya with astonishment.) 'Go forthwith, go this very moment to the nearest public place, prostrate yourself, kiss the earth you have stained, bow down in every direction, and proclaim at the top of your voice to the passers-by, "I am a murderer!" and God will give you peace again! Will you go? Will you go?' she asked trembling, while seizing his hands with tenfold strength, and fixing on him a burning glance." Though he struggles against the pathetic naïveté of the girl who loves him, it is to her that he reveals the truth behind the truth: "I wished to commit murder, without casuistic argument—to do so only for myself, and nothing else! Even in so terrible a thing, I scorned beguiling my conscience. When I committed murder, it was not to relieve my mother's misfortunes, nor to devote to the well-being of humanity the power and wealth which, in my opinion, such a deed ought to help me to acquire. No, no; such thoughts were not mine. At that moment, I did not in any way care to know if I should ever benefit anyone, or if I should continue for the remainder of my life a social parasite! Neither was money the main factor in the deed—no, another reason induced me to commit it. I see that now. Understand me, if the past could be recalled, I should most probably not do so again. But at that time I longed to know if I was vermin, like the majority—or a Man, in the full acceptance of the word—whether, in fact, I had the power to break through obstacles."

The inquisitor Porphyry comes to Raskolnikov's room after this confession to Sonya. Porphyry, it seems, has been too stringent in his methods of investigation. But Raskolnikov must not regard him as inhuman. He had been suspicious, certainly, but had there not been cause for suspicion? This change of front produced a curious reaction in the other: "The thought that Porphyry Petrovitch considers him innocent begins to torture him." His visitor goes on to discuss his host's contribution to criminology. He had read and thoroughly understood the essay. He has a liking for its author. He is attracted by him, and that is exactly the real reason why he has been able to find his way through the maze of the other's concealed thoughts. Yes, that is how and why he is so absolutely certain. But an actual confession, a voluntary confession, does suggest the presence of extenuating circumstances, does it not? The barrel-like man who, only a few minutes ago, had apologised for his suspicion has now become overwhelming in his gentle certitude. The unyielding Raskolnikov, in an outer sense, yields to the obviousness of truth. But, in an inner sense, the man is to remain stubborn even as a convict in Siberia. Like a tameless wolf—Dostoevsky himself had appeared like that when a convict—he avoids even Sonya who has accompanied him. The duality in Raskolnikov's nature remains too strong for the naïveté of love, of kindness and, above all, of faith. But at last he is dominated by this prostitute who has remained pure while so many of the good have become so deeply contaminated. When questioned by the murderer about her prayers, the sad prostitute, whose sin is born of self-sacrifice, had answered with a strange bewilderment: "What could I be? What should I be without God!"

There has been no set academic thesis to explain Sonya. One is only asked to understand her, just as one is only asked to understand her drunken father, who, in a tavern, pours out the strange mixture of triumph and despair which is the very essence of Dostoevsky's tortuous simplicity. "Crucify me," the poor old drunkard cries out in his confused anguish, "judge, but pity me as you do it! I will go to meet my punishment, for I thirst not for pleasure, but for sufferings and tears. Do you think, publican, that your half-bottle has given me any pleasure? It was sadness, sadness and tears, that I sought and tasted at the bottom of this flagon; but He who has had pity on all men and sees all hearts will have pity on us; He alone is Judge. At the last day He will come and ask: 'Where is the girl who had compassion on her earthly father, and did not turn away in disgust from the habitual drunkard? Where is the girl who sacrificed herself to an unkind, consumptive stepmother, and children who were not of her own flesh and blood?' . . . He will forgive my Sonya, He will forgive her, I know. I felt convinced of it when I was with her just now. We shall all be judged by Him and He will forgive us all; the evil and the just, the wise and the gentle. And when He has finished with the rest, our turn will come, too. 'Draw nigh,' He will say to us, 'draw nigh, ye drunkards, ye cowards, ye dissolute men.' And we shall draw nigh without trembling. And then He will say unto us: 'Ye are sots! Ye bear the mark of the beast on your foreheads, yet come unto Me.' And the wise and intelligent will say: 'Lord, wherefore, dost thou receive these?' And He will answer: 'I receive them, O ye wise and intelligent men, because not one of them thought himself worthy this favour.' And then He will hold out His arms, and we shall throw ourselves into them; and we shall burst into tears; and then we shall understand everything. All the world will understand, and Catherine Ivanovna also, Thy Kingdom come O Lord!"

But the last word of *Crime and Punishment* is by no means confined to the Christianity of *Tout comprendre c'est tout pardonner*. In this book, as indeed in all his great novels, there is a figure that remains impenetrable even to the compassionate faith for which Dostoevsky struggled all through his life. Svidrigailov thinks that he sees in Raskolnikov a kinship with himself, but he is mistaken. There is no Sonya on earth who can save this man who has worn out the capacity even for grief. He is one of those victims of complete isolation which appear among Dostoevsky's creations not as mere insoluble problems but as human beings who have fled from humanity never to be reclaimed by humanity. Svidrigailov has grown weary of lust, just as he has grown weary of himself. He has experimented with good deeds as with evil deeds, but he can no longer feel the faintest distraction in either. For Dostoevsky, he is one of those who have died long before their coffin is nailed down. This man who has severed his ties with the God-man can no longer even faintly rely on the Man-god.

The whole life of the man, as in a mirage, comes before us in a dream just as the whole life of Marmeladov flashes out in a single drunken outburst. It is Svidrigailov's last night alive. He has dreamt that he had rescued a poor beaten waif of the streets and placed her between the blankets of his bed. Then, just as he was going to leave the house, he had glanced back at the child to see that she was comfortably asleep:

"He carefully raised the coverings which hid her head. The child was sound asleep. She had become warm in bed, and her pale cheeks had already regained their colour; and yet, how strange! the colour of that complexion was much redder than is usual with children in a normal state. 'It is the flush of fever,' thought Svidrigailov. 'Can she have been drinking? These purple lips seem burning.' Suddenly he fancies he sees the long black lashes of the little sleeper gently move; beneath the half-closed eyelids there seemed a tendency to some cunning, sly, in nowise childish twinkle. Can the child be awake, and only pretend to sleep? Yes, her lips smile —they quiver as with desire to check a laugh. But now she throws aside constraint—she merrily laughs —there is, in that small face, a bold, brazen, luring look, without one trait of youth, for it is the face of a French harlot. Suddenly she opens both her eyes wide—they gaze on Svidrigailov with a lewd and amorous look—they ask, they smile. Nothing so repugnant as this childish face whose youthful traits betoken lust. 'What! at such an age?' he cries, a prey to horror. 'Can such things be?' And now she turns on him her painted face with outstretched arms. 'Accursed thing!' exclaims Svidrigailov with a cry of horror; he raises his hand to strike her, and at the same moment wakes."

It is not one man who is poisoned by the miasma of life. It is not one man alone who is menaced by the doom of his own making. The horrible secrets of Petersburg stir in his dreams, the secrets which come oozing out of fetid cellars. They seem to be escaping through the gratings and through the very icy sweep of the north wind. All these blend with the last loathsome thoughts of this man who hears suddenly, as in a dream, the two cannon-shots signalling the rising of the Neva.

This lonely and terrible figure belongs essentially to Dostoevsky. Luzhin, the miserable fiancé of Raskolnikov's sister Dunia, does not belong to Dostoevsky in the real sense any more than does, for example, Smerdyakov in *The Brothers Karamazov.* The novelist has not looked at either of them with that second pair of eyes with which Chestov has so persuasively endowed him. Infinitely inferior novelists might have presented Luzhin endeavouring to "plant" a crime upon Sonya on the very day of her father's funeral. Svidrigailov, though, belonged to the great writer because he was capable of finality even if it was only that of despair. No gleam of any sort comes from Luzhin, but his meanness brings from Catherine Ivanovna, the widow, an outburst which is strangely arresting in view of the fact that it is this woman, and no one else, who has forced Sonya upon the streets of Petersburg:

" 'Sonya, Sonya, I do not believe it! You see that I do not believe it!' repeated Catherine Ivanovna." She was blind to the evidence because she, too, belonged to Dostoevsky just as her dead husband had belonged. "These words were accompanied by a thousand caresses, while showering kisses on the girl, seizing her hands, and straining her in her arms like a child. 'You to have stolen something? But how stupid these people are! Good heaven! You are idiots, idiots, every one of you!' she cried out to those present. 'You do not as yet know this loving young heart! She rob! She? I tell you, she would sell her last garment, she would go barefooted rather than leave you without help, if you were in need—she has sold herself for us, that is what she is! She even accepted the yellow ticket because my children were dying with hunger—she has sold herself for us!"

That indeed is the manner of Dostoevsky, who passes judgment on none but allows each to realise himself, if there is anything in him to realise. The old duality is there, but the antics of Goliadkin in *The Double* have been left behind. The novelist had penetrated to depths of humiliation beyond the range of *Injury and Insult*. The early influence of Gogol had slipped away, though it may be urged that the founder of the Russian novel has been, and is being, too hastily belittled by critics no longer under the sway of *Dead Souls*. Mr. Meier-Graefe, for example, has gone so far as to maintain that Dostoevsky is to Gogol as Delacroix is to Gros. Well, did not Delacroix himself call Gros *le Homère de la peinture?* Be that as it may, and accepting the interpretation of literature through the medium of painting as tolerable, and quite unlike the dreaded interpretation of painting through the medium of literature, the champion of El Greco and the revealer of Van Gogh is interesting when he presents Dostoevsky as the Rembrandt of fiction. The comparison will strike many as grotesque, but viewed superficially, as if the ravages of time on painting—so close to its ravages on the human face—could really be applied to literature, the *souches* in Dostoevsky do resemble after a fashion the endless *souches* over the work of the Flemish master. There is, indeed, layer after layer in the Russian novelist above the glazed surface, and when one thinks that one has penetrated to the last layer of all, one meets again and again only a note of interrogation. No one can afford to be doctrinaire over Dostoevsky, who was doctrinaire over nobody and nothing, in spite of all his Slavophil tenacity.

In Siberia he had learned the last lesson of humility as distinct from that of humiliation; it was learned actually in a church: "Arrived, we stood herded together by the door—that is to say, in the lowest place of all. And as I stood there, there came back to me the reflection how, when in church during the days of my boyhood, I had been wont to gaze at the common people near the entrance, and to feel that somehow they must be praying in a different way from ourselves—that they must be praying in a more humble, more grovelling fashion, and with a fuller sense of their abasement. And now it had befallen me to stand in the very same place as they had done—albeit with this difference, that I and my companions stood there cowed and fettered! Every one in the church drew away from us, as though all were afraid of us; yet at the same time we were given alms, and I remember that somehow the circumstance communicated to me a sort of pleasure, and something subtly resembling a sense of relief."

That mingling of pity and humility was to flower in his attitude towards Sonya and her father and in his sorrow for all the disinherited and oppressed in a great city. But, besides painting to the heart and to the mind, this creative writer painted to the eye and, in an outer as well as in an inner sense, his portraiture in the great novels is unerringly exact. It may be urged, though, that the ethics of compassion and grief can no more indicate—one must avoid the word "explain"—the content of a creative writer than do the ethics of indifference and gaiety. Dostoevsky's hold on mankind was remote from ethics of any sort, no matter how hard he struggled to be strictly ethical. He certainly retained the political dream of Byzantium, but Soloviev is abundantly right—against general opinion—in asserting that in his work Dostoevsky was the very reverse of a mystic. But in Siberia he had become deeply conscious of the inner association of crime with punishment, as an incident in the eternally haunting problem of original sin. It was by no accident, then, that the series of his great novels began with a murder story which, in a sense, might be accepted as an alluring contribution to detective fiction.

By no possibility could Nietzsche have accepted with sincerity the rebel Raskolnikov, at long last repentant and subdued, as an incarnation of his own superman to be. But he was surely won over by the intricate windings of the human brain as revealed by Dostoevsky in *Crime and Punishment*. The German philosopher, like the Greeks before him, accepted action as the goal of thought, but also, like the Greeks before him, he realised that suffering itself belongs to action. It is not surprising, then, that the solemn creator of the Blond Beast was in truth stirred by the protagonist of Rodion Raskolnikov. Would Dostoevsky have been so stirred by Nietzsche? I think not. Many have denied to the Russian writer, for no discernible reason, the saving grace of humour, which is not necessarily *l'humour britannique*. But assuredly the Russian would have seen through the undisguised mechanism of the Blond Beast who illustrates so admirably, for all his tragic import, the *raideur* of Bergson's treatise on laughter. We in England were inclined to laugh at the well-heralded Prussian brute as at a bogy rather than a robot, for we rather admire *la raideur;* a duchess cannot be too much a duchess nor a bishop a bishop for the English stage. In any case, for Dostoevsky the roar of the Blond Beast would have meant precisely that bloodthirsty roar of Western Europe against which he continued to warn his compatriots for the greater part of his life. Far from being akin to Nietzsche, he was his antithesis, and Rodion Raskolnikov was equally the antithesis of that mass-murderer—the Blond Beast.

But all that is aside from the real point. Dostoevsky had a hold over a vast audience because he was interesting to the Continental mind. He would be also interesting to the English office-boy in very much the same sense that a penny dreadful is assumed to be still interesting to him. And when the Russian novelist is bored, when he becomes perfunctory, he admittedly sinks to the level, or almost to the level, of a popular concoctor of thrills, so that, after all, it is not so astounding that the eminent English novelist, to whom I have referred, dismissed him airily as a better writer than Hall Caine. *Crime and Punishment* itself betrays more than one trick of the expert serial writer, but it also reveals the real Dostoevsky at the zenith of his power. And in the book there is nothing whatever—any more than in *The House of the Dead*—to justify Turgenev's scornful allusion to Monsieur de Sade.

The novelist had already descended far down into that well of the unconscious from which laughingly he had long ago extracted the boyish figure of Goliadkin. In that well he was to discover amazing figures, always fantastic and yet always true to that inner core of humanity which bides its time under the conscious cloak of seemliness and order. *Crime and Punishment* is of the greatest significance, if only because the first of these strangely symbolic figures appears in its pages. His name is not Rodion Raskolnikov, the poor murderer who was to be dragged back mercifully to the "slave morality" from which he had sought to escape. His name is Svidrigailov, who killed himself because he could no longer bear to face the ultimate loneliness of life.

Chapter VII

A SIGNIFICANT INTERRUPTION

THE great novel was not yet finished when there came an interruption which exasperated the author. Careless as ever, in spite of the bite of experience, galled as he was by what Cézanne used to call the *grappins* of life, Dostoevsky had delivered himself into the willing grip of Stelovsky. This publisher had acquired, at a wretched price, the first collected edition in three volumes of his works. The affair was treated as negligible at the time, for Dostoevsky had found some unusually agreeable friends, the same friends to whom he related those grim happenings in Semyonovski Square of seventeen years ago. M. Korvin-Kronkovsky, who belonged to the Lithuanian noblesse and claimed descent from a semi-mythical king of Lithuania, had two daughters, Anyuta and Sophie, aged respectively nineteen and fourteen.

The elder girl happened to be making her first plunge into literature and, like so many others, was eager for the stimulus of the novelist's approval. Dostoevsky appreciated on his side the stimulus of "a literary friendship as necessary to a writer as love itself," in the words of his daughter, who denies that her father was ever in love with this engaging young girl; she was actually the first to congratulate him when he became engaged to Mlle Snitkin. But Dostoevsky made himself at home in the household, just like the hero of *The Idiot* in that of the Epanchin family. Mme Kovalevsky, the world-famed mathematician, tells us that he was at his best when

A SIGNIFICANT INTERRUPTION

they were quite by themselves; but at a party his rôle was almost exactly that of Prince Mishkin. So close, indeed, is the resemblance that the reader of Mme Kovalevsky's *Memiors* expects to hear the crash of a certain vase which appears in the Epanchins' drawing-room:

"The evening was unusually dull. The guests took not the slightest interest in one another; but as well-bred people, for whom such dull evenings form an essential part of existence, they bore their tedium stoically.

"One can easily divine how poor Dostoevsky felt in such company! In his personality and appearance he was frightfully alien to everybody else. He had gone so far in self-immolation as to put on a dress-coat; and this dress-coat, which fitted very badly and made him uncomfortable, ruined his temper for the whole evening. Like all neurotic people, he was very shy in the company of strangers, and it was clear that his ill-temper was to be displayed on the earliest possible opportunity."

When he was introduced to the other guests the novelist merely muttered something inarticulate and turned away. What was still worse was the fact that he monopolised Anyuta until the girl's mother lost patience and protested. Dostoevsky sulked and began casting furious looks all round the room. He had become again, seemingly, the boy of twenty-three who had just written *Poor Folk*. And, just like the Dostoevsky of so many years ago, he presented himself the day after the party, expecting to to forgiven by his hostess. He was forgiven, but the elder daughter refused point-blank to be browbeaten by the author of *Crime and Punishment*. Their antagonism deepened when Anyuta declared that Pushkin was out of date. Besides, the girl's advanced political opinions grated on this Slavophil: "Dostoevsky would often spring up in a rage, seize his hat, and depart with a solemn asseveration that he did not want to have anything more to do with a Nihilist, and would never again cross our threshold. But next evening he would come again, as if nothing had happened." On one occasion he attacked Anyuta savagely: "You are a poor, insignificant thing! How different your sister is! She is still a child, but how wonderfully she understands me! *Hers* is a delicate sensitive soul!" The little Sophie listened to this with deep interest: "In the depths of my soul I was well pleased with this change in the relation of Dostoevsky to my sister; but I was ashamed of the feeling. I accused myself of treachery to my sister, and took great pains to make up for my secret sin by being very nice to her. But despite all pangs of conscience. I was always glad of every fresh quarrel between Dostoevsky and Anyuta."

Anglo-Saxon novelists as a rule snatch from their lives and their loves, from their hates and from their disasters, slices well cooked if not precisely in the manner of Maupassant. They deal with these slices lovingly, for the most part, and at all events with self-respect. They avoid, as so few of us succeed in avoiding sin, anything derogatory to themselves. If they deepen the rawness of their enemies they are but little likely to accentuate the delicacy of their friends. Briefly, their records of reality are touched up exactly as the author's photographs are touched up before being ladled out for publicity. Now, the exact opposite appears to take place in the life of this Russian novelist. His biography only too often demands the old "C'est du Dostoevsky" either in the key of insolence or that of mere bewilderment. His books often strike one as less a part of his life than his life is a part of his work. At all events, he presents the illusion of this being so in some of his very greatest works.

At this particular stage, indeed, Dostoevsky conveys the impression of living a novel that he will soon transcribe, just as in Siberia he was living the dreadful record that was to appear as *The House of the Dead*. Consider his position in this year, 1866. Only three years ago, while accompanied by the capricious Pauline, he had been playing roulette at Wiesbaden in the hope of supporting his sick wife in Russia. He had lost at Wiesbaden; in Petersburg he was to find himself with his wife and favourite brother dead, while he was deserted by his mistress. He was to be burdened with his brother's debts and by the support of his brother's family. And yet at this same Wiesbaden he was to become penniless and seemingly hopeless once more. No wonder that he claimed for himself the vitality of a cat. Never was he more eager for literary triumph than just now when he was preparing to write the final chapters of the great novel that was to bring him what *Poor Folk* had not achieved—permanent success. But just at this time the publisher Stelovsky cracked the whip. Dostoevsky must write a short novel to be finished at a certain prescribed date. Exasperated as he was, the novelist had no choice but to obey. Stelovsky, according to his daughter, had her father on one occasion visited by a police officer. This official was touched by the great writer's story of real life; instead of acting for the publisher he gave Dostoevsky very useful advice by which he was enabled to avoid the usurer's craft. What is still more important, he enabled Dostoevsky to treat from inside knowledge the police court episodes in *Crime and Punishment*.

But he had to throw aside his uncompleted masterpiece in favour of a work of which Pauline is the admitted heroine. His eyesight began to trouble him, and an oculist warned him that if he persisted in working under this pressure he would become blind. It was now the beginning of October and he had only a rough draft ready when A. Melinkov suggested a stenographer. Dostoevsky accepted the suggestion and, in the capacity of a stenographer, the one woman in the world who was to bring some sort of order into the chaos of his life confronted "a sick man, weary, badly fed, badly lodged, badly served, hunted down like a wild beast by merciless creditors, and ruthlessly exploited by selfish relatives."

Mlle Snitkin, with her near Swedish strain and her distant English strain, was for all that wholly Russian at heart. She had nothing but sympathy for the writer whose work she had so long passionately admired. Unfortunately, Dostoevsky was at his very worst at their first meeting. Only the night before he had had an epileptic attack. In his daughter's words, he treated her future mother "as a kind of Remington typewriter. He dictated the first chapter of the novel in a harsh voice, complained that she did not write fast enough, made her read aloud what he had dictated, scolded her, and declared she had not understood him." Finally he dismissed her without ceremony, telling her to return the next day at the same hour. Mlle Snitkin went home in a rage, determined never to see the novelist again, and it was only from a sense of duty

A SIGNIFICANT INTERRUPTION 125

that she continued her unpromising task. But very soon she produced an impression quite remote from the Remington typewriter. What is more, she begged the novelist to prolong the hours of dictation, and when she went home she would spend the night copying out what she had taken down during the day. The book was finished, to the publisher's astonishment, at the prescribed date. Dostoevsky became a guest at her mother's house. Though about the same age, she was in fact very much younger in her mind than Sophie Kovalevsky's elder sister. She would laugh and talk almost like a child, and the great writer would listen to her indulgently. Doubtless, he would have hesitated long over a project as yet only half formed if he had not had one night a curious dream.

Now, anyone who reads the novels of Dostoevsky is aware of the fact that dreams, quite beyond the range even of that once famous Viennese clinic, are to be found scattered through their pages. But this dream of real life is, in every respect, one of such disarming innocence that the late Sigmund Freud might well have hesitated to detect in it the faintest gleam of putrescence. The dreamer had lost something and was rummaging all over his room through a mass of useless things. Suddenly, he discovered in a drawer a minute diamond that lit up the whole room with its brilliance. How could it have got into that drawer? Who had put it there? The psychologist, whether from wishful thinking or not, read into it the most important decision of his whole life. The small diamond was no other than his stenographer! On waking up, he said to himself: "I will ask her in marriage to-day." In his daughter's words, he "never regretted his decision." It was a very swift courtship, as this note indicates: "The first time I saw F. M. was on October 4th, 1866. On November 8th of the same year I became engaged to him."

The following month Dostoevsky was in Moscow. His correspondence with his fiancée begins in much the same key, and with the same excessive attention to detail, that is to be found all through his letters to his future wife. There are the usual scraps of news about those relations who were to become such terrors in the life of the young bride. Above all, there is the old question of the likelihood, the possibility, the very faintest hope, of an advance from a publisher. Here is a typical fragment from a letter dated January 2nd, 1867: "Now, my precious Anya, this is how the matter stands. Our fate has been decided, the money is there and we will get married as soon as possible, but at the same time, there is a terrible difficulty before us. The payment of the second thousand has been postponed to such a late date, whereas we need the *two thousand* now, down to the last kopeck. (You remember how we worked it all out.) How we are to settle this—I don't yet know, but, at any rate, whatever happens, our wedding can take place. And thank goodness, thank goodness! I embrace you and kiss you a hundred times."

On February 15th, 1867, the marriage to Anna Grigorievna Snitkin was duly celebrated in spite of the opposition of Dostoevsky's relations. After the marriage, these people seem to have done their very best to separate the bride and bridegroom: "My father was hurt when he was assured that he was too old for his wife; my mother was indignant at the thought that the great man she had married considered her silly and tiresome. . . . My mother saw with alarm how rapidly the admiration she had felt for Dostoevsky before their marriage was diminishing." The relations began to dominate the bride's home. Her husband did not interfere. In the end she told the novelist that they must escape from this environment or they would lose their happiness. Dostoevsky, who imagined that he had been cured of his passion for roulette, agreed.

But he refused to apply to his Aunt Kumanin, the Grandmother of *The Gambler,* as so shortly before she had given him that ten thousand roubles for the "Epoch." He fell back on the publisher Katkov of Moscow, who willingly advanced a few thousand roubles. But the relations at once clamoured for money and, when he had satisfied their requirements, there was too little left for the journey abroad. The bride's mother, however, considered the escape imperative and urged her daughter to pledge her furniture. "In the autumn, when you come back to Petersburg," she assured her, "I shall be able to find the money to redeem it. Just now the essential thing is to get away as soon as possible, and to remove your husband from the fatal influence of all those schemers." The bride took her mother's advice without hesitation, so intent was she in saving her husband from the vortex that always seemed to be threatening him. There is a passage in *The Gambler* that lights up a state of mind which neither this marriage, nor any other event in the novelist's winding life-story, could permanently change: "I find myself taking no thought for the future, but living under the influence of passing moods, and of my recollections of the tempest which recently drew me into its vortex, and then cast me out again. At times I seem still to be caught within that vortex. At times the tempest seems once more to be gathering, and, as it passes overhead, to be wrapping me in its folds, until I have lost my sense of order and reality, and continue whirling and whirling and whirling around."

Again and again on this difficult but merciful honeymoon he was to whirl in a vortex of his own creation. He, the most generous of mankind, was to be perpetually haunted by money. In his work roubles and kopecks are even more significant than francs and centimes in the *Comédie Humaine*. But it is an error to include the Russian novelist in the ranks of those creative writers who, while nonentities all around them are flattered and even highly paid, have themselves lived from the cradle to the grave in penury. One thinks of Edgar Allan Poe as one example out of so many, of the American poet who was rewarded for his masterpiece by the sum of five dollars while its manuscript was to be sold for twenty thousand pounds. Yet Poe's contemporaries, wholly innocent of the taint of genius even if guilty of perennial flatness, were considered well within their rights when they belittled both the man and his work. Such, however, was not the case of Dostoevsky. It is true that he protested against being paid at a much lower rate than were his wealthier rivals, Turgenev and Tolstoy. But comparatively large sums were frequently passing through Dostoevsky's hands, and in time the firm practical grasp of this lady, with the Swedish and English strains in her blood, was to drag the Slavophil out of that perpetually threatening vortex before it could finally close on him.

Again, Dostoevsky's enemies were not at all the

nincompoops who, under the guidance of Rufus Griswold, tormented the American poet. Bielinsky was not only a just and penetrating critic but, despite the scorn expressed for him by Dostoevsky, particularly in later years, was also a tolerant and generous soul. Turgenev was, admittedly, one of the most consummate artists who ever expressed themselves in fiction, besides being a man who never wearied in kindness. There was not at any time against Dostoevsky the familiar whoop of crowned inanity. What prejudice there existed was the result of those Slavophil tendencies which, undoubtedly, aroused antagonism among such Westerners as Turgenev, who accepted Europe whole-heartedly even to the croupier as its lowest symbol. Yet Dostoevsky was never doctrinaire in the Anglo-Saxon sense. He was undoubtedly passionate, vehement, rhetorical, insistent, but he was without the sin of *morgue*. He had nothing of that quiet superiority which puts foreigners' teeth on edge more surely than the loudest brag. Since his return from Siberia students had flocked to him for counsel, but no one has ever accused him of having become pontifical. Thomas Carlyle was so very different in this respect. One remembers the case of an English lady who brought her son to visit the sage. After the interview the mother anxiously probed the great man for his verdict on her offspring, only to be told that he ought to have been much more impressed by him, Thomas Carlyle, than he appeared to be.

What the Russian was in essence, Siberia had failed to change permanently. He has been accused of complaining frequently, yet he did not complain of the stupidly cruel sentence to Siberia. To all appearances, he had actually felt himself no more an exile in Siberia than he did afterwards in Europe. His native country was necessary to him as oxygen. He was doubtful of ever being able to recapture abroad the real Russian feeling, as Turgenev was so unerringly to recapture it. The eternal introvert of *Crime and Punishment* was inside the novelist who created him: "We may note in passing, one peculiarity in regard to all the final resolutions taken by him in the matter; they had one strange characteristic; the more final they were, the more hideous and the more absurd they at once became in his eyes. In spite of all his agonising inward struggle, he never for a single instant all that time could believe in the carrying out of his plans." But there was another side to Raskolnikov, and that, too, belonged to his creator. The student murderer was minutely observant as well as introspective. Nothing escaped him in the evil, secret, menacing street life of Petersburg. He was at home in the lowest taverns, in the environment of rags and broken boots and brimless hats. Yet he was strangely superstitious, again like Dostoevsky, who, having seen a diamond in a dream, had the wisdom to capture for himself an infinitely more precious one in real life.

The start was made three days before Easter 1867. "My mother," observes Dostoevsky's daughter, "would have been very much startled if someone had told her that day" that she would not cross the Russian frontier again for four years. Her husband unburdened himself to Maïkov in the summer of the same year: "The burden was unbearable. I departed with death in my heart. I had not faith in foreign lands—rather, I believed they might have a bad moral effect upon me. I was wholly isolated,

A SIGNIFICANT INTERRUPTION 131

without resources, and with a young creature by my side, who was naïvely delighted at sharing my wandering life; but I saw that that naïve delight arose partly from inexperience and youthful ardour, and this depressed and tormented me. I was afraid that Anna Grigorievna would find life with me a tedious thing. For up to the present we have been literally *alone*. Of myself I could hope little: my nature is morbid, and I anticipated that she would have much to bear from me." This anticipation proved only too well founded, but the young wife very soon showed herself "finer and stronger than I had guessed." Dostoevsky was in Katkov's debt, to the extent of three thousand roubles, and it was necessary for him to plunge into work at once, as "only what stands written in black and white is valid and money-making."

They stopped only one day in Berlin: "the tiresome Germans made me nervous and irascible, and I had to take refuge in the Russian baths." The next move was to Dresden, and there, more than ever, the novelist experienced a sensation of being a slice of bread severed from the loaf. The Germans got on his nerves increasingly. But what exasperated Dostoevsky, more than anything else, was the meeting with Russians who lived permanently abroad and regarded their native land with contempt. He asked one such Russian bluntly: "Why actually did you leave home?" The reply came with equal bluntness: "Because here is civilisation, and with us is barbarism." This attitude of mind inevitably suggests the author of *Smoke*, to whom there is a long reference in this same letter to Maïkov. Dostoevsky had met Goncharov at Baden. He had borrowed sixty francs from the author of *Oblomov* and had received, in addition, a lecture on gambling and a dissertation on Turgenev. Dostoevsky determined to pay a visit to his old enemy in spite of the fact that he was in his debt to the extent of fifty thalers. In this letter to Maïkov he is quite frank as to his prejudice: "I can't stand the aristocratic and pharisaical sort of way he embraces me, and offers his cheek to be kissed. He puts on monstrous airs; but my bitterest complaint against him is his book *Smoke*." Turgenev, it seems, told the great Slavophil to his face that if Russia were to be destroyed by an earthquake the loss would not even be noticed.

This visit at Baden was inevitably unhappy. Turgenev had been attacked by the Russian Press and was feeling more than usually hostile to the leader of his political opponents: "Frankly, I never could have imagined that anyone could so naïvely and clumsily display all the wounds in his vanity as Turgenev did that day; and these people could go about boasting that they are atheists. He told me that he was an uncompromising atheist. . . . Amongst other things he told me that we are bound to crawl in the dust before the Germans, that there is but one universal and irrefutable way—that of civilisation, and that all attempts to create an independent Russian culture are but folly and pigheadedness." Turgenev was in the very act of attacking the Russophils and Slavophils in an article. Dostoevsky advised him to order a telescope from Paris to aid him in this enterprise. Asked for the meaning of this advice, he answered, "The distance is somewhat great, direct a telescope on Russia and then you will be able to observe us; otherwise you can't really see anything at all."

Not unnaturally, Turgenev became angry, and Dostoevsky changed the conversation. But before leaving he managed to express his hatred for the Germans: "Do you know what swindlers and rogues they are here? Verily the common people are much more evil and dishonest here than they are with us; and that they are stupider there can be no doubt. You are always talking of civilisation; with what has your 'civilisation' endowed the Germans, and wherein do they surpass us?" Turgenev turned pale with anger and took the last words as a personal insult: "You know quite well that I have definitely settled here, that I consider myself a German and not a Russian, and am proud of it." No reader of Turgenev's novels can accept this statement as serious or as meaning anything at all beyond a renewal of his old wish to exasperate the younger novelist. But Dostoevsky took it seriously: "Although I have read your *Smoke,* and have just talked with you for a whole hour, I could never have imagined that you would say such a thing. Forgive me, therefore, if I *have* insulted you."

Dostoevsky took his leave very politely, promising himself never to visit his rival again. At ten o'clock the next morning Turgenev left his card with Dostoevsky's landlady. During the seven weeks that followed, Dostoevsky saw him only once more, and that was at the railway station: "We looked at one another, but no greeting passed. The animosity with which I speak of Turgenev, and the insults we offered one another, will perhaps strike you unpleasantly. But, by God, I can no other; he offended me too deeply with his amazing views."

But the old question of the incompatibility between Dostoevsky and Turgenev but little concerned the young bride when she settled down with her husband in the Dresden lodgings. She had to cope with the windings and caprices of a temperament with which she had to deal for fourteen years and to which she brought always faithfulness, compassion and solace. "As for me," she wrote to O. A. Kashin while on this difficult honeymoon at Dresden, "I can only assure you I am very, very happy. Who would not be with such a husband as Fyodor? He is the sweetest, best person in all the world. How few people there are who really know him. To the world he shows himself morose and irritable; but if they only knew what lay behind it all, the warmth of heart, the goodness and the humanity! The longer one knows him, the longer one is drawn to him. We are the greatest friends, living together inseparably, the one bone of contention betwixt us is the Germans. Fyodor rails at them, and I take their part; but our disputes always end in laughter and good-humour, as I am the first to recognise the absurd side of the German character." She was soon enough to recognise the more sinister side of the Fatherland, and her husband had already begun to conceive a positive hatred for that Western Europe of which Ivan Turgenev was becoming, for his compatriots, the accepted representative.

Chapter VIII

THE HONEYMOON

ANNA GRIGORIEVNA, at all events, was far from having death in her heart during those early Dresden days of which she has left such a kindly and, at the same time, strictly objective record. She had to cope, as already shown, not only with her husband's vagaries but with the persistent claims of his relatives. Besides, there was a delay in the expected letter from Katkov. This produced a typical entry: "We simply are at our wits' end to know what to do. Poor Fyodor is in a very morose mood, full of worry and irritable over trifles which at other times he would scarcely notice. This mood of his has its inevitable effect on me."

It naturally had, but what is peculiarly pathetic about this diary is the almost light-hearted manner in which the young wife accepts responsibility for her husband's losses during an expedition to Homburg: "I was intensely miserable about the lost money, and all the more so as Fyodor made it all out to be my fault." On the subject of another loss her husband was still more emphatic: "Why hadn't I told him that the money ought to be used for paying our rent; I ought to have reminded him, while now he had played it all away and lost it! It really is dreadful of him trying to fasten his own guilt on the shoulders of others." But at the beginning of her roulette troubles the poor lady seems to examine her conscience to see if, by any chance, she has interfered with her husband's much extolled system for roulette. "Really it is too idiotic," she allowed herself to exclaim just for once, and appears to think that she has gone rather too far.

In Dresden at least roulette seemed to be far away. Lovers' tiffs passed swiftly enough. Even the discovery at the post office of a letter from Pauline Suslova caused only a passing excitement. But the bride acted promptly on Edgar's maxim in *King Lear*:

> Leave, gentle wax; and, manners, blame us not:
> To know our enemies' minds, we'd rip their hearts;
> Their papers, is more lawful.

"In a great state, I took a knife and cautiously opened the envelope. It was a very stupid, clumsy letter, and says but little for the understanding of the writer. I am quite sure she is furious about Fyodor's marriage, and her annoyance is easy to see from the tone of her letter. I read it twice over; she called me Brylkina (very stupid and not at all clever). I went over to the looking-glass and saw how my face was covered with little red spots through excitement." For all that, the diarist, according to her habit, makes a note of her small purchases, ranging from a notebook to glass buttons for her blouse. She had just seen her husband off on one of those disastrous expeditions which only too soon were to become familiar enough. The very next day a letter came from him, expressing regret for his folly but at the same time insisting that it was entirely due to the mercilessness of his creditors. Still, he acknowledges the idiocy of daring to tempt fortune at Homburg: "I was terribly sad yesterday. If you had been with me, I would have embraced you. But I did not turn back, although I had the fleeting thought of doing so. When I remember all those Vrangels, Latkins, Reislers and many other matters more important than them, then I become quite upset and muddled. I am doing a foolish thing, a foolish thing (this is folly, folly!), and above all it is evil and weak, but here there is the tiniest chance and . . . damn it, I will stop!"

But he did not stop. The letters that follow are only too typical of the honeymoon with Pauline in real life and of the scenes in fiction snatched equally from life itself in *The Gambler*. He had left for Homburg on May 16th, intending to be away four days, yet there was no Fyodor in Dresden on the 20th. But there was a letter from him: "Fyodor writes he has lost everything, and Mama has sent only thirty-five roubles. Full of misery, I went home and cried bitterly; then I wrote to Fyodor, telling him to come back as quickly as possible and not stay there any longer, taking the letter immediately to the post. At the same time I wrote Mama, begging her secretly to pawn my fur coat and send some money." An entry on May 21st shows that the diarist anticipates an appeal for more money from her husband but is not in the least censorious: "I was all the more glad to realise how he loved me in that he was so distressed not to have got a letter from me. It must indeed be real love that makes him feel like that! I had some money on me, and started off at once to send it through to Homburg by means of a banker."

The very next day her husband was writing a letter giving the real explanation of his continued losses at the tables: "The whole mistake is that we ever separated and that I did not take you with me." Then, on May 24th, comes this only too typical confession: "Anya, my dear, my friend, my wife, forgive me, don't call me a blackguard, I have committed a crime, I have lost everything you sent—everything, to the last kreutzer. Yesterday I received it and yesterday I lost it. . . . Our circumstances are bad enough as it is, and yet I have wasted money on this journey to Homburg and lost more than a thousand francs—nearly 350 roubles. It is a crime!" Obviously he must return to Dresden, and he implores his wife to send him money for the journey, "even if it is your last." On May 25th she was at the station, but had almost given up all hope of seeing her husband when she suddenly caught sight of him: "For a moment I couldn't believe my eyes, then I rushed up to him, and was oh, so glad, so happy! He looked a teeny little bit different, most probably from the dust of the journey, but the joy of our meeting again was immense!"

The forgiving attitude of Dostoevsky's second wife is positively a consolation for the rancour of the first. This kindliness extended even to her husband's stepson. On one occasion, after she had added a few lines to Dostoevsky's letter to Paul Issayev, the novelist sealed the envelope, "but as I afterwards told him he had said something unkind in it, he opened the envelope again and struck out the offending sentence." Yet, even on this difficult honeymoon of hers, Pasha is a dread worse than roulette itself. They expected to return to Petersburg in the summer, but the thought of Pasha, and the exasperation in her husband produced by Pasha, filled the young wife with dismay: "Then he will be just as touchy as before, and Pasha will keep on grumbling at me for nothing. Even the thought of it makes me perfectly wretched, and I long and long that things may continue between us just as they

THE HONEYMOON 139

are. Directly we get back to Petersburg my eternal feud with Pasha will begin all over again, and he will hurt me without Fyodor even noticing, let alone taking my part."

But in the spring of this difficult year, 1867, Pasha at all events was far away both in space and in time. There were little squabbles between the married couple, little scenes of tears and forgiveness and so on. There were visits to restaurants, conflicts with waiters eager for abnormal gratuities, shopping, sight-seeing, the sharp fresh enchantment of a foreign land seen through fresh young eyes. Fyodor's exasperation begins to slip away: "At first he used to be so dreadfully touchy, and now he positively eats out of my hand! He used to get into such dreadful rages, and scream so at the people in the house with him, that I used to tremble to think of what the future would be with such a husband and think that if it went on like that my life would become nothing but a torment. But now all that is over, though our domestic affairs cannot be said to be anything like propitious."

The bride had always, at the back of her mind, not so much roulette, not so much even Pasha, not so much the host of other dependents, not so much even the creditors who were a constant threat—not so much the combination of all these things together, as the shadow of Pauline. Though she tried to keep her secret, her husband was not slow in divining it. Once in an aquarium, while his bride was intent on goldfish, molluscs, water-snails and tortoises, the novelist seems to have dissected her innermost thought: "Then we went on to the Gardens. On the way Fyodor told me it was an ugly thing to be jealous of one's husband. But as a matter of fact I am not, the whole thing is perfectly immaterial to me, and the last thing in the world I want to do is to torment him with jealousy."

She was quite right, for really all through his merciful second marriage Dostoevsky appears to have remained singularly faithful and devoted, in spite of all those scenes of nervous irritability, which were, of course, associated with the torment of epilepsy. Under the most peaceful conditions one of his seizures, without any sort of preliminary warning, might come upon him: "At ten minutes past five, when I was not in the least expecting it, Fyodor suddenly cried out; I sprang up and hastened to him, but he never stopped screaming, having been taken suddenly with an appalling attack of cramp that twisted up both his hands and his feet. Then he began groaning as I had never heard him before, opening his eyes and lying there for minutes on end without any expression whatsoever like he sometimes does before a fit, while I prayed God to preserve him from another." But this attack was not followed by any further seizure, and a few hours later the novelist was standing on a chair so as to get a better view of the picture he loved best in the world—the Sistine Madonna. Warned by an official to desist, he bided his time, told his young wife to go into another room, and rejoined her with the information that he had seen his favourite picture in spite of the commissionaire.

On another occasion, just after one of his attacks, Dostoevsky was enraged at the behaviour of a Government clerk: "He brooded on it the whole evening, and got into such a frenzy of rage that I really was quite afraid for him. He told me, moreover,

THE HONEYMOON

that during this episode his brother Misha had quite suddenly appeared, head and shoulders in the doorway. He says he is afraid lest he should go mad, my darling, darling Fyodor! Oh, how I do grieve for him!" This strange hallucination recalls the time when as a child he had cried out to the peasant Marei, "There goes a wolf."

But the life at Dresden, broken only by that expedition to Homburg, was singularly peaceful compared with the days to come. For in July the diary plunges us directly into the hectic atmosphere of roulette. But now the scene is laid at Baden-Baden and the newly married couple are, at all events, together. Just as in *The Gambler,* we have glimpses of winning from time to time. Here is a glimpse of the wife watching her husband's famous system: "We had nothing but this single ducat, and it was just on closing time. Fyodor staked his gold piece on red and won, then on *passe,* and won, so that now we had three gold pieces. The third time we won again and now had five gold pieces, that being as much as Fyodor had taken with him first. We were ever so surprised, and, I need hardly say, delighted, although it can't be called winning, at least it means getting back what we have lost, for to-day. We were so pleased about it, we laughed the whole way home, and Fyodor kissed my hand, saying there was no luckier man in the whole universe." But the very next day the novelist returned home with the news that he had lost everything but must try his luck again with just two more ducats. He knelt at his wife's feet imploring her to give him just the two gold pieces. She yielded, and back he went to the tables. After a long interval he returned with the news that, having lost the money, he had pawned his wedding ring and lost the proceeds. He must have three more ducats to redeem the ring. He was given the money "without useless words."

Quite soon he came back to inform her that he had redeemed his ring and won five gold pieces. He returned three to his wife and saved the rest for the tables: "We went now to get a meal, as I was terribly hungry. I had suffered beyond words, waiting for Fyodor. I cried, and cursed myself, Roulette, Baden-Baden and everything on earth; I am ashamed now to confess it, and never remember to have been in such a state before. After I had wept my fill, I felt better." She assumed, when her husband went back to the tables after dinner, that his money would be lost, but in actual fact he returned with winnings amounting to several gold pieces, "so that altogether we have now, together with the extra five in my trunk, twenty-one gold pieces—which, in comparison to our income of the last few days, is quite an amazing fortune."

On July 10th there came that clash with Turgenev which Dostoevsky described at such length to Maïkov. Incidentally, it seems to have made very little impression on Mme Dostoevsky. Her only comment is to the effect that after the interview with his rival her husband went off to the Rooms. On this occasion he returned with the only too familiar news that he had lost everything. However, he started off again with exactly five gold pieces in his pocket. When he came back he looked so pale that his wife began to comfort him. Then, to her astonishment, he produced, as in a veritable fairy-tale, a purse crammed with gold. "It was a habit of

THE HONEYMOON 143

Fyodor's," she notes after further experience, "to make one feel first terrified and then delighted. When we were abroad, suffering so terribly from want of money, and waiting for it to be sent with such impatience, he would come back from the Post Office with a countenance of the utmost woe. I would begin to comfort him and he would then go out into the hall or to the landlady and bring in the sweet things and the fruit which we had been promising ourselves for so long directly we once had the money to get them with." After these particular celebrations, the novelist went back to the tables with ten gold pieces, which he quickly lost. But very soon afterwards he won another purse full of gold, went out to shop, and returned with his pockets crammed with the delicacies loved by his young wife: "What other husband in the world would have found *ryzhiki* for his wife in Baden-Baden? Really it is an achievement on his part never to be forgotten! Then he produced some bilberries out of his pocket that he had also discovered here, then caviar, then some French mustard—in short, all the things I like best! Wasn't it sweet of him, and haven't I the dearest husband in the world? This alone that he has done would make me the happiest person in all the world, and what lots of other things besides has he got to capture my whole heart with! I simply can't say how pleased I was about it!"

Not so very long ago the poor lady had found her ideal novelist miserably lodged in Petersburg. Here in Baden-Baden she was sharing rooms with him above a smithy. The noise, harmonising with the screams of children, maddened the bride, who implored her husband to leave Baden-Baden. The landlady, nearly always such a familiar figure in the novels, was in frequent conflict with Anna Grigorievna. As for the novelist, he would get angry not only with the landlady but with his wife for making a fuss about the small miseries of the household. In their wretched rooms, as the heat of summer grew more fierce, while the children sprawled all round them, and with the prospect of actual starvation drawing nearer and nearer, the noise of the smithy became the very last straw: "It is difficult to think of a more desperate state of things; Heaven forbid it should get any worse, for then I really know not what we should do. Fyodor went, later on, to Weissmann, and as he was coming back with the porter he saw our landlady talking to another woman, pointing up at our windows and at the porter, too. No doubt she had gone to her husband, after Fyodor had gone out, and said to him: 'Our lodgers are starting to pawn their things, and therefore we shall be done out of our rent probably.' " Her husband had secured fourteen gulden from Weissmann and had gone with them to the Rooms. He had lost and came back dreadfully pale. It was then that the young wife uttered that daring reproach: "Really it is too idiotic."

By degrees everything was going, from clothes to jewels. The novelist had become, as was his habit, furious rather than cowed. His exasperation would betray itself even at the tables. He would make scenes if anyone jostled him in the Rooms. His wife was inclined to think this absurd. When things seemed quite unbearable Dostoevsky determined to explain his position to Goncharov and apply for a loan. Then he would think of Katkov. But how could one write a letter, urging a further advance, from such a place as Baden-Baden? He did secure a small loan from the creator of *Oblomov* on the ground that he wanted the money not for gambling but for necessities, "Goncharov at once produced his purse and took out the three coins. Both were very embarrassed at parting. Only a few days ago Fyodor had asked him if he would convey the money to Turgenev which he owed him, and he had at once said he would. Ah . . . if only they had done it! Now Fyodor hasn't got a single kopeck!" A little later in the whirligig of the novelist's life there was another application to Goncharov, but this time he impressed Dostoevsky as hardly in a position to pay his own hotel bill. Dostoevsky had to fall back once more on Weissmann. The porter was summoned, and the young wife's two frocks, one green and the other lilac, were duly displayed. They were pronounced shabby and old-fashioned. An offer of twenty francs was made while the great writer begged for forty, "and after, so Fyodor told me, he had almost gone on his knees to him, Weissmann agreed to the sum of thirty francs for one month, Weissmann stipulating that the payment was made punctually, or else the goods would be forfeited."

Life was becoming more and more a nightmare both inside and outside of the fatal Rooms. Here is an entry which gives, after a fashion, both the high-water and the low-water marks of their little inferno: "Scarcely had we reached shelter when a terrific storm came down, with thunder and lightning, like that evening we won the hundred and sixty-eight gold pieces—but what a difference between then and now! Dear God, how difficult everything is—so much so that sometimes I want to lie down and die!" But that was only on the surface. Anna Grigorievna had no intention of yielding. When they had been married exactly five months, though the anniversary was marked by further losses at roulette, the bride decided to celebrate the occasion. Far from moaning over their position, she went into fits of laughter because she noticed that the heel of one of Fyodor's shoes had become loose. The small miseries of life swelled and multiplied: "Good-bye, my poor clothes; for you are past saving, now. We shall never be able to redeem you."

Baden-Baden had become a quicksand. She began to picture her husband playing and playing as in some nightmare of eternity, playing but never winning enough to break free. Then suddenly, as though the poor woman had not enough to endure, particularly now that she was enceinte, Dostoevsky had another seizure: "I was terrified to death, and wanted to get him back to his bed, but this I could not do, so I propped him up against mine, standing him between the bed and the wall, for I had not the strength to lay him on my bed, so that there he was, in convulsions, half standing, half sitting. His right foot, too, was paining him, for he had knocked it against the wall. After his cramp had passed away, he began to fling himself about so violently that it became impossible for me to hold him. I put two pillows down on the floor, and gradually let him down on to them, so that he could lie on the floor and have room to stretch his legs, which would be better for him. Then I undid his waistcoat and trousers that he might breathe more freely. For the first time I now noticed that his lips were quite blue,

THE HONEYMOON

and his face much redder than usual, which made me very unhappy."

The novelist lay for a long time unconscious, and Anna mused on the fact that everything that he said while in this state was in German, a language which he had not mastered. Then he addressed his wife and begged her pardon but could not understand in the least what she said. Finally, he asked her for money with which to go back to the tables: "And a fine piece of work that would have been—I could imagine to myself the sort of figure he would have cut, and yet, none the less, I had a feeling he would have won." But within a very short time, after a sleep of just three-quarters of an hour during which there were many wakeful periods, he was able to go out with his wife, and the diary drifts into one of its oases of tranquillity, concerning itself with big cups of chocolate, the Austrian band and the flowers and flags that celebrated its winning of the first Gold Medal at the Paris Competition.

Dostoevsky continued to dream of his own big win to come, particularly when the money arrived at last from Katkov. Anna Grigorievna, for her part, had expected they would die of hunger before that event, and that, if they didn't, her husband would lose the publisher's advance like everything else: "I daresay I said it rather sharply, but I was at my wits' end what to do. For a whole month I had borne it and said not a word, even when there was nothing else left to us, for still I could hope for some help from Mama, or on pawning our clothes and valuables, but that now everything was finished; it was impossible to ask Mama for any more, and I would be, moreover, ashamed to do it. And just because I was so miserable and impatient, Fyodor couldn't stop thinking of that great big win of thousands he was going to make."

And so it went on and on until the moment came when they said farewell to the smithy. The landlady never came up to say good-bye to them. Only the deplorable smithy children, who had disturbed their nights so often, gave them any sort of farewell as they drove away to the station with a hundred and forty francs as their joint fortune.

Chapter IX

ESCAPE

THEIR little capital of a hundred and forty francs was insufficient; further pawning before leaving Baden-Baden was imperative. But the expectant mother left the dreaded place in that amused frame of mind which, in spite of everything, so often displays itself in the diary. There was still no question of death in her heart. She was exactly what her husband called her, "a young, warm-hearted, pretty creature" who had the enigmatic privilege of being in the custody of this erratic man of genius. She had developed, on the testimony of her husband, "a great talent for travelling; wherever we went, she discovered everything that was worth seeing, and at once wrote down her impressions; she has filled countless little notebooks and so on with her hieroglyphics." Clearly, she had shaken off the depression of Dresden and the madhouse atmosphere of Baden-Baden.

Geneva indeed must have seemed at first to both of them a veritable escape, not only from the trials of this protracted honeymoon but from the shadow of Siberia. In the great novel that had brought Dostoevsky fame, as distinct from the malady of feeling famous, the acid memories of Siberia had been almost as insistent as in *The House of the Dead*. This passage from *Crime and Punishment* might well have been taken word for word from the earlier work: "In prison, of course, there was a great deal he did not see; he lived as it were with downcast eyes. It was loathsome and unbearable for him to look. But in the end there was much that surprised him and he began, as it were involuntarily, to notice much that he had not suspected before. What surprised him most of all was the terrible impossible gulf that lay between him and all the rest. They seemed to be a different species, and he looked at them and they at him with distrust and hostility." But Raskolnikov, like the central figure of *The House of the Dead*, was quick to realise that these dark-minded convicts were in many ways superior to the political prisoners who scorned them.

From the first Anna Grigorievna appreciated Geneva, but her husband, in this respect like Turgenev, felt oppressed by mountains. In his correspondence he has very few good words for Geneva, "a horrible town like Cayenne." Then further on in the same letter to Maïkov: "And the people are so self-satisfied and boastful! It is the mark of quite peculiar stupidity to be so self-satisfied. Everything is ugly here, utterly rotten, and expensive. The people are always drunk! Even in London there are not so many rowdies and 'drunks.' Every single thing, every post in the street they regard as beautiful and majestic." Obviously it was no real escape, and that same month, October 1867, the novelist is writing from "Bains-Saxon" to his wife describing his little journey minutely after his fashion and proposing to leave for Geneva the next day. But on the next day he is writing from Saxon-les-Bains in a quite different key: "Anya, My Dear, I am worse than a beast! Last night by ten o'clock I had won 1300 francs. To-day—I have not a sou. I have lost absolutely everything, everything! And all because that rascal of a servant at the Hôtel des Bains did not wake me

ESCAPE

up, although I had told him I wanted to leave for Geneva at 11 o'clock."

On the 17th of the next month, we are frankly back in the old atmosphere of *The Gambler*: "I arrived here at a quarter to four and I discovered that the roulette did not close until five o'clock (I had thought it was four). So I had an hour. I ran there. I lost fifty francs straight off, then suddenly I began to win. I don't know how much I won, I didn't count; after that I lost heavily almost to the last coin. And suddenly with my last bet I *won back* the 125 francs I had started with and an additional 110 francs. So now I have 235 francs in all. Anya, my dear, I thought very seriously of sending you 100 francs, but, after all, that is too little. If only it had been 200 francs." He assures his wife that for three hours that evening he will play cautiously like a Jew, and that if he wins anything in addition to what he has won already he will dispatch money to her. But the very next day he commences his letter from Saxon-les-Bains: "Anya, my dear, my precious, I have lost everything, everything, everything! Oh! my angel, don't be sad, don't worry. Be confident, a time will come when I shall be worthy of you and I shall stop robbing you like a wretched low thief!" He is convinced that, just as in 1865 he had been saved by *Crime and Punishment,* so now he will be saved by the new novel that is taking possession of him perhaps even to the exclusion of roulette. No system, seemingly, can be relied on, but in any case there is always Katkov who will not refuse a further advance: "There will be scarcely anything left, but instead, we shall have our things. By not paying for our rooms we shall be able to live on the diamonds and the rings until we receive our money. On the 15th December we can get them out and pawn them again, and this will continue for *three* months, and in *three months' time* I shall send Katkov the novel for 3000 roubles and then he will surely send, at my request, at least 300 to cover the expense of your confinement, and another five hundred two months later." His first child, Sonya, was born on February 22nd, 1868, and died on May 12th of the same year.

The novelist was devoted to his little daughter and expresses his devotion whole-heartedly to Maïkov in a letter from Geneva of May 30th, 1868: "She was just beginning to know and love me, and always smiled when I came near. And now they tell me, to console me, that I shall surely have other children. But where is Sonya! Where is the little creature for whom I would, believe me, gladly have suffered death upon the cross, if *she* could have remained alive?"

For all his irascibility and for all his seeming weariness and disillusion, Dostoevsky preserved to the very end of his life the youth of his heart. "I could never understand," admits his daughter, "this love of a young girl of nineteen for a man of forty-five." She questioned her mother on the all-important topic, only to receive this protest: "But he was young! You can't imagine how young your father still was! He would laugh and joke, and find amusement in everything, like a boy. He was much gayer, much more interesting than the young men of that period, among whom it was the fashion to wear spectacles and to look like old professors of zoology."

In the meantime, Dostoevsky continued to send money to Michael's widow and the old burden of Pasha lay like a dead weight. He was affectionate to

Pasha, to whom he exclaims in a letter from Geneva dated March 3rd, 1868: "Know once for all that you will always be my son, my eldest son; and not duty bids me say so, but my heart. If I have often scolded you, and been cross to you, that was only my evil disposition; I love you as I have seldom loved anyone." And to this deplorable stepson the great writer expresses fear for the future of *The Idiot,* the first part of which was appearing in the "Russky Viestnik." If only it were a success then indeed all would be well for the novelist's little world, including P. A. Issayev.

But the very next month there is a desperate letter to his wife from Saxon-les-Bains: "I took the ring to the pawnbroker, she took it with great disgust but did not give me any money for it. She said *she hadn't any,* but she told me to come for an answer at 7 o'clock. It is now 6.15 p.m. But she said she would not give me more than 10 francs. It is quite obvious that she is frightened and has been forbidden usury by the local authorities. She almost said as much." Dostoevsky assures his wife that he will plead for 15 francs, instead of 10, as he has nothing left but a few centimes.

They moved to Vevey. Here the novelist's depression deepened, and also the longing to get back to his own country. "I have nothing to tell you," he exclaims in that letter of June 10th to Maïkov, "no news of any kind. I get duller and stupider every day that I'm here, and yet I daren't do anything until the novel's finished. Then, however, I intend in any event to go back to Russia. To get the book done, I must sit at my desk for at least eight hours daily. I have now half worked off my debt to Katkov. I shall work off the rest." He anticipates a hostile reception for *The Idiot,* in which he is in the act of depicting the ideal Russian of the future. But Anna Grigorievna's loneliness had been broken at Vevey by a long visit from her mother, and all three of them took mountain walks together. Dostoevsky, the writer who is always credited with having been saturated by the miasma of cities and who, admittedly, rejected what seemed to him the general oppressiveness of the Alps, none the less yielded to the beauty of the scenery around Vevey. For all that, he found the place enervating and he suffered more frequently from epilepsy and less specific nervous attacks. He was haunted, too, by the fact that for some time he had suspended his payments to Michael's widow and the eternal Pasha. The next move was to Milan, and here once more he was seized, only much more poignantly than his rival Turgenev with nostalgia. "I am very heavy-hearted," he wrote to his niece Sofia early in November, "homesick, and uncertain of my position; my debts, etc., deject me terribly. And besides I have been so alienated from Russian life that I find it difficult, lacking fresh Russian expressions as I do, to write anything at all: only think—for six months I haven't seen a single Russian newspaper. And I still have the fourth part of my novel to do, and it will take about four months more."

The famous cathedral greatly impressed Dostoevsky, who went up on the roof to see the view over the Lombard plain. On his first visit abroad, this cathedral had been the sight which had captivated him perhaps more than anything else in Europe. But when the autumn rains came they settled down for the winter in Florence. The new novel remained to be finished. Anna Grigorievna was once more acting as his stenographer. Besides this, she studied thoroughly the artistic treasures of Florence. Their talented daughter maintains, in spite of several passages in the correspondence, that her parents were really happy in Florence. Certainly Dostoevsky, who is usually so harsh towards foreign countries, was fond of Italy and even maintained that Italians reminded him of his compatriots. Already the young wife had become what she was to remain to the end —the buttress against life for this man of genius who was, in spite of all his acute sensitiveness to the secrets of others, so easily deceived: "Young and strong, she desired to protect the famous writer, who was approaching his decline. His debts and his numerous obligations might have frightened a timid soul. But my mother's Norman blood braced her for conflict; she was ready to do battle with her whole world." That had been her attitude when she was taking down *The Gambler,* and now it was intensified as she watched the creation of that extraordinary figure, Prince Mishkin. She had not only to contend against the world for her husband but to contend against his own bitter self-criticism.

Small articulate people, all over the world, have jeered confidently at the formlessness of much of Dostoevsky's work. Even Strakhov, who was, to all appearances, so sympathetic to the novelist, commented frankly on this and met with an equally frank admission some three years later in a letter from Dresden: "Yes, that was and ever is my greatest torment—I never can control my material. Whenever I write a novel, I crowd it up with a lot of separate stories and episodes; therefore the whole lacks proportion and harmony. You have seen this astonishingly well; how frightfully have I always suffered from it, for I have always been aware that it was so. And I have made another great mistake besides: without calculating my powers, I have allowed myself to be transported by poetic enthusiasm, and have undertaken an idea to which my strength was not equal. (N.B.—The force of poetic enthusiasm is, to be sure, as for example with Victor Hugo, always stronger than the artistic force. Even in Pushkin one detects this disproportion.) But *I* destroy myself thereby." But he was essentially a realist, though his conception of realism was remotely different from that of his contemporary, Zola. "My God!" he exclaims in a letter to Maïkov towards the close of 1868, "if one could but tell categorically all that we Russians have gone through during the last ten years in the way of spiritual development, all the realists would shriek that it was pure fantasy! And yet it would be pure realism! It *is* the one true, deep realism; theirs is altogether too superficial."

Doubtless, Mme de Staël would have shrunk from this formlessness. But a disconcerting clarity emerges unerringly from the seeming chaos so that the old gibe, "C'est du Dostoevsky," became, as the years passed, more and more puerile. Examine the labyrinths of *Crime and Punishment* which are so close to the labyrinths of the old Petersburg. Consider the swarming mass of derelicts who slink in and out of those mean flats, impregnated with the physical reek and the moral putrescence of a great city. Each one of them has his place exactly as each mean street has its place. The contradictoriness even of the principal characters is as true to nature as the city itself to its inhabitants. No one can argue more persistently, and inconsistently, about the motive of Raskolnikov than he does about it himself. Could

Sonya's step-mother, who had driven her out upon the streets for the sake of her own starving children, explain her love for her step-daughter? All one knows for certain is that it is not sham love Porphyry himself is contradictory in his attitude towards his prey in a sense that Sherlock Holmes, for instance, would never have been remotely ambiguous.

But the essential lucidity in confusion of the great writer dwarfs the mere neatness of any well-cut novel from such a finished cutter as, for instance, his contemporary Octave Feuillet. Glance for a few seconds at Monsieur de Camors and then turn to Prince Mishkin. Certainly you see both figures, but with what a difference in intensity of light! You remember the Frenchman with an effort, but no effort will rid you of the memory of the Russian. But why mention Octave Feuillet? In the whole gallery of the *Comédie Humaine,* from him who exclaimed to Paris, "A nous deux maintenant," to Père Goriot himself, there is no more irradiated and irradiating figure than the hero of *The Idiot.* Had he written only this one book, Dostoevsky would have proved himself to be the writer who would indeed reveal to his compatriots what was "most intimate and real in their own souls." Yet, even for Dostoevsky's daughter, who is as sympathetic to her father's work as she is to the man himself, Mishkin remains quite frankly a degenerate. The novelist, however, defended his creation precisely from the charge. He had heard this work pronounced at least fifty times the best of his books, and he maintained that "all those who spoke about it, as being my best work, had something particular in the organisation of their intelligence, which struck me and gave me a great deal of pleasure." It was Dostoevsky's view in this novel that though there may be weakness in certain cells of the brain, the brain as a whole may none the less remain both morally and intellectually superior to that of those who would deride it.

The significance of the Prince lies in the fact that he is not only an interpreter of those national tenets which, as the years passed, were to become the frank propaganda of the Slavophils; he is important as revealing in his own person that inner cohesion of all Dostoevsky's seemingly inchoate art. In one book after the other the breaking down of barriers, separating human beings, is the very essence of the narrative. In *Crime and Punishment* the barriers between the murderer and the prostitute seem to be too strong to be broken down by the tears of Sonya's pity. Yet it is not until they are broken down and the man's pride humbled to the dust that the redemption of Raskolnikov can begin. This for him is the first necessity and the last. Now, Prince Mishkin is a breaker down of all such barriers. He is a veritable touchstone of character. No matter who confronts him in the swarm of people on that vast canvas, each one of them when in contact with him reveals his true self beneath any mask. It may be Rogozhin, the savage with murder in his heart, or Ganya, who frankly admits himself to be a blackguard. It may be the strong-willed Aglaya, or Nastasya who hesitates too long between the Prince's dream of beauty redeeming the world and Rogozhin's doom of killing what he loves best on earth.

Not for a second does Mishkin hesitate about the real meaning of Nastasya. For him she is one of those strange beings who are permeated by the desire for vengeance on themselves. "This unhappy woman," he says to Aglaya Epanchin, "is persuaded that she is the most helpless, fallen creature in the world. Oh, do not condemn her! Do not cast stones at her! She has suffered too much already in the consciousness of her own undeserved ignominy! And wherein is she guilty?—oh God! every moment of her life she bemoans and bewails herself and cries out that she does not admit any guilt, that she is the victim of circumstances—the victim of a wicked libertine. But whatever she may say to you, remember that she does not believe it herself—remember that she will believe nothing but that she is a guilty creature." The duality of Nastasya with its deep rendering of the *odi et amo* motif is only too plain; but it is reserved for the acute, child-like Aglaya to penetrate the duality of the Prince just as unerringly as he had penetrated to the core of her own startled simplicity: "I consider you the the most honest and upright of men—more honest and upright than any other man; and if anybody says that your intellect is—that your wits are—sometimes affected, you know it is unfair. I always say so and uphold it, because even if your surface intellect be a little affected (of course you will not feel angry with me for talking so—I am speaking in all good faith), yet your real intellect is *far* better than all theirs together; such an intellect as they have never even *dreamed* of, because you have, as it were, two intellects—a real one and an unreal one."

The Prince is only too close to the tormented novelist, particularly just before an epileptic fit. Mishkin would be seized by the desire to look for something, without knowing what it was. He would forget about that and then start searching again. On one particular walk, impossible to forget, something quite definite fixed itself in his memory. He had seen a particular object recently in a shop-window. He was anxious to know whether, or not, he had become the victim of hallucination. But on retracing his steps he found the actual shop and the actual article, marked sixty kopecks. Sharply it came back to him that it was precisely at this place that he had felt the tragic eyes of Rogozhin fastened upon him. Then the vague contradictory thoughts of this stricken man whirl round and round one concrete object—a knife. All the evil of the city seems to be pouring down upon this dreamer mastered by a Demon more formidable than the approaching would-be assassin. Parfen Rogozhin's face is lit up with the smile of insanity and there is something gleaming in his right hand.

"Parfen, I won't believe it!" the Prince exclaims, and the next instant his whole being becomes strangely illumined: "This lasted perhaps half a second, yet he distinctly remembered hearing the beginning of the wail, the strange, dreadful wail which burst from his breast of its own accord, and which no power or effort of will on his part could suppress." Mishkin had been saved from Rogozhin's knife by one of his seizures. "As is well known," the novelist comments with the knowledge of bitter first-hand experience, "these fits occur instantaneously. The face, especially the eyes, becomes terribly disfigured, convulsions seize the limbs, a terrible moan or wail bursts from the breast of the sufferer, a wail in which his whole being seems to disappear and be blotted out, so that it is impossible to believe that the man who has just fallen is the same who emitted the dreadful cry. It seems more as though some other being, inside the stricken one, had cried.

Many people have borne witness to this impression; and many cannot behold an epileptic fit without mysterious terror and a feeling of mysticism and dread." In that dehumanised cry is registered once more the duality of Dostoevsky the man and Dostoevsky the creative writer; in it one begins to understand that realism which resembles that of no other author. Not even the Greeks conveyed more profoundly the calamity that, because of necessity, none can avert. Certainly, the charm of dead rose-leaves seems remote from this writer who claimed not only suffering but sin itself as a necessary ingredient of human experience. For all that, it was Dostoevsky's persistent dream, no less than Mishkin's, that some day beauty would yet redeem this soiled planet.

Nothing will convince Mishkin that the Russian can ever really find an escape in the dryness of materialism: "It is so easy for a Russian to become an atheist, far more so than for any other nationality in the world. And not only does a Russian 'become an Atheist,' but he actually *believes* in Atheism, just as though he had found a new faith, not perceiving that he has pinned his faith to *nil*. Such is our anguish of thirst."

In the Epanchins' drawing-room he is exactly like Dostoevsky in Sonya Kovalevsky's home, though he makes considerably more strenuous attempts to adapt himself to the other guests. But it is not in the Epanchins' drawing-room but in a far different setting that this strange drama plays itself out in the final tragedy. Rogozhin, remotely different from Raskolnikov in all other ways, is a victim, like the hero of *Crime and Punishment,* of the *idée fixe.* He plays with the idea of killing; he is drawn by a curious magnetism to the actual concrete knife, a form of attraction perfectly comprehensible to the apache of Paris. Just as the familiar magnetism of Dostoevsky has been able to confront Aglaya with Nastasya—both women being loved, without consciousness of any inner clash, by the Prince—so that same magnetism brings Mishkin to a silent forbidding house with the question: "Where is Nastasya Philipovna?" Rogozhin made no answer but motioned to him to look for himself behind a curtain. In the dim light Mishkin could see upon a bed, covered from the "head down, in a white sheet," a motionless figure: "The gazer could just make out by the elevation of the sheet, that a human being lay outstretched beneath it. All around, on the bed, on a chair beside it, on the floor, were scattered the different portions of a magnificent white dress, bits of lace, and rich ribbon. On a small table at the pillow glittered a mass of diamonds, torn off and thrown down anyhow. From under a heap of lace at the end of the bed peeped one small white foot, which looked as though it had been chiselled out of marble; terribly still and white it seemed. The Prince gazed and felt that the more he gazed, the more deadly became the silence. Suddenly a fly awoke somewhere and buzzed across the room, hovered over the bed, and settled in silence on the pillow. The Prince shuddered."

Side by side, close to the dead woman, the murderer and the dreamer felt towards each other neither hatred nor fear. All through the night they guarded her as nuns might have guarded her, as if, indeed, the spirits of good and evil had been fused at last in an immense regret. But the Prince is doomed no less than the murderer is doomed. There is no "happy ending," no soothing of his readers' strained nerves, no de-crescendo of comfort and security in the Anglo-Saxon manner. In some ways the novel is almost too close to autobiography. Mishkin is speaking through the novelist's own lips when he tells Adelaida Epanchin, just as he had told Anyuta in the famous mathematician's old home, of the excessive sensitiveness of the brain when expecting death second by second. The whole book, indeed, is permeated by personal memories apart from epilepsy and the experiences of Siberia. And the foreboding of the book which strikes at one in the opening pages is humanised by the novelist's love of Nature, his fondness for trees, his understanding of animals, and those less conspicuous traits that have been too often denied to him. Then, just as in *Crime and Punishment,* we are confronted with an analysis of suffering before which that of Victor Hugo pales, with an interpretation of criminal motive that makes the criminologist of fiction appear almost infantile, with the old passionate belief in a national Christianity, with the peculiar psychology of the Russian capital, and with Dostoevsky's permanent love for and veneration of childhood.

There is in this book not the faintest trace of what he had come to regard as the enthusiastic political aberration of his youth, for which he had paid so cruel a penalty. Of one of his old fellow "conspirators" he wrote to Maïkov towards the end of 1868: "I must confess that I have heard nothing of Danilevsky since the year 1849, though I've often thought of him. What a frenzied Fourierist he was at one time; and now that same Fourierist has turned himself back into a Russian who loves his native soil and customs!" Dostoevsky had become, apart altogether from his genius, just such a type of Russian, but he could not accept the notion that Bielinsky, had he lived, would ever have joined the Slavophils: "No; with Bielinsky that was quite out of the question. He was, in his day, a remarkable writer, but could not possibly have developed any further." Slavophil propaganda—one cannot avoid the word—had become an integral part of Dostoevsky's material; and it is no wonder that his art was not infrequently unequal to its dead weight. Even in *Letters from the Underworld,* published three years after *The House of the Dead,* we read from the lips of "a rat gifted with an intense consciousness" these typical words: "Civilisation develops in man nothing but an added capacity for receiving impressions. That is all. And the growth of that capacity further augments man's tendency to seek pleasure in blood-letting. Nothing else has civilisation conferred upon him." In the novels, just as in the correspondence, Dostoevsky attacked the "spirit of Euclid" as illustrated in positivism. He maintained that if Bielinsky had lived he would have realised his error but would never have repented of it.

In the letter to Maïkov from Florence towards the end of 1868 the novelist refers to a work on atheism. Already the germ of *The Brothers Karamazov* was working and, though the novelist published several books before his final masterpiece, it was always this idea of atheism and, undoubtedly, his own inner struggle against atheism which at once afflicted and sustained him. But he assures Maïkov that it will be necessary to absorb a whole library of works dealing with atheism from both Catholic and Orthodox-Greek sources: "In the meantime I've got to live somehow. I don't mean to hurry my 'Atheism' on to the market (I have such lots to say therein about Catholicism and Jesuitry as compared with Orthodoxy). . . ." But the work simply cannot be written out of Russia. In a letter to his niece, Sofia Alexandrovna, he rails against his exile: "In three months, we shall have been exactly two years abroad. In my opinion, it is worse than deportation to Siberia. I mean that quite seriously; I'm not exaggerating. I cannot understand the Russians abroad. Even though there *is* a wonderful sky here, and though there are—as, for example, in Florence—literally unimaginable and incredible marvels of art, there are lacking many advantages which even in Siberia, as soon as I left the prison, made themselves evident to me: I mean, especially, home and the Russians, without which and whom I cannot live." He has become very interested in the "Zarya," a new journal the first number of which has reached him in Florence. He had, however, borrowed some seven thousand roubles from the "Russky Viestnik," and so he anticipated difficulty in contributing to any other paper. In the same letter he alludes to a plan for an annual periodical which was eventually to emerge as his famous *Diary of a Writer*.

His mind has become more than ever creative. He suggests literary ideas one after another: "But the chief thing is this next big novel. If I don't write it, it will torment me to death. But I can't write it here." The return to Russia, however, was impossible until an instalment of at least four thousand roubles had been paid on those debts in Petersburg which he had assumed so recklessly. In the following month he writes to Strakhov in allusion to *Smoke*: "Of Turgenev's novel I don't wish even to speak; the devil knows what he may mean! But is not my fantastic *Idiot* the very dailiest truth? Precisely such characters *must* exist in those strata of our society which have divorced themselves from the soil—which actually are becoming fantastic. But I'll talk of it no more! In my book much was written in haste, much is too drawn-out, much has miscarried; but much, too, is extremely good. I am not defending the novel, but the idea."

In a letter to Sofia Alexandrovna the following March he again alludes to his rival, maintaining quite wrongly that Turgenev had lost his talent through long residence abroad. For Dostoevsky there is no such danger because of his dislike of the Germans, though he is afraid of Italian influence. He has now received an official request to contribute to the "Zarya," but the unfortunate fact is that he cannot appeal to Katkov for more money while he is working for another journal. For the rest, he is delighted with the new periodical, and particularly with an article by Danilevsky on the rôle of Russia. For Dostoevsky there is but one single goal for his country, namely, to "reveal to the world her own Russian Christ, whom as yet the peoples know not, and who is rooted in our native Orthodox faith." That is the very core of this strange writer's "propaganda," which is never wholly absent even from such relatively trivial contributions as, for instance, the story entitled *The Landlady*.

He had found no real peace in Switzerland after that hopeful escape from Dresden. As the days passed, Florence became more and more distasteful to the distracted exile. The young wife had been so grateful for that escape from Dresden, but now in the distance Dresden itself was to appear yet another escape. Anna Grigorievna was once more enceinte, and so her husband was anxious about the long journey, which, however, passed off quite pleasantly. They stayed two days in Venice, and Anna Grigorievna "almost screamed with delight" when she saw for the first time the Piazza of St. Mark's and the palaces. They went on to Vienna, which Dostoevsky found more beautiful than Paris. Prague was the next halting-place before the return to Dresden, where, shortly afterwards, a little girl came into the world. The novelist rushed to the registry office to announce the birth. The authorities asked him to give his wife's maiden name. He could not remember it, and went home in an exasperated frame of mind.

" 'What is your name?' he asked his wife severely.

" 'My name? Anna,' replied my mother, much surprised.

" 'I know your name is Anna. I want to know your maiden name.'

" 'Why?'

" 'Oh! It is not I who would know it, but the police here. These Germans are so inquisitive. They insist on knowing what you were called before your marriage, and I have completely forgotten!'

"My mother instructed her husband, and advised him to write the name on a bit of paper."

But now that Florence was far away it began to appear strangely attractive. "For the present we are not doing so badly," he assures Sofia Alexandrovna, "but I am badly 'sold,' for it seems now that the hot, dry air in Florence was extraordinarily beneficial to my health, and even more so to my nerves (nor had Anya anything to complain of, rather the contrary). It was precisely on the *hottest* days that the epilepsy was least perceptible, and my attacks in Florence were much slighter than anywhere else. But here I'm always ill (perhaps it may be only the effect of the journey). . . . I have fever at the actual moment, and think that in this climate I shall write feverishly—that is, incoherently."

He is still overwhelmed by the idea of his great novel, but it will be necessary for him to write fresh stories before attacking his real work: "And to me that is terrible. What lies before me, and how I shall arrange my affairs, is to me an enigma!" At all events, the enigma could no longer be solved by Katkov the publisher. It is now a question of Kachpirev, the editor of the "Zarya." As usual, the novelist is perfectly frank to Maïkov, to whom in this autumn of 1869 he pours out the very depths of his misery: "Does he think that the letter in which I described my destitute condition was a piece of fine writing and nothing more? How can I work, when I am hungry, and had to pawn my very pantaloons to get the two thalers for the telegram? The devil take me and my hunger! But she, my wife, who now is suckling her infant, *she* had to go herself to the pawnshop and pledge her last warm woollen garment! And it has been snowing here for the last two days (I am not lying: look at the newspapers!). How easily may she catch cold! Isn't he capable of understanding, then, that I am *ashamed* of telling him all these things?" And there are so many more things of which he is ashamed to speak. Neither the midwife nor the landlady has been paid. Kachpirev has insulted not only Dostoevsky but Anna Grigorievna by taking the letter of appeal for aid so casually. The whole thing is unbearable in the novelist's eyes: "And then they demand of me lucid art, effortless and untroubled poetry, and point me to Turgenev and Goncharov! If they but knew the conditions under which *I* have to work!" In this atmosphere (almost the old atmosphere of the roulette tables but without the roulette) the year 1869, one of the most important years in the artistic life of Fyodor Dostoevsky, came to a close. But the greatest of his novels would not allow itself to be written in any foreign land, and the escape to Dresden was in reality just as ineffectual as had been the escape from Dresden.

Chapter X

BACK TO DRESDEN

IT became more and more difficult for the novelist to interpret Russian life at a distance from Russia. Yet, abroad, he was just as much obsessed by his belief in Russian progress on national lines as he was obsessed by it in his own country. He was now in the act of interpreting this conviction which runs in his own words: "No country will renounce its own life; it will consent rather to live in poverty, but at all events to live, rather than to live in the fashion of other nations, which is not to live at all." But before dealing with the destroyers of Russian life on national lines Dostoevsky was too busy himself with a short work entitled *The Eternal Husband,* an interruption to *The Possessed* exactly as *The Gambler* had been an interruption to *Crime and Punishment.*

Dostoevsky has often been accused of presenting novels rising in their motif but little above the shocker which is still supposed to thrill the London office-boy. The charge is, of course, spitefully grotesque. The "juicy" murder theme that, even in these murderous days, fascinates so powerful a section of our island public is remotely different from this Russian's work. But murder is certainly very significant even in the greatest of Dostoevsky's novels, from *Crime and Punishment* to *The Brothers Karamazov.* Even in the minor stories, even in *The Landlady* and *A Gentle Spirit,* the threat of murder seems to be lurking in every page. At first glance, this would appear to be disconcerting. How is it that this great novelist rejected so absolutely the calm mellow atmosphere which gave Turgenev, in spite of all his irony, his undying charm?

On the surface again, this question is not difficult to answer. Murder was not so remote from Dostoevsky as it may be assumed to have been from his contemporaries in Europe, including his Westernised rivals. His father had been murdered. An aunt of his had been murdered. He himself had been incarcerated in close association with murderers. But not only in Siberia but in his life prior to his sentence, enforced poverty had brought him quite close to that underworld which of necessity is brought, almost as a matter of daily routine, in contact with criminals or potential criminals. He himself, under any sort of conditions, seemed for long years incapable of escaping from the disease of poverty, as though it were an integral part of the disease of epilepsy. Until his second wife took charge of his affairs, poverty, quite unconnected with gambling, never deserted him for very long. But his diatribes against publishers and editors, and even his diatribes against himself, need never be taken too seriously. His fits of despair, though infinitely deeper than those of Dickens's Micawber, vanished within almost equal celerity. He was wholly right in claiming for himself the vitality of a cat. But one cannot be too much on one's guard against his over-simplification of himself.

Though apparently he confesses everything, nothing in the whole world of imaginative fiction is more deceptive than the naïveté of Dostoevsky. The very duality, which at times he admits so significantly, is possibly even more subtle than that found in any one of his novels. Never, by any chance, must one accept whole-heartedly any reading by Dostoevsky of his personal problem. For in one and the same person there continued to exist, as it were side by side, the inquisitiveness of a police inspector and the inquisition of an alienist. Against his mysticism, with the dark background of the Bosphorus, the enigmatic and sometimes equivocal gravity of long Byzantine faces, the awe of icons, the undying faith in a flight of stronger eagles over the renewed city of Constantine, there stood out in stark perspective a concrete personal world of hypochondria, jealousy, the plague of debt, the plague of temperament, the actual torment of epilepsy, the ever deepening consciousness of the gulf between aspiration and achievement. It is no wonder that so many of his creations are, literally from moment to moment, uncertain of themselves, swayed by a duality even of intention. In none of his books is this last phase of hesitation more persistent than in *The Eternal Husband,* and in this book, as in nearly all the others, there are hints of such bitter personal reminiscence that the work cannot be labelled an overelaborate *jeu d'esprit* as too many, perhaps, are inclined to label it.

Briefly, the dead woman Natalya Vassilyevna seems to be hovering between a lover of long ago, Velchaninov, and Pavel Pavlovitch the widower who lost her nine years before. These two men, hurled at each other after the manner of Dostoevsky, illustrate excellently the attraction of hatred. In spite of all the incongruity of the situation, they are endowed with all the fantastic realism of this author. The dead woman herself is at least equally real even to minuteness of detail suggesting minuteness of memory: "She was not exactly pretty; perhaps she was actually plain. She was twenty-eight when Velchaninov first knew her. Though not altogether beautiful, her face was sometimes charmingly animated, but her eyes were not pretty: there was something like an excess of determination in them. She was very thin. On the intellectual side she had not been well educated; her keen intelligence was unmistakable, though she was one-sided in her ideas. Her manners were those of a provincial lady, and at the same time, it is true, she had a great deal of tact; she had artistic taste, but showed it principally in knowing how to dress. . . . In difficult positions her firmness and stoicism were amazing. She was capable of generosity and at the same time would be utterly unjust." Besides, she is the type for whom the first lover is the husband, "but never till after the wedding." As one reads these lines, and between these lines, it is impossible not to recall a fantastic parting in the moonlight under the kindly observation of a certain Baron Vrangel.

To deepen the complications, there is a child of eight years old, the little Liza, whom the widower ill-treats. Velchaninov rescues the child, though he is uncertain as to whether he is, or is not, her father. Then he is taken ill in close proximity to the widower. Something grotesque, inevitably, insinuates itself into the murderous atmosphere which is so genuine. Velchaninov is in great pain and the potential assassin ministers to him with hot plates. Later on in this nightmare within a nightmare, Velchaninov sees Pavel Pavlovitch brandishing a razor with obvious intent. He rouses himself in time and overpowers the would-be murderer. The real point of this, one of the most interesting although comparatively unimportant works, is that Pavel Pavlovitch illustrates the "instinct" for vengeance, of which from first to last he is never wholly conscious, as a veritable reflex.

As for his intended victim, he ponders, just like Dostoevsky himself, on whatever clue there may be to motive: "If it is settled that he tried to murder me *accidentally,* had the idea ever entered his head before, if only as a dream in a vindictive moment?" Velchaninov decided that the foiled assassin certainly wished to kill him though the actual impulse to murder had never come into his mind: "Pavel Pavlovitch wanted to kill him, but didn't know he wanted to kill him. It's senseless, but that's the truth." And with that genius of his, born of veritable intuition and not of "taking infinite pains," the novelist has conveyed exactly that swaying between antagonistic impulses which Velchaninov has detected. But, more than ever in the manner of Dostoevsky, Velchaninov examines the workings of his own mind, asking himself if in reality he had expected an attempt upon his life: "I began, as it were, to expect something . . . but, of course, not that; but, of course, not that he would murder me." All the same, in his heart of hearts, Velchaninov had realised from the first that this man who fawned upon him without hypocrisy—that is the extraordinary part of it, without hypocrisy—loathed the very sight of him: "Yes, it was from hatred that he loved me; that's the strongest of all loves. . . . Why, he rushed to heat plates for me in the night, thinking to create a diversion—from the knife to pity and tenderness! . . . He wanted to save himself and me, too—with his hot plates! . . ."

The anticlimax comes a little later, when Velchaninov meets Pavel Pavlovitch by accident at a railway station. He has married again, and Velchaninov has been the means of saving his young wife from an unpleasant scene. In the course of conversation she invites him eagerly to her country home, and the eternal husband is tortured by the thought that his old enemy will become his guest again. With complete indifference his enemy assures him that no such fear is necessary, and on this note, almost of *opéra bouffe,* a really arresting study of criminal intent closes abruptly.

But murder, not merely in intent, was by no means remote, as already indicated, from this Russian writer who had offended the students of Petersburg by his presentation of Raskolnikov. Anna Grigorievna's mother, who had been with her daughter at the death of the little Sonya, had not returned to Russia and was present during the confinement of her daughter in Dresden. Both she and her daughter were devoted to Anna Grigorievna's brother, Jean, who got leave from the Petrovskoi Academy near Moscow to visit his mother and sister. Now Jean had a great friend named Ivanov who did everything in his power to hasten his departure and persuaded the Director of the Academy to grant his friend leave for two months. Only a few weeks later, Ivanov was found murdered in the park that surrounded the Academy. After some time a political plot was unravelled, and in it most of the students were involved. Instead of attending to their studies in agriculture, they had been working against the Government. Ivanov had been one of their leaders, but he had changed his mind and had given notice of resignation from membership of their secret society. This resignation proved to be his death-warrant. He was enticed into a solitary corner of the park and killed by a certain Netchaiev while his arms were being held by other students. This murder created a sensation all over Russia and was known as the Netchaiev Case.

The affair naturally made a deep impression on the novelist; readers of *The Possessed* will remember how very closely Chatov's death follows what actually took place in the precincts of the Academy of Agriculture. Besides Chatov, Aimée Dostoevsky assures us, many other characters in this novel are taken from life, though for fear of compromising his brother-in-law her father kept his sources hidden from his critics. But the family understood now perfectly well why poor Ivanov had hurried Jean out of Russia.

The year passed almost tranquilly, except for this cloud, and the novelist was able to work during a comparatively long respite from epilepsy. In a letter to Maïkov of February 24th he is almost enthusiastic about his new novel: "I hope to earn at least as much money with it as I did with 'Raskolnikov'; and so look forward to having all my affairs in order by the end of the year, and returning to Russia. Only the theme is almost too intense and thrilling. I have never yet worked so easily and with such enjoyment." But he is still more interested in the great imaginative work to come. Only a fortnight later he is assuring Strakhov that he has a really great theme in his head: "I won't enlarge upon that; I will only say that I have never had a better or a more original idea. I may say this without incurring the reproach of lack of modesty, because I speak only of the idea not of the execution of it. *That* lies in God's hands; I may indeed spoil all, as

I have so often done; still, an inward voice assures me that inspiration will not fail in the execution, either. Anyhow I can answer for the novelty of the idea and the originality of the manner, and I am, at the present moment, fire and flame." That letter is dated Dresden, April 5th, and on the 29th of that month there is a letter to his wife with the ominous heading "Homburg." But, instead of the old railings against the system and the tables, we read only of a cold railway journey and the untidiness of a hotel bedroom.

In spite of his numerous anxieties and the pressure put upon his literary work, Dostoevsky and his family were comfortable enough this time in Dresden and wholly devoted to the small Lyuba. But now both the novelist and his wife became victims of the same nostalgia. His daughter, for her part, maintains that her mother was far the more homesick of the two. But, to his sisters Vera and his niece Sofia, Dostoevsky acknowledges for the nth time his longing for his native land: "My affairs are in the worst conceivable condition. We certainly have quite enough to live on, but we cannot even think of returning to Russia. Nevertheless, I must get back somehow, for life here is to me quite unbearable." But his creditors barred the way. When he had left Russia three years before, after the genuine success of *Crime and Punishment,* he had made a payment to three of them, an effort which maddened all the rest, who protested against preferential treatment: "They indicted me, and I took to my heels, but in the hope that I should manage to write another novel in a year and pay off all my debts. That hope was mistaken." There follows one of the usual hints about the great novel which he was planning as a cycle of five complete stories, and then, with reference to *The Possessed,* he writes: "For the moment I am writing a very odd story for the 'Russky Viestnik'; I have to work off an advance from them." On July 14th of the same year he pours out his heart to his niece Sofia. His creditors will have him imprisoned if he sets foot in Russia, in the belief that one journal or another will pay them so as to get him out of jail. "I find it very hard to have to look on and see Anna Grigorievna consumed by homesickness and longing as she is. That troubles me more than aught else. The child is healthy, but has not yet been weaned. Return is now my one fixed idea."

In this letter he expresses complete disillusion in regard to *The Possessed,* the idea of which had attracted him at first. In reality the novelist is too much obsessed by *The Brothers Karamazov* to be quite whole-hearted over any other work. In the very next month he is telling Sofia of the small household difficulties and, particularly, of his wife's longing for Russia: "How unbearable are the anxieties about my family alone! I see clearly how Anya longs for home, and how terribly she languishes here. At home, too, I could earn much more money; here we are absolutely impoverished. We have just enough to live on, it is true; but we cannot keep a nursemaid. A nursemaid here requires a room to herself, her washing, and high wages, three meals a day, and a certain amount of beer (of course only from foreigners). Anya is nursing the baby, and never gets a full night's rest." There are no amusements for the young wife. Her health is becoming troublesome, the small miseries amount to an accumulated burden. A series of epileptic fits have made life still more difficult and work has had to be put aside. Then "I suddenly saw quite clearly why the book had gone so ill, and where the error lay; as if possessed by sudden inspiration, I saw in an instant a quite new plan for the book. I had to alter the whole thing radically; without much hesitation I struck out all that I had written up to that time (about fifteen sheets in all), and began again on the first page. The labour of a whole year was destroyed." And once more he urges that if only he could give two or three years to a work after the manner of Turgenev, Goncharov and Tolstoy he could produce something that would be talked of for a hundred years. "I am not boasting; ask your conscience and your memory if I have ever yet boasted."

In a letter to Strakhov, towards the end of October, there is a further allusion to the trouble caused by the writing of *The Possessed,* which its author had been more and more inclined to view with a certain amount of contempt: "But later I was overtaken by a real enthusiasm, I fell in love with my work of a sudden, and made a big effort to get all that I had written into good trim. Then, in the summer, came a transformation: up started a new, vital character, who insisted on being the real hero of the book; the original hero (a most interesting figure, but not worthy to be called the hero) fell into the background. The new one so inspired me that I once more began to go over the whole afresh." In regard to this sudden change of heroes—quite different from the change of heroes in the

Aeneid, or indeed in *Paradise Lost*—his daughter has a significant note: "A curious thing happened to the novel *The Possessed.* When Dostoevsky began it, he had taken Nicolaï Stavroguin for the hero, but when he had nearly finished the book, he realised that Verhovensky was much more interesting, and decided that he must be the hero." For all that, Julius Meier-Graefe seems to me right in claiming that though Verhovensky is the principal actor he is too nearly a robot to convince, whereas Stavroguin might well have become a tragic figure.

At the outbreak of the Franco-German War, the novelist's credit came to an end and life became still more difficult. But, contrary to what one might expect, Dostoevsky protests against his niece's contempt for war: "Without war, people grow torpid in riches and comfort, and lose the power of thinking and feeling nobly; they get brutal, and fall back into barbarism. I am not speaking of individuals, but of whole races. Without pain, one comprehends not joy. Ideals are purified by suffering, as gold is by fire." He believed that France had become brutalised by well-being and pleasure, and that new life would come to her through the ordeal. Like his old enemy, Turgenev, he believed that the French would win if only they did not hasten to make peace. What struck him as extraordinary at the time was that the pride of war found no expression among the ordinary crowd but was confined to the professors, the doctors, and the students. He encountered the professors every evening in the public library and found them astonishingly arrogant: "A very influential scholar, with silver-white hair, loudly exclaimed, the day before yesterday, 'Paris must be bombarded!' So that's the outcome of all their learning. If not of their learning, then of their stupidity. They may be very scholarly but they're frightfully limited! Yet another observation: all the populace here can read and write, but every one of them is terribly unintelligent, obtuse, stubborn, and devoid of any high ideals."

Only too soon he was to be plunged back into his own affairs, including a transaction looming up between him and Stelovsky, the publisher. In the meantime, the first part of *The Possessed* was appearing in the "Russky Viestnik," and Dostoevsky, in spite of all his prejudice against the author of *Smoke,* expressed his delight in Maïkov's verdict on the Demons: "They are Turgenev's heroes in their old age." For the rest, the novel progresses laboriously and Dostoevsky's seizures have become frequent. Under these conditions, one is not altogether astonished at the ominous heading "Wiesbaden" in a letter to his wife written the very next month and dated April 28th. It opens without preamble: "Anya, for God's sake, for Lyuba's sake, for the sake of our future, don't worry, don't be upset, and read this letter carefully to the end. You will then see that the trouble is not actually worth such despair. On the contrary, something will be gained and will be worth more than was paid for it. And so, my angel, keep calm, listen and hear me out. For God's sake, don't kill yourself." But, he indicates, she must know well what has actually happened: "I have lost everything, everything. All the 30 thalers which you sent me. Do remember that you are the only soul who can help me and there is no one else in the whole world who loves me."

In the next paragraph there are three words of immediate significance, "Write to me." These words, conveyed in a telegram, meant that he had lost at the tables and was to be sent a sum arranged beforehand with his wife. Dostoevsky was sure things were likely to go against him because he had dreamt of his father: "The dream," Mme Dostoevsky notes, "was an omen of grief or misfortune, and I was a witness several times that after such a dream (two or three days later) someone who had been quite well would fall ill or die in the family, or F. M. would have a bad epileptic fit, or we would suffer some material loss." She goes on to admit thankfully that nothing particular occurred on this occasion to their respective families. But the novelist himself was struck when, in spite of the warning, he stood in front of the selected table: "Should I be able to guess correctly or no? And what do you think, Anya? About ten minutes running I guessed aright. I even guessed the zero. I was so impressed by this that I began to play, and in five minutes I had won 18 thalers. Then, Anya, I forgot myself. I made up my mind I should leave by the last train and spend the night at Frankfort, but at least I would bring some money home. I was so ashamed of having *robbed* you of those 30 thalers."

He had been longing to make his wife a present of a pair of earrings to replace those that he had failed to redeem from a pawnbroker: "You have pawned everything for me during these last four years and you have been roaming about abroad with me and longing to be at home. Anya, Anya, do remember I am not a cad, I am only a passionate gambler. . . . By half-past nine I had lost everything and I left the tables in a stupor." In the same letter he alludes to "the hideous illusion" by which he has been tormented almost ever since his brother Michael's death. Mme Dostoevsky states that then and there her husband was definitely cured of "the hideous illusion." Though there are two more letters from Wiesbaden which express the necessity of borrowing, the regret for lost pledges at the pawnshop and so on, there is not a single reference to the tables. "I am only thinking," he exclaims in the letter of May 1st, 1871, "of how I could possibly get back to you quickly. I am living in a fever— and it is very upsetting. Yesterday was a very difficult day for me, and to add to it all—it was raining. It cleared up towards the evening and I went out for a walk. But I am always much more unhappy in the evenings for I am always thinking of you. I keep imagining how it has all affected you." He assures and reassures the anxious woman that, even if he does not come home the next day, it will not be because he has gambled away his journey money: "*That will not, that cannot happen.*"

The cure was indeed complete, so far as gambling was concerned. In a letter to Strakhov from Dresden in that same month he is back on the familiar Slavophil track, condemning the representatives of the West, particularly the dead Bielinsky and the living Turgenev. "Know this," he exclaims in allusion to the author of *Smoke,* "all that school is no more than "landed-proprietors' literature.' And that kind of literature has said all it had to say (particularly well in the case of Leo Tolstoy)." In other moods no one knew better than Dostoevsky that the author of *Fathers and Sons,* to which at this very time he was opposing *The Possessed,* was an artist who would live not by the favour of this or that political group but by right of art.

It had become overwhelmingly necessary for Dostoevsky to return to his own country. His wife was enceinte for the third time and, at first, she had wished that her confinement should take place at Dresden. Then, for fear of being detained yet another year abroad, she changed her mind and they started precipitately for Petersburg only a few days before the birth of Fyodor.

Chapter XI

THE DARK LEGEND

IT WAS on the 8th of July that the little family reached the Russian capital, more or less deserted as usual for the summer holidays. It was then that they learned from Paul Issayev's wife that she and her husband proposed living with and on them indefinitely. Foiled in this direction, Paul turned to the novelist's relatives for moral support. But Anna Grigorievna had become more experienced after her travels. She could now cope with people who had been too much for her in the early days of her marriage. She was very soon to cope with the more complex world of publishers, editors and booksellers that had always been too much for her husband. Apart from all this, the relations themselves had improved their position during the last four years. The younger generation had begun to earn their living. Some of the girls had married and their husbands were helping their mother. One of the aunts, Alexandra, had married a rich man. The only members of the family now actually dependent upon the novelist, besides Paul Issayev, was the luckless Nicolaï. In the meantime, *The Possessed,* like *Crime and Punishment* before it, was arousing the anger of the students as it appeared in the "Russky Viestnik."

It is not such a great novel as either *Crime and Punishment* or *The Idiot,* but it is peculiarly important for other reasons. The chief of these perhaps is that in spite of all its looseness of form, which blends so naturally with the disorder that it describes, it crystallises Dostoevsky's whole attitude towards any form of revolution on Western lines. Then, it is permeated by the old conflict—hardly ever wholly absent from the work of this novelist—the conflict between the God-man and the Man-god. But even more significant than this is the repeated clash of duality all through its pages. There are in *The Possessed* two gods, two forms of aspiration, two dominating demons; there is, too, what is perhaps the fiercest clash of all, that of *odi et amo*. Even the possessed ones themselves seem to believe at one instant, only to deny the next.

Since the publication of Turgenev's *Fathers and Sons* the revolutionaries had been called Nihilists, but there is very little kinship between Stavroguin and Bazarov. There is no duplicate of the murderer Raskolnikov in this book of murder, but there is much of Svidrigailov in the man Stavroguin of whom Kirilov, the engineer (claimed not by Dostoevsky but by Léon Chestov to be the hero of the book), observes: "If Stavroguin believes, he does not believe that he believes. If he does not believe, he does not believe that he does not believe." The arch-revolutionary indeed believes in nothing, perhaps least of all in revolution. "I have experimented in debauch," he confesses quite in the manner of Svidrigailov, "on a grand scale, and I have exhausted my strength; but I do not care for it, and it was not my aim." He cannot believe in disbelief; he cannot accept negation. But his companion Peter, the robot of denial, is unconscious of any uncertainty. He has not need of the Man-god but he must lean on Stavroguin as the brute leans upon its master. "I am a buffoon," he admits to this master, "but I do not wish that you, who are the better part of myself, should be one also."

But the engineer, Kirilov, the god-tortured semi-madman, clings to the belief in the superman to be in a manner altogether beyond the dreams of the ape Peter. "The man of the present," he argues, "is not yet what he ought to be! There will come a new man, happy and proud. He who will be indifferent as to living or not living, he will be the new man. He who will conquer suffering and fear, he will be God. And the other god will no longer exist." Kirilov insists that all history falls into two periods, the one ranging from the gorilla to the annihilation of God, and the other ranging from the annihilation of God until the day when "Man shall be God and change physically." This emotional Nietzscheism is specifically formulated in the following fragment of dialogue in which Kirilov is the first speaker:

"He who will teach men that they are good, he will finish the world."

"He who did teach them it, Him they crucified."

"He will come, and his name will be the Man-god."

"The God-man?"

"The Man-god: there is a difference."

But even in the moment of asserting the rise of the superman he is keeping a lamp burning before his icon and, underneath his rejection of the discarded truth, there vibrates a longing for it to be restored. It is to the ape Peter, however, and not to Stavroguin, that the engineer reveals the very passion of his unbelief: "Listen, listen! a great idea: there was a day when three Crosses were erected in the middle of the earth. One of the crucified had such faith that He said to the other: 'You will be with Me to-day in Paradise.' The day ended, both died, and they found neither Paradise nor Resurrection. The prophecy was not fulfilled. Listen; this Man was the greatest of all the earth, it owes to Him what makes it live. The whole planet, with all that covers it—without this Man—is only madness. Neither before nor after Him has His like been met with, and that itself is a miracle. Yes, it is a miracle, the solitary existence of this Man in the flight of ages. If it is so, if the laws of Nature have not even spared *Him,* if they have not had pity even on their Masterpiece, but have made Him also live in the midst of a lie, and die for a lie, then the planet is a lie, and rests on a lie, on a stupid derision. Consequently the laws of Nature are themselves an imposture and a diabolical farce."

But it is Chatov, the Christian, always on the verge of doubt, rather than Kirilov, the unbeliever, always on the verge of belief, who expresses Dostoevsky's conception of the primary national truth: "With every people, at every period of its existence, the end of the whole national movement is only the search for God, of a God for it, in whom it may believe as the one true God. God is the synthetic personality of a whole people, considered from its origin until its end." Yet, pressed by Stavroguin to answer yes or no as to whether he really believes in God, Chatov answers: "I believe in Russia, I believe in her orthodoxy. . . . I believe in the Body of Christ. . . . I believe that a new Advent of the Messiah will take place in Russia. . . . I believe—" Here Stavroguin interrupts, "But in God? In God?" Chatov can only stammer out: "I—I—shall believe in God."

Yet this hesitancy of Chatov does not link him for a moment with the demons of denial. His is the deep experience of compassion which is the secret of one side of Dostoevsky's power. No other novelist could have presented the scene in which Chatov's wife, who has deserted him, returns to her husband for sanctuary for herself and the child of Stavroguin. The naturalness and simplicity of Chatov make this incredible position credible, without any special pleading on the part of the novelist. But it is precisely Chatov who has pity for all who must link together, with the supreme bond of guilt, the demons from whom he had thought to escape. The character of Chatov is admittedly taken from Netchaiev's victim, Ivanov, but Dostoevsky protested against the general view, more or less accepted by Mme Dostoevsky herself, that his brother-in-law Jean influenced him in this study of character. He has stated specifically what his actual sources were: "I will at once assert that my only source of knowledge about Netchaiev and Ivanov and all the circumstances of the murder is newspapers." He insists that he works only on the complete fact, that he can detach himself from the actual event and that no resemblance is to be found between the actual murderer and his Pyotr Verhovensky. In the same statement he goes on to cast an interesting sidelight, not only on the writing of *The Possessed,* but upon his method of work as a whole: "I believe all the same that by dint of imagination I shall create in my mind, which has been affected by this occurrence, a person and a type capable of such a crime. Undoubtedly the portrayal of such a type is not futile; even so it was not he alone who attracted me. To my mind examples of this deplorable species of humanity are not worthy of literary handling." Then, as though to settle the disputed point as to who is the central figure of *The Possessed*, claimed to be Verhovensky by Mme Dostoevsky herself, he adds: "To my own astonishment this person appeared to me half humorous, which accounts for the fact that, although the incident occurs right in the foreground of the novel, the figure is valid only as accessory to the sphere of activity of another personality; it is the latter who is to constitute the principal character of the novel."

There are murderers in this novel, but Raskolnikov has no place in it. Stavroguin is not remotely a superman, while his ape Peter is a self-confessed buffoon. The girl Liza, swayed between love and hatred for this man, offers herself to him only to be cast off almost at once. "And so that is Stavroguin," she mocks, "the 'drinker of blood Stavroguin,' as a lady of this place, who is in love with you, calls you! Listen. I have already told you: I placed my life in an hour, and I am content. Do the same. . . . Or rather—no, for you it is useless, you will still have so many 'hours' and 'moments.'" And Liza confesses the duality of her own impressions: "I ought to confess to you that in Switzerland I was already persuaded that you had something horrible upon your conscience: a mélange of mud and blood, and —and, at the same time, something profoundly ridiculous."

The half-witted cripple, whom Stavroguin married out of pity, has also detected the duality of this man. She has read the threat of murder in his heart, but she refuses to believe that this is really the hero of her life: "As for resembling him, yes, you resemble him a great deal, you might be even his relation—crafty fellow! But my one is a falcon with piercing eyes and a prince, while you are a screech-owl and a merchant." She reminds him of the fact that Chatov once struck him in the face and that the blow was not returned. She reminds him of the fear in his eyes that she had once read when he entered the room. "When I saw your miserable face, at the moment that I fell, and when you picked me up, I felt as though a worm were gliding into my heart.—'It is not he,' I said to myself; 'It is not he!' My falcon would never have blushed for me before a young girl in society! My God! For five whole years my solitary happiness has been to think that my falcon was somewhere yonder, behind the mountains, that he was living, that he was flying and facing the sun. . . . Speak, Impostor; have they paid you well for playing this rôle?"

In this strange book there is not only the antagonism between the Man-god and the God-man but the old clash between the European God and the Russian God. Karmazinov, a malicious caricature of Turgenev, admits frankly that he has no faith whatever "in the Russian God." Asked if he believes in the European God, he replies categorically: "I believe in no God. I have been calumniated in the eyes of the Russian youth." The portrait of Karmazinov is amusing as a caricature, but unfortunately so many other characters in *The Possessed* suggest unintentionally the caricaturist's art. In Bazarov, Turgenev had presented a normal human being, a man amongst men. That figure, "sombre, untamed, only half-emerged from barbarism, brave, wayward, and honest," is a complete contrast to these convulsed demons whose hiding-place should not be in the hearts of human beings but rather, as the whole novel suggests, in the bodies of swine. But it is Stavroguin who admits in the words of

Chatov: "When one is no longer attached to one's country, one has no more god, that is to say no more aims in existence." It is impossible for this hero *manqué,* this hero who belongs to Freud rather than to Sophocles, to be anything but suspicious of negation. He is incredulous of everything, particularly of incredulity: "One can discuss infinitely on everything, but from me there has only issued a negation, without grandeur and without force." As presented in this novel, Stavroguin seems to stand half-way between the sinner Svidrigailov and the greater sinner to come, by whom the novelist has been so long obsessed.

But whereas Svidrigailov is impervious to the urge of confession and the oldest of the Karamazov family seemingly ignorant of its very existence, Stavroguin is disconcertingly prepared to merge his pride in his sin through the medley of acknowledged guilt. This is due, as Janko Lavrin has been quick to detect, not to Stavroguin's delight in any self-torment, nor to any desire for a tragic pose, but solely in order to escape, if only for a few moments, from the void that can indeed be evaded only by the road that this strange hero ultimately took. A series of questions by Chatov beat almost meaninglessly on the arch-demon. "Is it true that when you were in Petersburg you belonged to a secret society for practising beastly sensuality? Is it true that you could give lessons to the Marquis de Sade? Is it true that you decoyed and corrupted children? Is it true that you declared that you saw no distinction in beauty between some brutal obscene action and any great exploit, even the sacrifice of life for the good of humanity?"

Chatov does not pretend to explain why evil is

odious and good beautiful; but he knows well why that distinction between good and evil is utterly effaced in the Stavroguins. He thinks that Stavroguin's mad marriage was the result of a passion for martyrdom: "It was a lacerating of the nerves. Defiance of common sense was too tempting. Stavroguin and a wretched half-witted, crippled beggar!" Stavroguin does not agree to this analysis. Whatever else he knows about himself, he realises that he is more complex than that. In reality, he is much too complex for the Nihilists whom he joins as a relief from the boredom of the sinners. This experiment was a failure like so many others. "Do you know that I looked upon our iconoclasts with spite," he acknowledges in a letter, "from envy of their hopes? But you had no need to be afraid. I could not be of them, for I never shared anything with them. And to do it for fun, from spite, I could not either, not because I am afraid of the ridiculous—I cannot be afraid of the ridiculous—but because I have, after all, the habits of a gentleman and it disgusted me."

He might, though, have joined the party wholeheartedly if only he had felt more spite and envy towards them. Then, like Raskolnikov before him, though differing so deeply from the hero of *Crime and Punishment,* he allowed himself to experiment with the theory of power. He brought himself to the pitch of enduring public insult, to openly announcing his grotesque marriage, to facing, with utterly unfeigned indifference, a loaded pistol. The idea of power having failed him, he sought the idea of a nobler love. Liza, who had deserted her fiancé to spend one solitary night with him, learned the bitter truth in the morning: "I knew I did not love you, and I ruined you. Yes, I accepted the moment for my own; I had a hope. . . . I've had it a long time . . . my last hope. . . . I could not resist the radiance that flooded my heart when you came in to me yesterday, of yourself, alone, of your own accord. I suddenly believed . . . perhaps I have faith in it still. . . ." Before leaving him for ever, with a regret that has passed beyond mockery, the girl insinuates the fantasy of poisoned illusion: "I won't be your nurse, though, of course, you need one as much as any crippled creature. I always fancied that you would take me to some place where there was a huge wicked spider, big as a man, and we should spend our lives looking at it and being afraid of it. That's how our love would spend itself."

Liza could not fill the void. It was perhaps possible for his "nurse," Darya Pavlovna. For either he must accept his burden or elude it for ever. Perhaps Darya will accompany him to Switzerland, where he had recently bought a house. "It is a very dull place, a narrow valley, the mountains restrict both vision and thought. It is very gloomy. . . ." But, after all, he decided against this final experiment and hanged himself, brushing "himself off the earth like a nasty insect" in his own phrase of final self-condemnation.

Such is Stavroguin as he appears in *The Possessed*. But there is a certain chapter containing his so-called Confession which was withheld from publication at the time of the book's appearance in the "Russky Viestnik." Unfortunately, the publication of these pages years afterwards has increased the number of people who insist on confusing the morals of a writer with those of one or other of his characters. The very fact of Dostoevsky's police-court intimacy of detail, which pierces far more deeply than the notebook realism of Zola, makes this dangerous confusion all the more infectious. The dynamo of the Russian novelist worked imaginatively with tremendous force on any selected material. He could tear from any setting every secret or, on the other hand, he could free himself from it as completely as though it had no existence. That charming story, *The Little Hero,* was written in the Petropavlovsky Fortress. The extraordinary sensibility of the little boy, as though from the very heart of the writer when he was on the eve of being tried for his life, is probably as good an example of detachment as any to be found in literature.

One could cite many other examples from the pages of Dostoevsky, but for some reason or other that detachment, that separation of the author from the material in which he has merged himself, has always been regarded with a certain amount of suspicion in the case of the principal character in *The Possessed.* In *Crime and Punishment* there had been an allusion to a peculiarly loathsome form of crime, the same sort of crime that taints further the deeply tainted life of Stavroguin. The actual crime is given in the withheld chapter which deals with the violation of a child victim of Stavroguin. He knows, afterwards, that she is in the very act of hanging herself in the next room, and yet he waits until life has left her. Now, admittedly, the burden of this guilt might well prove too much even for Stavroguin; he seeks out the Bishop Tikhon to confess to him in his cell.

Admittedly, too, there are several episodes in *The Possessed* that seem to be integral to the author himself, many fragments that appear to be torn from personal memory. The torment of epilepsy threatens Kirilov, the engineer, who describes an ecstasy of feeling almost too intense for endurance. "If this state were to last more than five seconds," he tells Chatov, "the soul would be unable to resist it, and would disappear. During these five seconds, I live through a whole human existence, and for these seconds I would give all my life, and it would not be paying too dearly for them. To endure that for ten seconds, one would have to be physically transformed." Chatov asks him point-blank if he is not an epileptic and, when the other replies in the negative, warns him that he is in danger of the dread disease that Dostoevsky knew so well: "Take care, Kirilov; I have heard it said that this is precisely how it begins. A man subject to that malady has given me a detailed description of the sensation which precedes the attack, and while listening to you, I seem to be hearing him. He also spoke to me of the five seconds, and told me that it was impossible to bear this state for any longer time."

Then, all through the book, there vibrates the passionate acceptance of the *credo quia incredible*. And, though the whole tenor of *The Possessed* is a denunciation of the demons of destruction, Dostoevsky is almost equally hostile towards the tepid type of man who reaps the reward of others' audacity while he avoids danger in the name of goodness. This is almost the only type of sinner for whom the merciful Dostoevsky shows himself without mercy. The novelist of cities had never lost faith in the Russian peasant; he had not forgotten Marei; he had not forgotten the servant in his boyhood home who, when the family was informed suddenly that their little country house had been burnt down, offered the novelist's mother five hundred roubles, the savings of years of toil. His belief in the *moujik,* indeed, was much closer to Tolstoy's than is generally believed: "We come directly from him, from the people, as from an independent *point d'appui,* from the people as they exist now, savage, after two centuries of a sombre servitude, but we believe that they carry in them all the means of their own development. We have not gone back to the ancient Moscow to search for ideals. We have not said that it is necessary to commence by changing everything, in the German fashion, before considering our people as an element fitting for the future eternal edifice." That is the message of Dostoevsky's nationalism, and it is no wonder that he rejects *à outrance* the terrible innovators of his creation. Then, in this novel, more clearly perhaps than in any other of his works, he has signified his innermost convictions as to the destiny of his well-loved country.

Because of this seemingly indivisible union between the man and the book, there have not been lacking eager little souls only too willing to interpret the ulcers of fiction as the ulcers of fact in the life of a man of genius already so cruelly punished. Nor has there been lacking a public sedately willing to feed upon these same ulcers with a certain ravenousness. Now Stavroguin is peculiarly tempting to these grave-diggers of literature. Because of Stavroguin's elaborate Confession it has seemed unfitting to dismiss him with the familiar "C'est du Dostoevsky," so he has been strapped on to the author in the most hideously personal sense. Even that distinguished writer M. André Gide, whose admiration for Dostoevsky's power is unstinted, allows himself to write, with an almost cynical begging of the whole question of authenticity: "And more curious still, an anecdote from Dostoevsky's own life, which I have from a Russian in his intimate circle." This person is not named, but the "anecdote," as every student of Dostoevsky knows very well, spread rapidly all over Europe.

M. Gide proceeds in a faintly apologetic vein: "I was imprudent enough to tell it to several individuals and already it has been made use of; but in the form I found it retailed, it was fast approaching unrecognisability. Hence my anxiety to give the exact facts here." M. Gide proceeds to give "the exact facts," once more begging the question in the opening sentence: "There are, in Dostoevsky's life, certain extremely obscure episodes. One, in particular, already alluded to in *Crime and Punishment* and which seems to have served as theme for a certain chapter in *The Possessed*. This chapter does not figure in the novel, having been so far withheld in Russia even." He then gives the terrible narrative of the little girl hanging herself while Stavroguin waits in an adjoining room. "What measure of truth is there," M. Gide asks, "in this sinister tale? For the moment, it is not for me to say." But apparently it *is* the moment, for the French novelist continues with perfect assurance: "The fact remains that Dostoevsky, after an adventure of this nature, was moved to what one must needs describe as remorse. This remorse preyed upon him for a while, and doubtless he said to himself what Sonya said to Raskolnikov. The need for confession became urgent, but confession not merely to a priest. He sought to find the person before whom confession would cause him the acutest suffering. Turgenev, without the shadow of a doubt! Dostoevsky had not seen him for long, and was on uncommonly bad terms with him. M. Turgenev was a respectable man, rich, famous, and held in wide esteem. Dostoevsky summoned up all his courage, or rather he succumbed to a kind of giddiness, to a mysterious and awful attraction."

After this prosaic interpretation of the Russian *otchaianie,* the Frenchman continues his completely undocumented verbal fantasy: "Picture Turgenev's comfortable study: the author himself at his desk.—The bell rings.—A man servant announces Feodor Dostoevsky. What is his business?—He is shown in, and at once begins to tell his tale.—Turgenev listens, dumb with stupefaction. What business of his is all this? No doubt the other man is mad!—After the confession, a great silence. Dostoevsky waits for some word or sign from Turgenev, believing no doubt that, like in his own novels, Turgenev would take him in his arms, kiss him and weep over him, and be reconciled. . . . But nothing happens:

" 'Monsieur Turgenev, I must tell you how deeply I despise myself. . . .'

"He pauses again. . . . The silence remains unbroken until Dostoevsky, unable to contain himself any longer, bursts out in wrath: 'But *you* I despise even more! That's all I wanted to say to you,' and off he goes, slamming the door behind him."

The tragedy of the scene is amply relieved by jocosity, but what evidence is there that it ever took place? How is it possible to accept, without any direct evidence of any sort or kind, (1) the sin of Stavroguin as being the sin of Dostoevsky; (2) the alleged confession to Turgenev as being anything else than a concoction of private friendship? Admittedly, in Dostoevsky's life fact has the ring of fiction while in his work fiction has the ring of fact. Admittedly, there are in many of the novels and in many of the short stories echoes of the novelist's personal convictions and personal aspirations. As I have already indicated, these echoes vibrate all through *The Possessed*. Admittedly, there are things in the record of the monstrous Stavroguin that account for, even if they do not justify, the application of Turgenev's bitter gibe "Monsieur de Sade" to the work of his rival. There are, in fact, many other bitter references to Dostoevsky scattered among the *obiter dicta* of Turgenev, just as there are equally scornful comments on Turgenev in the correspondence of Dostoevsky. But I defy anyone to produce a sentence originating from Turgenev which reveals Dostoevsky in the act of confessing to the crime of a character in his fiction.

In his arresting study of Dostoevsky, Meier-Graefe gives us a reasonable note on this peculiarly malicious libel: "The person responsible for the Paris legend is a Russian writer living in Paris at the moment, a contemporary of both Dostoevsky and Turgenev, who seeks to associate Stavroguin's confession with the poet's own transgressions." In regard to André Gide's sketch of the imaginary interview, Meier-Graefe adds: "If this fantastic confession was ever made, one might go still further and assume that for the sake of self-debasement Dostoevsky put himself in Stavroguin's place without having perpetrated the crime." Equally Dostoevsky might have put himself, and indeed actually did put himself, in Raskolnikov's place, without having committed the crime of murder. Mr. Meier-Graefe continues: "Nötzel has shown the improbability of the legend and has rightly condemned the careless methods of such 'research.' He asserts that he has followed up reports of this nature and invariably found them 'untenable gossip.' "

There is no doubt that a communication by the trusty Strakhov to Leo Tolstoy, dated November 28th, 1883, entirely changed Tolstoy's attitude towards the dead writer. "I never saw the man," Tolstoy wrote on hearing of Dostoevsky's death, "and never had any direct relations with him, yet suddenly, when he died, I understood that he was the nearest and dearest and most necessary of men to me. Everything that he did was of the kind that, the more he did of it, the better I felt it was for men. All at once I read that he is dead, and the prop has fallen from me." Strakhov's letter, which had so utterly changed Tolstoy's attitude towards the dead man, was not only printed in a Russian periodical in October 1913 but was reprinted in the *Reminiscences* of Mme Dostoevsky. The trusted Strakhov, who doubtless wished to exalt Tolstoy at Dostoevsky's expense, appears to have heard the wretched anecdote from Professor Viskovatov, who had been at no time an intimate friend of the dead novelist. As for the letter itself, written by the friend of his youth, Mme Dostoevsky has shown up the stupid felony for what it is worth. It is rather surprising why one or other of Dostoevsky's old friends, in view of Svidrigailov's rumoured crime of exactly the same sort, never sought to identify the novelist with the monster of *Crime and Punishment*.

It is submitted that the crime belongs not to real life but to fiction, and not to one novel only. The sin of Stavroguin is undoubtedly to be found in Svidrigailov, and it must be remembered that the novelist was at work on *Crime and Punishment* at the period when he was an habitué in the drawing-room of Mme Kovalevsky's old home. In this drawing-room he would behave exactly like Prince Mishkin at the Epanchins, now mute and now declaiming. He would doubtless do exactly what he most wished not to do, exactly like the Prince who illustrated so unerringly the law of reversed effort. The Prince, it will be remembered, was unwise enough to sit down close to that "handsome China vase, which stood on a pedestal almost at his elbow and a little behind him." Mishkin's agitation increased: "At his last words he suddenly rose from his seat, and incautiously waved his arm, somehow twitching his shoulder and . . . there was a general scream of horror!" The vase, from which at first Mishkin had sat as far away as possible, fell in ruins. But free from the presence of strangers the novelist in the family circle would discuss, often perhaps with too great freedom, not only the problems of his difficult life but the problems of his novels, which were undoubtedly inextricably mixed with real life in one sense, however remote from it in another.

His realism was certainly sometimes alarming, and it must be remembered that the celebrated mathematician was only a little girl at the time: "Our mother used sometimes to be terrified," Mme Kovalevsky admitted frankly some twenty years later. "In this way he once told us a scene out of a novel he had planned in his youth. The hero was a landed proprietor of middle age, highly educated and refined; he often went abroad, read deep books, and bought pictures and engravings. In his youth he had been very wild indeed, but had grown more staid with years; by this time he had a wife and children, and was universally respected. Well, one morning he wakes very early; the sun is shining into his bedroom; everything about him is very dainty, pretty and comfortable. He is penetrated with a sense of well-being. Thorough sybarite that he is, he takes care not to awake completely, so as not to destroy this delightful state of almost vegetable felicity. On the boundary between sleep and waking, he enjoys in spirit a series of agreeable impressions from his latest trip abroad. He thinks of the wonderful light on the naked shoulders of a St. Cecilia in one of the galleries. Then some fine passages from a book called 'Of the Beauty and Harmony of the Universe' come into his mind. But in the midst of these pleasant dreams and sensations he suddenly becomes aware of a peculiar feeling of discomfort, such as that from an internal ache or a mysterious disturbance."

It is like a Freudian complex which has been buried for twenty years. "What he remembers is how once, after a night of debauchery, egged on by drunken companions, he had forced a little girl of ten years old.

"When Dostoevsky uttered these words my mother flung her hands above her head, and cried out in terror: 'Feodor Mikhailovitch! For pity's sake! The children are listening!'

"At that time I had no idea what Dostoevsky was talking about, but from my mother's horror I concluded that it must be something frightful.

"Mama and Dostoevsky became good friends, all the same. She was very fond of him, though he gave her much to bear."

"The passions," as Talleyrand observed, "were

not meant for the drawing-room," but it is rather futile to attack the great novelist at this time of day on the score of good taste. The point is that it never occurred to anyone in that little group to associate Dostoevsky with that criminal landed proprietor of his brain. But André Gide, for his part, is so certain about the alleged confession to Turgenev that he accuses Dostoevsky not only of being, like Stavroguin, a self-condemned monster but of a real lack of humility. What he does grant him—just as life itself granted him—is an abundance of humiliation. And, quite rightly, the French writer urges that every one of those wounded people in the Dostoevsky novels might trace the origin of his wound to a specific humiliation. Stavroguin himself was no exception. His own mother describes him as "A proud man who has suffered humiliation early in life and reached the stage of 'mockery'," in the phrase of Stepan Trofimovitch. And she goes on to give her own deep distinction between humility and humiliation: "And if Nikolai had always had at his side (Varvara Petrovna almost shouted) a gentle Horatio, great in his humility—another excellent expression of yours, Stepan Trofimovitch!—he might long ago have been saved from the sad and sudden demon of irony, which has tormented him all his life."

What is really strange is that the author of *The House of the Dead* has never fallen into the prison-house of irony. For, long before his experience in Siberia, he had felt the unforgettable stabs of humiliation. It is idle to expect from this Russian the naïveté of humility, untainted by the infection of long memory. It is like demanding from Dante the chuckle of Dickens. Above all, it is idle to contrast the stricken figures in Dostoevsky's novels, as Gide contrasts them, contemptuously, with the alert heroes of the *Comédie Humaine*. It was a curious choice for the future author of *Poor Folk* to fasten on his very antithesis Balzac, the *demiourgos* of the bourgeoisie as Æschylus was of Greek heroes. The whole swarm of Parisians leaped to life under the touch of Balzac—the soldier, the doctor, the clerk, the notary, the women who added beauty to force and the women who rebuked force by elegance. Such as it was, the dream of nineteenth-century France came sparkling and alive from Balzac, clearcut as the Æschylean dream of gods. And in his masterful way Balzac did indeed reveal, in that strong if often distorted torrent of French prose, very many of the guarded secrets of the human heart. But his way was not the way of Dostoevsky. How indeed could it be? Consider the difference of the setting: the one in the City of Light whose very defeats had been admittedly glorious; the other in the sombre atmosphere of that Russian capital which denied to its citizens the very suggestion of liberty. And Dostoevsky, be it never forgotten, was soon to bear upon his own body the impress of that terrible denial. Not for him was the early poverty of Balzac illumined and redeemed by the impulse towards *la gloire*. Not for him the sunlit world of the boulevards and the cafés, the world of disputations, freedom of thought and speech, gaiety, light mockery and the eternal challenge of logic, the eternal appeal to human reason. No, no, it was different for Dostoevsky in that swarm of lodgers, students, prostitutes, policemen, waifs and strays, in that setting of police courts, coffin-like rooms, in that atmosphere of filthy restaurants reeking with cold veal, cabbage soup, flies and cognac.

Dostoevsky had experienced at first-hand far too much of humiliation to grope his way easily to any sanctuary of humility. Whether or not he ever actually reached such a sanctuary, he undoubtedly gave in Zosima the arch-type that has arrived through the fullest experience at the wisdom of the ultimate resignation. But surely it is almost as fanciful to identify the novelist with Zosima as with Stavroguin himself. The golden legend is often almost as foolish as that "dark legend" which, as V. Komarovich has shown, grew up round that ninth chapter which was excluded from the publication of *The Possessed*. The existence and even the content of this chapter was by no means a secret confined to the author and to the publisher Katkov. There was an allusion to it undoubtedly in a letter from Turgenev to Schedrin, dated September 24th, 1882, apart from Strakhov's letter to Leo Tolstoy of November 28th, 1883. What was the origin of the persistent rumour concerning a man who was so far more sinned against than sinning from the cradle to the grave? M. Komarovich has attempted to analyse something at least of the enmity that lurked in the background: "Indeed, the dark legend that Dostoevsky was a sensualist is based (by N. Strakhov chiefly) either on an obscure calumny, or on coarse and callous surmises as to the mystery of that troubled and too exacting conscience which was the mark of Dostoevsky's character. And we believe that the surest way of freeing Dostoevsky's memory from those false accusations is by means of open enquiry and the fullest understanding of Dostoevsky as an artist." It is perhaps because the repellent motif persists from novel to novel, particularly in the notebook sketches for that epic of a great sinner which was to appear as the uncompleted *Brothers Karamazov,* that private friendship to saddle Dostoevsky with an infamous charge.

The identification of characters in fiction, perhaps a rather childish pastime, still seems to appeal to people of all nationalities. Asked by some busybody who Mme Bovary actually was, Flaubert replied "Moi." Had Shakespeare been asked who Caliban was, he might well have given the same monosyllable in reply. Asked who Stavroguin was, Dostoevsky might have echoed that "moi" of Flaubert, but merely in the French novelist's sense. In reality, Stavroguin has emerged from a certain Speshnyov, a member of the Petrachevsky circle, blended with an impression of no less a person than Marx's formidable rival. Michael Bakunin was Turgenev's friend when he was a student in Berlin, in the days when that Oath of Hannibal was sworn for the freedom of the serfs, actually accomplished, some years later, through the publication of the *Annals of a Sportsman.* Undoubtedly, Turgenev drew Bakunin as Dmitri Rudin. No one has accused him of self-portraiture in that book, though it is in many ways far closer to actual memory than is *The Possessed* of Dostoevsky. Rudin, as Bakunin, is a lonely and impressive figure dying gallantly on the barricades of Paris for a cause in which he does not believe. Stavoguin, far more horribly disillusioned of life and hope, dies by his own hand. But why has the accusation of self-portraiture been fastened on the one author and ignored in the case of the other, while both were, to no small extent, drawn from precisely the same model?

Apart altogether from the libel of the "dark legend," Dostoevsky has been charged with injustice.

He himself, however, was the victim of prolonged injustice. He was rejected by Bielinsky and his circle on the charge of illiberal views; he was sentenced to penal servitude in Siberia for serving the cause of revolution. He was accused of ruining his brother Michael's life. In reality he sacrificed some of the best years of his own life, already so mutilated, to Michael's family, Michael's debts, the support of Michael's mistress. He had been grossly calumniated by the former Mme Issayev, but he accepted without complaint the burden of her son. He yielded to the rapacity of his own relations, receiving by way of thanks, almost invariably, insulting complaints and demands for more. He had been eager to accept as friends his rivals in literature, only to find himself, as he believed, shunned and at the very best patronised. In one human being alone, in the person of Anna Grigorievna, his second wife, had he found mercy from the merciless bed of Procrustes in which his life had been so long warped.

Chapter XII

HOME LIFE IN RUSSIA

THE second marriage more than atoned for the purgatory of the first. The little Fyodor had scarcely commenced to crawl when Mme Dostoevsky began the task of protecting her husband against the rapacious creditors who were already threatening him with imprisonment. After his experiences with Stelovsky, considerable wariness towards the publishing world seemed to be an elementary precaution. Now, when proposals were made to the novelist in regard to publication he would say quietly, "I cannot decide anything for the moment. I must consult my wife." But the most rigid economy had become necessary: "For many years we had to live in very modest dwellings; we had only two servants, and our meals were extremely frugal. My mother made her own dresses and her children's frocks. She never went into society, and very rarely to the theatre, in which she delighted." Not unnaturally, this austerity clouded the already sorely tried youth of Dostoevsky's consoler. When assured by the novelist that money would be forthcoming somehow, she would ask almost with the despair of the old days in Germany, Switzerland and Italy: "But where is it to come from?"

The attitude of the Russian students at this time was openly hostile to Dostoevsky. Long before he had ruffled them by the publication of *Crime and Punishment,* there had been that episode in November 1861, when so many of them in their turn had been imprisoned in the Fortress of St. Peter and

Paul. During the course of the episode they had been roused by one of the professors who was arrested and banished from Petrograd. Then, when his colleagues had supported him, their lectures had been suspended and they had finally been forbidden to lecture in public. Towards all these struggles in the name of liberty, and particularly towards the Polish revolution which occurred almost at the same time, Dostoevsky showed very little sympathy. He considered the students unreasonable and their policy of destruction useless and ill-timed. It is for this reason that he was regarded, quite wrongly, as an enemy of Poland. As for the students of Petersburg, if they were disconcerted by Raskolnikov, it may be judged how stupefied they were by Stavroguin and his companion demons who were being presented to them in number after number of the "Russky Viestnik."

Certainly the troubles of the Dostoevskys were very far from being over in this year, 1871, the same year that Turgenev was commencing the Parisian period of his life. Two years before, the final instalment of *War and Peace* had delighted the Russian public which, in another two years, was to welcome *Anna Karenina*. The unfortunate Dostoevsky, for his part, was forced to apply to his publisher for delay in the last instalment of *The Possessed;* it was not completed until 1872. In a letter to his wife, dated January 2nd, 1872, there is a significant note on an interview with the publisher Katkov: "It was only after great difficulty that I was able to see him. There were three other people waiting. At last I went in and stated quite frankly my request for money and a settlement of **our** (former) old accounts. . . . I think Katkov will give me something—I am sure he will." But he is much more doubtful about two of the creditors: "I am wondering whether Polyakov has harmed you in any way, but for God's sake don't worry! He will not have time to make any false move before I come even if he would wish to hurt you. But we ought to have come to some understanding with Hinterlach; that worries me far more."

In 1872 commenced the family's habit of spending the summer months at Staraya Russa in the Government of Novgorod. Here they rented a villa, of which the novelist's daughter gives us a minute sketch almost in her father's manner: "Everything in this house was on a small scale: the low rooms were furnished with old Empire furniture; the green mirrors distorted the faces of those who had the courage to look into them. Paper scrolls, pasted on linen, hung on the walls, presenting to our childish eyes monstrous Chinese ladies with claw-like nails and feet squeezed into tiny shoes. A covered verandah with coloured glass panes was our delight, and the Chinese billiard-table, with its glass balls and little bells, amused us on the long rainy days so frequent during our Northern summers. Behind the house was a garden with comical little flowerbeds. All sorts of fruits grew in this garden, which was intersected by tiny canals."

During their wanderings in Europe, when the novelist was under the spell of roulette, he would always buy his young wife's favourite dainties when he happened to win. Now in the sleepy little Russian town, where there was no question of gain or loss at the tables, he clung to his old delight in shopping. When there was any sort of family festival in view he would always offer to go out and buy the hors-d'œuvres: "I always smile when I read how Dimitri Karamazov bought provisions at Plotnikov's, before starting for Mokroé. I seem to see myself at Staraya Russa, in that self-same shop where I sometimes went with my father, and observed with all the interest of a greedy child his original manner of providing for himself. When I went with my mother, she would come out carrying a modest parcel in her hand. When I accompanied my father, we left the shop empty-handed, but several small boys preceded or followed us to our house, gaily bearing big baskets and reckoning on a good tip."

Their little villa is in existence no longer, but while it existed it was beset by curious visitors who gazed at the table on which *The Brothers Karamazov* had been written and at the old armchairs where the novelist had once sat: "Among these pious pilgrims was the Grand Duke Vladimir, who came one day when he was in the neighbourhood holding a review of young soldiers. He told my mother how greatly he admired Dostoevsky. 'This is not the first domicile of his I have visited,' he added. 'Passing through Siberia, I stopped at Omsk to see the prison where he suffered so greatly. It is entirely changed now. The memories of *The House of the Dead* effected a vast reform in all Siberian prisons. What a genius your husband was! What a power of touching the heart he had.'" The speaker was the grandson of Nicholas I by whom the novelist had been condemned among others to penal servitude with the added torture of a sham condemnation to death, "to teach those young people a lesson."

Like Dickens, the Russian in his later years was very popular as a reader of his own works. He became a great attraction in the most aristocratic circles of Petersburg. The Cesarevna (Mlle Dostoevsky corrects our English usage in regard to this title) expressed a wish to talk to him about his reading. He was then literally pushed into a little boudoir and the door closed after him: "Dostoevsky was astonished at these mysterious proceedings. The little room was dimly lighted by a shaded lamp; a young woman was quietly seated by a small table. At this time of his life my father no longer looked at young women; he bowed to the lady, as one bows to a fellow-guest, and thinking some joke was being played upon him, went out by the opposite door. Dostoevsky knew that the Cesarevna was to be at the party, but he believed, no doubt, that she had left, or perhaps, with his usual absence of mind, he had forgotten that she was among the audience." However, a special reception was arranged by an old friend of the novelist, the Grand Duke Constantine.

Dostoevsky on this occasion was on his very best behaviour: "He was delighted with the Cesarevna. She was a charming person, kindly and simple, who had the art of pleasing. Dostoevsky made a great impression on her; she talked so much of him to her husband that the Cesarevitch also wished to make his acquaintance." So Dostoevsky, who had once stood stripped to his shirt in Semyonovski Square, duly presented himself at the Anitchkov Palace: "The imperial pair received him together and were charming to him. It is very characteristic that Dostoevsky, who at this time was an ardent monarchist, disregarded Court etiquette and behaved in the palace as he was accustomed to behave in the *salons* of his friends. He spoke first, got up to go when he thought the conversation had lasted long enough, and after taking leave of the Cesarevna and her husband, left the room as he always left it, turning his face to the door." Though this must have been the very first time that the future Alexander III had been treated quite so simply, Dostoevsky's daughter assures us that he was not in the least offended and always spoke of her father afterwards with sympathy and appreciation: "He saw so many bent backs in his life! Perhaps he was not sorry to find in his vast empire one spine less supple than the rest."

Long ago, in 1859, Dostoevsky had appealed to the Tsar on behalf of his stepson Paul Issayev in these words: "You would thus assure the happiness of his mother, who teaches her son every day to pray for the prosperity of Your Imperial Majesty and that of Your Illustrious Family. Majesty, you are as the sun which shines on the good and the evil. You have already secured the happiness of millions of your subjects, be yet again the providence of one poor orphan, of his mother and of a wretched sick man whose excommunication has not been lifted and who is ready to sacrifice at once his life for the emperor, the benefactor of his people." That there was no hypocrisy in this appeal is proved again and again in fragments from the novelist.

The well-known Englishman, Mackenzie Wallace, once by chance heard Dostoevsky, a complete stranger to him, discussing enthusiastically the late Emperor Nicholas I. He had entered the room without knowing that the novelist was there; but he listened carefully as the conversation continued. As soon as Dostoevsky had left, the Englishman asked if this was really the author of *The House of the Dead*. On being told that it was, and that Dostoevsky had been a convict in Siberia, he expressed astonishment: "How can he then extol a sovereign who condemned him to penal servitude and made him suffer atrociously and unjustly?" Still, in spite of all his sincere veneration for the royal family, the great writer did allow himself on one occasion at least to make this comment: "I shall be still more the servant of the Tsar when he learns that his subjects are his children. But really he takes a great deal of time to understand this."

Dostoevsky has been, too often and too carelessly, labelled the novelist of suffering; his correspondence has certainly lent itself to this caption, though, it must always be remembered, he never regarded his unjust sentence as unjust. As for his quite natural complaints, his daughter has warned us that it is a common thing for neurotic people to seek consolation for its own sake: "For my part, I think that persons may have both very strong wills and feeble nerves. In their actions they are guided by their strong wills, but from time to time they soothe their unhealthy nerves by cries and tears, and complaints to those of their friends who are indulgent to them." The novelist himself has commented on this egotism of suffering: "I call this the intentional sharpening of suffering, this enjoyment that the greater part of those whom destiny overwhelms and who are conscious of its injustice actually experience." In more than one of his early works he elaborated this odd phrase. "I am reviled and I expressly keep silent; I am beaten and I maintain my silence. I shall not cry at any price: they will be still more enraged because I do not cry," declares the little heroine of

Injury and Insult, who illustrates forcibly the positive enjoyment of suffering. But in a letter to his wife from Staraya Russa, in the June of 1872, the novelist exclaims without any subtlety or any *arrière pensée* whatsoever: "What a gipsy life this is, full of pain and sorrow, without the slightest joy and nothing but suffering, suffering, suffering!" Yet Dostoevsky disliked any gush about suffering. Strakhov recalls a lady who one evening at a reception rushed up to the novelist and gazed at him for a long time. Then, breaking the silence, she exclaimed: "The more I look at you, Fyodor Mikhailovitch, the more I seem to read on your face the sufferings that you have endured." Visibly irritated he replied: "Of what sufferings are you speaking?" And he at once deflected the conversation.

Dostoevsky was utterly devoid of affectation. He never posed in his journalism. He was perfectly sincere in his crusade on behalf of his country in its relations with the West. In his opinion neither the German, nor the Frenchman, nor the Englishman began to understand the Russian, who, for his part, so easily understood each of them. But he is still more harsh towards his compatriots who insisted upon using the French language in their own country and who became, in their Europeanism, so much more Byronic than Byron. He insisted that for every Russian the essential question had become not "What ought I to do?" but rather "What ought I to be?" and he refused to accept even the *War and Peace* of Tolstoy as on a level with almost any work of Pushkin. For Dostoevsky, Pushkin in literature was exactly what the Russian himself was in life. In his opinion, Pushkin assimilated the culture of the West without losing the individuality of his own race. And for Dostoevsky, as for his rival Turgenev, the Russians alone were the true *gens de l'humanité*.

In his disagreement with the students of Petersburg, the Russian writer's attitude had been governed by the sincerity of his convictions. He had come from Siberia with his great Idea for a Russia that was to develop herself on Russian lines. It was natural, then, that he viewed with acute distrust a programme which seemed to him merely one of destruction. His daughter comments on the fact that her father's biographers have been puzzled by the deep interest shown by the novelist in the Slav question during the last years of his life. This ardour seemed to her to be the result of his long residence abroad. In her opinion, so widely different from Turgenev's, Russians in Europe are at first dazzled by Western civilisation and then, after studying it carefully, are struck not by its force but its dwindling power: "It is evident that in a few centuries the trembling hands of the Germans will no longer be able to hold aloft the torch of civilisation handed to them by the dying Romans. The Slav race will pick up the fallen torch and in its turn give light to the world." Much of her father's prejudice against Latin culture is revealed, perhaps quite unconsciously, in his daughter: "The incapacity of the Germans to rejuvenate the world is easily explained; the whole of their culture is based upon the Latin civilisation of the ancient Romans, a civilisation magnificent, no doubt, but essentially pagan. Try as they may, the Germans will never free themselves from their aristocratic, feudal ideas. The Slavs, whose civilisation is more recent, knew nothing of the Latins. Their culture, received from the Orthodox Church of the East, was profoundly Christian from the beginning." It is not difficult, then, to realise, from this point of view, Dostoevsky's dream of a unification of the Slav peoples without any attempt, or wish,. to impose their yoke on foreign nations.

Writing in the days when the peoples of Europe turned, with a sort of dubious hopefulness, towards the League of Nations, Mlle Dostoevsky noted, just as Dostoevsky himself would have noted, that the world was in the very act of entering a new phase of its evolution: "The ancient alliance between the countries of different races, the work of kings and diplomatists, has had its day. It was an anomaly, for the people in question generally hated each other the while they lavished compliments and marks of respect. The new confederations, based upon the fraternal sympathy of people of the same race, will be more durable." Whether they will or will not be more durable none but a madman, or an astrologer, would presume to prophesy. But there is no doubt that in the far-off world of the nineteenth century, in what was then considered not unjustly the most backward country in Europe, Dostoevsky, so often twitted with sixth-century ideas, was elaborating after his own fashion a League of Nations devoid of the foundation of force.

Rightly or wrongly, he believed that the Russian intellectuals had been on the wrong road and that the nations of the West, for exactly the same reasons, continued and would always continue on the wrong road. "Go where you will," he exclaims in recognition of repentant intellectuals, "in France, in England, in the United States of America, of even in Patagonia, and begin to preach the gospel that personal happiness is illegitimate, that egotism is a crime. Everyone will turn away from you. . . . Without the people which for thousands of years bears on its shoulders the whole of Russian history, without love for the people, without a love naïve, mystic, the Russian intellectual would not be conceivable. What anxiety, what scruples he throws into his constant search for the truth, the popular truth and above all the peasant truth! The Russian intellectuals are ashamed, yes, ashamed to live while forgetting the little peasant, and it is from him that they have borrowed their famous formula: 'Life according to truth' and not according to *right* or doctrine. If in the West science, the juridic or historic consciousness of necessity dominate, it matters little: in Russia it is *love*. We believe in it as in a mysterious force which breaks down at one blow every obstacle and installs in the same moment a new life." Such was the undying dream of Dostoevsky, who had brought it back with him from that abyss of elemental hatred, the convict prison of Omsk.

But, as already indicated, it is quite wrong to label him as a pan-Slav or, indeed, even a Slavophil in the ordinary sense. Dostoevsky, Strakhov and Grigoryev, the three best known collaborators on the "Vremya" and afterwards on the "Epoch," were called *territoriaux*. They did not reject European culture; they contented themselves with urging that, before being adopted in Russia, it shoud become Russian. His attitude, however, towards his country never assumed the uncritical attitude of Tolstoy. It never occurred to Dostoevsky to tell students in the sciences and arts to go to the *moujik* to learn. He would undoubtedly have sympathised with Countess Tolstoy in her complaint to Mme Dostoevsky:

"I tell my sons that they must study, learn foreign languages, and become distinguished men, and their father tells them to leave their schools and go and work in the fields with the moujiks."

But whether in his journalism or in his creative books, always excepting *Poor Folk* and *The Brothers Karamazov,* Dostoevsky worked under inexorable pressure. In his own words, "It happened to me very often in my literary life to give the beginning of a novel or of a short novel to the printer while the end was still only in my head and had to be ready for the next day. Accustomed to this way of working, I did the same for *Injury and Insult.* As a novel for the review, the success of which was more precious to me than anything else, was necessary, I proposed to work in four parts. I assured my brother that I had had a plot quite ready for a long time, which was not the case, that I would write it easily, that the first part was already finished, etc. I worked for money. I realised perfectly well that in my novel it is puppets who are acting and not real living beings; walking ghosts and not people animated by life; for that it would have been necessary for me to have time to ripen my ideas. But while I was writing I perceived nothing, so precipitate was my work. The result was a barbarous work, which, however, contains a hundred or so pages of which I am proud." Such a stricture might be made, possibly, against more of the novels than *Injury and Insult.* In sober truth, there is little to be said by the most lofty critic of the great Russian writer that has not been said by himself. It is claimed, by no means without a certain amount of truth, that in the whole world of art only form is permitted to survive. Yet, somehow or other it is precisely the seemingly formless writers who, one after the other, scramble apparently without the slightest effort into the hearts of posterity. Only too truly, Dostoevsky admitted the hurry of his work. It is not surprising that a fourth-form English boy could detect the breathless errors and even the occasional fatigue of his narrative, while a sixth-form English boy might well consider himself entitled to correct them. But the core of Dostoevsky would remain as impenetrable as before. His life remains, like his work, inexplicable through the process of the mere registration of facts.

A sort of explanation is, undoubtedly, to be found in the cerebral storms that followed an epileptic seizure. Repeatedly, the novelist has insisted on the ecstasy that preceded such a seizure. But when the crisis was over, the sensations became sharply painful while the impression-ability remained almost as intense: "It seems to me then that something infinitely heavy is weighing upon me, I seem to have committed an enormous sin, a monstrous crime." And in that cry dehumanised, separate, as the victim himself has noted, alike from his bodily frame and his inner spirit, all the opposites seem to unite so that he has become quite literally two people at once. Does not this state of mind in itself account for the atmosphere of the confessional-box that Dostoevsky has allowed to pervade so many of his novels? Does it not perhaps account for a great deal of those fictional horrors which private friendship sought to hand on to the world as actual facts? On the authority of the famous psychiatrist, Dr. Tchij, the penetration of Dostoevsky's analysis was largely due to this morbid state. The novelist, according to this authority, became a pathologist without having seriously studied pathology. And he quotes, as illustrating the extraordinary sensitiveness of Dostoevsky's introspection, these significant words which, indeed, explain his whole involuntary theory of Russian realism: "It is not the object that is essential, it is the eye; if the eye is there, the object will be found there as well. If you have no eye, if you are blind, you will not arrive at finding anything at all. Ah! the eye is an important thing; what for one person is a poem is for another a cloud."

Dr. Tchij dismisses the old idea of genius and madness being one and the same thing, insisting that genius is the exact opposite of madness. He maintains that when Dostoevsky's novels were written the real nature of epilepsy was unknown to science, and that the author, through his own personal experience, was in advance of the scientific knowledge of his day. Dr. Tchij studied closely the melancholy madness of the hero of the story entitled *A Feeble Soul*. This morbidity of Vassya advances stage by stage until the poor clerk is seen feverishly writing page after page with an empty pen. As in the novels of Dostoevsky so in real life, once more on the authority of Dr. Tchij, cerebral maladies do not begin with incoherent ideas or ridiculous actions but by a morbid transformation of the whole character with anomalies of the senses and states of mental agitation. Irrational fear, discontent, sadness, anxiety show themselves one after the other. And while it was considered a great merit in Shakespeare to have detected the law of progression in mental illness, this authority claims that Russians may be proud of Dostoevsky for having discovered it for himself years before its acceptance by scientific opinion.

Apart altogether from his stress on dreams, so

long before Freud, both in fiction and in fact, Dostoevsky remained a day-dreamer all through his life. At Staraya Russa, like Kant in this respect, he would take the same walk day after day. Beggars would naturally lie in wait for him and, without noticing them, he would give to the same applicants over and over again. On one occasion Mme Dostoevsky played a little practical joke on her husband: "My mother saw through the tricks of the beggars, and was much amused by her husband's absent-minded ways. She was young and fond of practical jokes. One evening, seeing him returning from his walk, she threw a shawl over her head, took me by the hand, and stood by the roadside. When he approached she began to whine plaintively, 'Kind gentleman, have pity on me. I have a sick husband and two children to support.' " Mlle Dostoevsky's father stopped and handed her mother some coins. She burst out laughing and he exclaimed angrily: "How could you play me such a trick—before the child, too?"

That was not a very serious contretemps in the life of a man who had once shuffled along in chains in Siberia. The novelist was happy in the quietude of his home. He would play and dance with the children; he was particularly fond of the mazurka, and his widow has assured us that he was delighted when she informed him that he danced it like a real Pole. What is curious, in view of the supposed and so often self-confessed irregularity of Dostoevsky's nature, is that his life at Staraya Russa was almost clock-like in its regularity: "F. M. always worked during the night, so he did not get up before 10-11 a.m. Then he would come out to drink coffee, he would call the children, who would joyfully run up to him and tell him all that had happened that morning and all about what they had seen on their walk. F. M. used to keep up an animated conversation." Then, after twelve, Mme Dostoevsky would become once more his stenographer and would take down at his dictation what her husband had written during the night: "As I have already said, I always enjoyed working with F. M. From my early girlhood (from the age of fifteen) he had been my favourite author, and I was very proud that it had fallen to me to be useful to him, to work with him, and that I was the first person to listen to what he had written from his own lips."

Lunch would follow, and then, no matter what the weather was like, a walk through the deserted streets of the little town: "He nearly always used to go into the Plotnikov shop where he used to buy a small quantity of sweets and delicacies which had come straight from Petersburg." He was well known in this shop where Mitya Karamazov bought the sweets on his way to Mokroyé. It would be hard to picture a simpler, more kindly figure than the famous writer as he appeared in the tranquillity of the Staraya Russa setting. He had become again almost what he had seemed to be to Mme Kovalevsky when she was a child, receiving with her sister Anyuta for the second time this strange being: "I was sitting in the same room, but taking no part in their conversation; I stared unwinkingly at Dostoevsky, and devoured every single word he said. This time he looked different from what he had at his first visit —young, frank, clever, and attractive. 'Can he really be forty-three years old?' thought I. 'Can he really be three-and-a-half times as old as I am, and twice as old as Anyuta? They say he is a great writer, and yet one can talk to him like a chum!' And all at once he seemed to me such a dear. Three hours went by in no time."

Yet here he was in the very midst of the personnel of his greatest and most terrible book, living in the very house of old Karamazov and with the lovely Grushenka a near neighbour. Even the drivers of those very *troïkas* used to be employed by the family and used to take them to Lake Ilmen in the summer: "Sometimes one had to wait there several days, and the sojourn in a big village on the lake is described by Dostoevsky in the last chapters of *The Possessed.*" The summers passed in a peacefulness that was such a sharp contrast to the turmoil of the Karamazovs. One day resembled another, but all the time there lurked grim watchers in the background, though it was not until the spring of 1875 that the great national writer realised that he was still under the supervision of the police. Why this should have been the case, it is difficult to understand. The novelist long ago in Siberia had become steeped in his own peculiar nationalism, and this had been strengthened by his prolonged sojourn abroad.

Neither in his private nor public utterances, neither by word nor by pen, was he remotely likely to attack the régime which had punished him so unjustly. And, as I have tried to show, his attitude was due not to servility, not to cowardice, but to a deep conviction. In short, he had remained faithful in the most literal sense to that Idea which he had brought back with him from Siberia. This was to flower finally in his famous address at the inauguration of the statue of Pushkin. In the meantime, he continued to be sorely driven. "We ought not to have whipped up F. Dostoevsky's great talent," admitted Apollon Grigoryev, "as if it were a post-horse, but it should have been cherished and taken care of." Attention was to be paid to this admission some years after the novelist's return to Petersburg, though he was to remain, in spite of all the efforts of his faithful wife, comparatively a poor man even at the moment when he claimed that his name alone was worth a million roubles to a publisher.

Chapter XIII

THE INHERITANCE

DOSTOEVSKY had certainly remained relatively poor, though freedom from the publisher Stelovsky had brought the hope of better things for the little family. The contract that under the menace of prison he had been compelled to sign was, in his own words, horrible, but now, in spite of the students who were still recalcitrant, he was as near to contentment as he had ever been in his life: "I think my father was happier in these early years of his return to Petersburg than later, in the agitated period of his great successes. His wife loved him, his children amused him with their infantine prattle and laughter; old friends often visited him, and he could exchange ideas with them. His health had improved, his attacks of epilepsy were no longer frequent, and the mortal disease which was to close his career had not yet declared itself."

The debts were paid at last. It was possible to give pleasures, so long denied, to his wife and family: "The first diamonds Dostoevsky offered to my mother were very small, but his joy in giving them was great." Both of them must have remembered the diamond in that dream of long ago that had brought about their marriage. Both of them must have remembered, too, their dealings in Dresden with the man Weissmann who had presumed to criticise Anna Grigorievna's cherished frocks: "F. M. was always sad that we were too poor to allow me to dress well, and that any clothes I had were nearly always in pawn. One of his dreams, therefore, was that when he would have money he would order some new clothes for me; but alas! to his great regret those dreams were seldom realised (and I was almost indifferent, for even later, when our circumstances did improve, I thought little of dress)." But things really were very different now, and there seemed to be, in this pleasant jog-trot of domesticity, but one unpleasant blot. It was once more Pasha. The whole family appears to have been victimised by this stepson of the novelist. There had been a loan advanced on Mme Dostoevsky's furniture when she and her husband went abroad. During the absence of the bride's mother from Petersburg money had been sent to Paul to pay the interest due. He had not paid it, and he had, needless to say, failed to return the money.

But the Dostoevskys were as forgiving as people in the novels, and Pasha was received as a guest at the villa in Staraya Russa. The young man, however, failed to conform even to the most elastic rules of polite society: "Although he was the son of an officer of good family, a member of the hereditary nobility, had been educated in the Corps of Cadets with well-bred boys, and had spent his holidays in the house of my uncle Mikhail, who received all the most distinguished writers of the day, Paul Issayev conducted himself much as his maternal forefathers may have done in some oasis of the Sahara; I have rarely encountered such a curious case of atavism." All the other guests were offended and would complain to the novelist, who would get angry and show Pasha the door; "but, metaphorically speaking, he always came back through the window. He clung closer than ever to his papa, continued to live in idleness and to depend upon him for money." Pasha had become a determined parasite and Dostoevsky's friends obtained post after post for him in the hope of ridding his stepfather of the burden, but always without success.

He was certainly a difficult visitor, but there came another visitor even more embarrassing. She, however, did not make her appearance until the students were flocking back of their own accord to Dostoevsky. It was the publication of *The Diary of a Writer,* with its gospel of patriotism and religion, that brought the youth of Petersburg back to the man who understood them as no one else perhaps in his generation understood them: "These poor young men and maidens came to my father weeping and sobbing and opened their hearts to him. Dostoevsky received them as if they had been his sons and daughters, sympathised with all their sorrows, patiently answered all their artless questions as to the life beyond the grave." In his daughter's opinion her father sacrificed his art to this journal exactly as Tolstoy may be said to have sacrificed his to the production of peasant literature. There was one ex-student, however, who did not view the great Russian novelist quite as these repentant students viewed him. It was a dramatic visit, and it may well have recalled old times both in Russia and in Euroue. During Mme Dostoevsky's absence from the house, a heavily veiled lady who had refused to give her name was ushered into the drawing-room by the maid. There followed this unsatisfactory dialogue:

" 'To what do I owe the honour of this visit?' he asked.

"The lady replied by throwing back her veil and

gazing at him with a tragic air. My father frowned. He disliked tragedy.

" 'Will you tell me your name, Madam?' he said dryly.

" 'What! You don't know me?' exclaimed the visitor in the tone of an offended queen.

" 'No, I do not know you. Why will you not tell me your name?'

" 'He does not know me!' sighed the lady. My father lost patience.

" 'What is the meaning of this mystery?' he cried. 'Please tell me the reason of your visit. I am very much occupied at present and have no time to waste.' "

The lady pulled down her veil and left the room and the house. Then a far-off memory came back. He had heard that melodramatic tone before. "Good heavens!" he exclaimed, "it was she—it was Pauline!" When Mme Dostoevsky returned her husband told her about this visit of his one-time mistress. To him the affair did not appear in the least trivial: "I have offended her mortally. She is so vain. She will never forgive me for not having recognised her. Pauline will know how dear the children must be to me. She is capable of killing them."

It is quite possible that such complete forgetfulness may have been assumed. For, in the whole sequence of episodes with Pauline, there seems to have been a quite unforgettable antagonism, the actual atmosphere of *odi et amo* on both sides had passed into the stage of *amo et odi*. Quoting from Apollinaria Suslova's diary, Professor Janko Lavrin writes in his latest arresting study of her enigmatic lover: "Thus on December 14th, 1864, she wrote: 'When I remember what I was two years ago, I begin to hate D. [Dostoevsky]. He was the first to kill all faith in me." And an entry on November 2nd, 1865 runs: "To-day we argued and contradicted each other for ever so long. For quite a time he has been offering his hand and heart to me, but he only annoys me." Dostoevsky, on his side, gave this characteristic analysis of her character: "If you ever marry, in three days you will hate your husband and run away from him. . . . You cannot forgive that once you gave yourself to me, and now you are taking your revenge for it; this is a woman's way." This, incidentally, is exactly the kind of hostility indicated in Nastasya, and it appears frequently in other novels besides *The Idiot*. But, on the authority of Dostoevsky's daughter, such hostility towards her father, in the rôle of first lover, is singularly out of place.

A more prosaic but very much more truthful reason for hostility is conveyed in an unstamped letter written by the novelist from Wiesbaden after Pauline had deserted him when he found himself absolutely penniless: "As soon as you had left me, the very next day, I was told in the hotel that it was forbidden to give me lunch, tea or coffee. I demanded an explanation and the fat German proprietor said that I 'deserved' no lunch, and that he would let me have only tea. So from yesterday tea has been my only food. And even the tea is extremely bad. . . . If you have reached Paris and if you can get something out of your friends and acquaintances, do send me a maximum of 150 guldens and a minimum of as much as you like. If I had 150 guldens I could be quits with these swine and change my hotel, while waiting for some money. . . ." Then, two days later: "My affairs are bad beyond words; it would be impossible for them to be worse. One step further, and I shall be in the welter of miseries and obscenities beyond imagination." A correspondence, however, between these two continued, as Anna Grigorievna discovered on her honeymoon, but it soon passed. The novelist's second marriage was indubitably a success, from the standpoint of both husband and wife. It is curious that Dostoevsky, who had sought consolation from the bitterness of his first marriage, should have found in Pauline a bitterness almost as poisonous as that of the former Mme Issayev herself. When he became a widower he is said to have been attracted for the time being by a certain Martha Brown who was actually a Russian by birth but passed as the wife of a Baltimore sailor. His interest, however, appears to have been one merely of pity; it was quite a different attraction from that which he experienced for the charming Anna Korvin-Kronkovskaya, the elder sister of the famous Sophie Kovalevskaya, who was to become the Aglaya of *The Idiot*.

Pauline was certainly eccentric, but her eccentricity did not extend to killing the little Dostoevskys. It did extend, though, to a marriage with the literary critic Vasily Rozanov, who was sixteen years younger than herself. He at least was a genuine enthusiast for the work of his wife's former lover.

In the meantime, the Life of a Great Sinner was progressing. From childhood Dostoevsky had been interested in the Russian monastery; he understood monastic life, and not merely from the outside, as he was soon amply to prove. To the *staretz* Zosima he gave much of his own autobiography, but he also made a special pilgrimage to the Monastery of Optima Pustin, not very far from Moscow: "My

THE INHERITANCE 233

father visited it in company with his disciple, the future philosopher, Vladimir Soloviev. Dostoevsky was much attached to him, and some persons supposed that he had described Soloviev in the person of Alyosha Karamazov." In the opinion of Mlle Dostostoevsky, however, Alyosha represents her own father in early manhood. But she insists on the realism that the novelist brought to the monastery, just as honestly as he did to the mean streets of Petersburg: "It is obvious that my father merely gave a literary form to the speeches of Zosima, Father Paissy and Father Iosef. In such a momentous matter as a religious question he preferred to let the monks speak, since they could speak with authority and knowledge." The *staretz* Ambrosius, the accepted model for Zosima, produced a great impression on the great writer who spoke of him with emotion on his return home.

But in that second villa in Staraya Russa another short-lived child had been born to the Dostoevskys. He was known as Alyosha and his father was devoted to him, just as he had been to Sonya years before. Preoccupied as he was by the portrait of the one sinless Karamazov, the novelist must have often brooded over the future of his little Alexey. But alas, like the little Sonya before him, the fourth and last child died while still a baby.

In the winter of 1872, the painter Vasily Grigorievich Perov asked the novelist's permission to paint his portrait for the Moscow Gallery. Dostoevsky agreed willingly and, before commencing the work, the artist visited the Dostoevskys daily for a week. "It can be said," Anna Grigorievna notes, "that in this portrait Perov managed to catch F. M.'s 'creative moment.' I have often seen this expression on

F. M.'s face: I would sometimes walk in and see him looking within himself as it were, and I would go away again without saying anything, and later on I would discover that F. M. had been so busy with his thoughts that he had not noticed my coming and he would not believe I had been in the room at all. V. G. was a clever man and F. M. loved to talk with him." But over this portrait private friendship came actively and vividly into play. When the picture was exhibited at the Academy of Arts V. S. Soloviev has stated that the editors of the "Grazhdanin" invited "the public to go and see Perov's portrait of Dostoevsky, which was a clear proof that Dostoevsky was a madman whose place was in a lunatic asylum." Mme Dostoevsky has added further evidence on this peculiarly cruel libel: "F. M.'s portrait was among Perov's works. His literary enemies, when describing the exhibition and praising the artist, did not hesitate to say it was obvious from the portrait that Dostoevsky was mad. That hurt F. M. very much, and I had great difficulty in dispelling the depressing effect it had on him. What hard hearts they must have had to write such a thing, especially as the critic could not have been ignorant of the terrible complaint from which Dostoevsky suffered! How cruel people are sometimes."

Long ago, on the 1st of October 1844, Dostoevsky had written to his brother Michael that he was willing to sacrifice his share of the paternal inheritance for the sum of five hundred roubles at once, with another five hundred roubles payable at ten roubles a month. He was afraid, even then at the age of twenty-three, of being thrust into prison for debt. And now he was to find himself entangled in legal proceedings over another inheritance. His rich aunt,

THE INHERITANCE 235

Mme Kumanin, had died before his return to Russia.. She was, as already noted, the Grandmother in *The Gambler,* and Fyodor was her godson. In a letter to Maïkov, dated August 14th, 1869, Dostoevsky dwells on the fact that during the last four years of her life his aunt was not in her right mind. Mlle Dostoevsky deals at some length with the quarrel that arose between the various heirs on account of this protracted lawsuit: "Aunt Kumanin died while my parents were abroad and left a very muddled will. The heirs spent several years in quarrelling among themselves, and only after my father's death did we at last get our share."

In his contributions to the "Grazhdanin" in 1873 Dostoevsky included under the title of *The Diary of a Writer* many of his articles; it was undoubtedly these contributions which effaced among the students the impression that had been produced on them by *Crime and Punishment* and *The Possessed.* He had regained all his old popularity in this year, but, in the March of 1874, he was arrested for infraction of the Censorship regulations. Soloviev has left this note on the incident: "In the Spring of 1874 . . . he [F. M.] once came to see me, and as I was out he left me a note in which he said among other things that in a few days' time he would have to serve a term of imprisonment as editor of the 'Grazhdanin.' During the morning of March 22nd, Apollon Nikolaevitch Maïkov came to see me. 'Do you know where I have just come from?' he asked —'From our prisoner; our Fyodor Mikhailovich is in prison. . . . Go to him, he is waiting for you.' 'What sort of a mood is he in?' I asked. 'In the best of spirits. Do go and see him.' I went to the famous corner of the Sennaya Square and was allowed in at once. I found F. M. in a spacious and fairly clean room, where, besides himself, there was some other young man in the corner, who was badly dressed and had the dullest face. F. M. was sitting at the small plain table, drinking tea, smoking his own cigarettes and holding a book." This innocuous incident of an imprisonment that lasted for exactly three days was the basis, undoubtedly, of yet another "anecdote" on the alleged turpitude of this man of genius. In actual fact, though, he was not responsible even for the infringement of the Censorship. It was the publisher of the journal, Meshchersky, who was really to blame. On July 5th, 1873, the novelist writes to his wife: "I received a fairly amiable letter from Meshchersky begging my pardon that I should have to sit in prison because of him." The publisher had certainly been extremely casual over this matter, and Mme Dostoevsky notes that he did not think it worth while even to mention it in his subsequent memoirs.

The novelist found himself in charge of the very journal whose editors had once asked people to examine his portrait, in order to see for themselves that his right place was a lunatic asylum. But apparently he was entirely preoccupied, not by attacking his enemies but by spreading far and wide the Idea of Russian nationalism that he had brought back to him from the convict prison. It was in 1874 that he resumed his long-interrupted relations with the poet Nekrassov. Numerous letters passed between them on the subject of the forthcoming novel known under the two English titles *A Raw Youth* and *The Hobbledehoy*.

Shortly after his return from that prolonged honeymoon of exile, he had made the acquaintance of

THE INHERITANCE

Constantin Petrovich Pobedonostsev, the Chief Procurator of the Holy Synod. They had become friends during the novelist's editorship of the "Grazhdanin"; there is no doubt that the famous ecclesiastic had a considerable influence of the great writer during the last years of his life. The day after Dostoevsky's death, Pobedonostsev wrote to Aksakov: "We were brought together during the editorship of the 'Grazhdanin.' Out of sympathy for his wretched position, I worked with him throughout the summer and we became good friends." Dostoevsky would frequently visit him in Staraya Russa and would discuss with him the tendencies of their country, in the novelist's own words, "alas! so like a mad house." He would also discuss his creation of Zosima. In that same letter to Aksakov, written, as stated, on the day after the novelist's death, there is full confirmation of this: "You write that you are sad, though you have not heard of the death of F. M. Dostoevsky, but it is twice as sad at his grave. I knew that man intimately. It was solely for him that I held those Saturday evenings, and he often used to come and spend them with me. He thought out his Zosima with the help of my advice. We had many heart-to-heart talks. . . . He lived just at the right time. And now he is irreplaceable for he stood alone." On the very day of the novelist's death Pobedonostsev had appealed to Alexander III, the heir to the Russian throne, in an effort to arrange a subsidy for the Dostoevsky family. In this appeal he gave it as his weighed opinion that "Dostoevsky's death was a great loss to Russia. Among literary men he was almost the only one—an ardent preacher of the fundamental principles of faith, rationalism and love of the fatherland. Our wretched youth, erring like sheep without a shepherd, had faith in him and he had a great and good influence upon them. Many . . . turned to him as to a father confessor, both in words and in letters. And now there is no one to take his place."

But this post of confessor to the Russian youth was very wearing to a man of Dostoevsky's frail physique. Mme Dostoevsky has told us that people would come to him with requests for an opinion on their works. They would leave bulky manuscripts in his charge; they would ask for the influence of his important friends; they would ask for work and for money: "F. M. could never refuse people anything, although these innumerable visits tired him, disturbed his work, took up time which might have been spent on looking after his health, which was then beginning to fail (how many times was he late at a treatment of compressed air in Dr. Siminov's Clinic which did him so much good, all because of some tiresome visitor!). And, finally, they used to rob F. M. of me and the children, of whom he was compelled to see less and less and who were his happiness." There is no doubt that it was largely to rid herself of this incubus that his wife decided to spend the winter as well as the summer in Staraya Russa in that second villa which was afterwards to become the Dostoevsky Museum.

It was in the summer of 1874 that Dostoevsky experimented with his first cure at Ems. His correspondence, from one foreign country after another, shows how very difficult he was to please. But he became almost ecstatic over the approach to Ems: "We sat packed like herrings, but, Anya my darling, as it began to grow light I had never seen anything like it in all my life! What is Switzerland, what is

Wartburg (do you remember?) in comparison with the last half of this journey to Ems? Everything that you can picture to yourself as being exquisite, tender and fantastic in a landscape, in the most ravishing landscape in the world; hills, mountains, castles, towns like Marburg, Limburg, with the most charming turrets in an amazing combination of mountains and valleys. I have never seen anything like it." But in the little town itself there begins almost at once the everlasting conflict with the world of reality, the fixed quantities of landladies and shopkeepers, the problem of board and lodging and above all the great central figure of Ems, so far as most of the visitors were concerned, the celebrated Doctor Orth. As a matter of fact, this doctor pleased the novelist at the very beginning by telling him that his cure would last only four weeks instead of six. But, as the correspondence progresses, Dostoevsky becomes frankly enraged against many of the visitors.

One woman, about forty with a daughter of fifteen, a cosmopolitan and an atheist, a worshipper of the Tsar but a scorner of Russia, particularly exasperated his torn nerves: "She is a chatterbox and is always arguing. I told her quite frankly that she was insufferable and that she didn't understand anything; of course, I said it jokingly and politely, but I really meant it. We parted amicably, but I shall never meet them again. And when I went to bed I had a nightmare." His moral condition, he assures Anna Grigorievna, is one of sadness and boredom and he is simply longing to get back to her and the family. There is no sort of need for jealousy: "You said that when I was abroad I might perhaps run after other women. My darling, I know from experience that I can't think of any other woman. I have no need for other women, I want you. And that is what I say to you daily. I am far too used to you and I have become too much of a family man. The past is past, and *in that respect* there is no one better than my darling little Anya. Don't be a prude when you read this: I must tell you. I hope you won't show this letter to anyone."

He was busy at Ems with the plan of *A Raw Youth,* the publication of which was to bring him once more into contact with Nekrassov. The novel, however, was not written at Ems; it was not commenced before his return to Staraya Russa. In regard to this work, nothing complete has been found in the Notebooks and many of the notes may be said to apply just as much to the last novel as to the one that preceded it. Mme Dostoevsky states that Nekrassov actually raised Dostoevsky's payment for the forthcoming novel which was to appear in the "Otechestvennia Zapiski." But she adds significantly that he had to be much more cautious in applying to Nekrassov for money than he was with Katkov. Apart from this, several of Dostoevsky's political opponents were on the staff of this journal and Dostoevsky feared that a demand might be made for him to make certain changes in his work. This, he assured his wife, he would not do under any conditions; he would rather that they went begging: "What we should do in such circumstances was a thought which greatly worried both of us, not to mention the fact that we should immediately have to return the money taken in advance; but this was already spent, and it would have been extremely difficult for us to return the money at once. Apart from that, what money should we have had to live on until such time when Fyodor Mikhailovich managed to place his novel?" It was the old, old question echoed as it were from Dresden, from Baden, from Vevey, from Milan, from Florence, from Dresden again, and then back again from Petersburg. But there was no hitch of this kind; the novelist returned to Staraya Russa, well satisfied with his cure, to write that curious novel so largely impregnated with personal memory, a novel which one might compare from this particular angle with the *David Copperfield* of Dickens, with *Le Petit Chose* by Alphonse Daudet, and perhaps even with George Eliot's *The Mill on the Floss*.

Only, the realism of the Russian writer was not to be softened by any forgiving mellowness of memory. "I remember," notes Mme Dostoevsky, "that once during the winter in Staraya Russa F. M. had just read a chapter he had written about how a young girl had hanged herself (*The Hobbledehoy*, Part I. Chap. 9). The reading over, he glanced at me and exclaimed, 'Anya, what is the matter with you, my darling, you are quite pale. Are you feeling faint?' 'It is you who have frightened me,' I replied. 'Goodness! does it really make such a terrible impression? How sorry I am, how sorry I am!'" This chapter, incidentally, made a profound impression on Nekrassov. In a letter from Petersburg to his wife dated February 9th, 1875, Dostoevsky mentions a visit from Nekrassov: "He considered the suicide scene and the story as 'the height of perfection.' . . . Nekrassov is altogether terribly pleased. 'I have come to discuss the future with you. For goodness' sake don't hurry and don't spoil your work, for you have begun far too well.'" Nekrassov then went so far as to discuss, of his own accord, the question of money: "You are entitled to about 900 roubles, you have had 200, and consequently there are nearly 700 roubles due to you. If we add 500 in advance—would that be enough?" Dostoevsky replied: "My dear friend, add a thousand." Nekrassov agreed at once.

It was the same Nekrassov, who had come to him in the grey of the morning to acknowledge the compulsion of *Poor Folk*. And now he was acknowledging the far more acid compulsion of this new record of experience. Before even partially completing that Life of a Great Sinner the novelist had glanced back, after his own individual fashion, at the festering humiliations of youth, which are, as M. Gide insists, so remote from genuine humility. Records of personal memory, however, are as a general rule curiously devoid of bitterness. They are mellow rather than vitriolic and tend to reject over-emphasis, particularly in the direction of caricature. *David Copperfield* shows us Dickens almost as aloof from actual caricature as he is in *A Tale of Two Cities*. In *Le Petit Chose* Alphonse Daudet presents neither the bubbling absurdity of Tartarin nor the solemn absurdity of M. Chèbe. In *The Mill on the Floss* George Eliot has deliberately avoided the tedium of moralising over the sad antics of *homo sapiens*. Even the ironical Turgenev, who was often enough more malicious towards himself than towards others, refuses to be harsh to Sanin. But Dostoevsky, for his part, is quite without tenderness towards the hero of his book of memory.

As he glanced back, there were not many oases in the desert of those early years. In a single flash he could bring the principal figures back to life: his gentle mother who taught him the alphabet, the terrible Army surgeon who made him stand to atten-

THE INHERITANCE 243

tion during those long hours of Latin, his loved elder brother Michael. The head of the French school at Moscow, M. Suchard, would come back to him, and Marei the peasant who had stroked his cheek, and the servant who had offered all her poor savings to his mother when the news came that their little house in the country had been burnt down. The pedagogue Tchermak would come back to him as a much less dreaded figure than his own father. But always there had been so very little money even on that spring day when the two brothers crawled from post-house to post-house on the way to the Petersburg School of Engineering. There the discipline had been infinitely harder than anything at home; there had been flogging for the slightest breach of discipline.

But for Fyodor Dostoevsky there had been no such breaches of discipline; there had been isolation; one had kept oneself in a remote day-dream of one's own. But one could not avoid humiliation. There had been much of that. One wanted so many things—tea, books, rough boots; one's soldier servant must be paid. One passed on from one phase of only half-comprehended activity to another. One entered the Army but somehow one did not belong to it. Always the destroying dream persisted, the servitude of Letters. But why had one turned to Balzac, to *Eugénie Grandet,* when *Poor Folk* was waiting to be born? The scamper of youth, though, had quickened before that; there had been more roubles, an actual allowance, a sense almost of security on the edge of quicksands. But the quicksands were to become more threatening, though certainly the poet Nekrassov had paid that wonderful visit lighting up all the greyness of night and morning.

How they had hailed him at last! For at twenty-three one is really old, much older than later on! How eagerly he had met them, longing to be one of them, to serve the cause as they served it. Ah, but the bite of mockery was to make itself felt only too quickly. It would have been better for him to have gone back to the life of coffee and rolls for subsistence on the guarantee of *Eugénie Grandet*. It was no wonder that one sought another circle where one might be understood. Then, suddenly, without even thinking dangerously, one spoke dangerously, and then the sequence quickened. Oh yes, it all came dancing hideously back—the arrest, life in that desolate Fortress whose very name suggests the shiver of apprehension. But even here his Little Hero had emerged so sensitively into life. But the Little Hero didn't save him from Semyonovski Square and from the convict prison that followed and from service in the Army as a common soldier and from the sad sense of exile, to be mitigated by the mirage of that first marriage. What a life it had been when one had time to glance back at it in perspective as it really was, stripped of the glamour of creation as though the Fortress of Peter and Paul had never been illumined by that beautiful story and as though *The House of the Dead* had never distracted one from the slow torment of Omsk. Pauline would emerge from the shadows only to return to them. The roulette tables, so intimately associated with her, would resume their clatter before dying away in less simple memories. But from first to last how intimately woven the man and his work had remained.

Dostoevsky knew every cobweb of memory that lingers after the spider is dead. He knew how humiliation scalded through the years. He knew that sense of sin without which tragedy, from Sophocles to Ibsen, must be for ever silent. He did not have to go out to study the humiliated, the oppressed and the despairing, because he himself belonged to them. That is why he was able to appeal to the whole world of men and women as perhaps no one, neither Balzac, nor Hugo, nor Dickens, nor Tolstoy, nor Turgenev, nor Ibsen, had ever or would ever appeal. Because he himself was stricken he understood the stricken, and because he himself, in spite of everything, believed in the unseen, in the incredible justice, he was able to speak—he the disorderly, incoherent, unpractical wanderer through life—as one veritably illumined. Oh yes, that old gibe, "C'est du Dostoevsky," was to have a very different ring in the after years and the inheritance of Dostoevsky was not at all the little fortune bequeathed to the family by the Grandmother in *The Gambler;* the inheritance was nothing less than the magic power of reading and healing the human heart.

Chapter XIV

THE RAW YOUTH

JUST as *The Gambler* had interrupted *Crime and Punishment* and *The Eternal Husband* had interrupted *The Possessed,* so *A Raw Youth* barred the way of *The Brothers Karamazov.* But to no small extent this book is closely associated with The Life of a Great Sinner, almost as closely associated indeed as *The Brothers Karamazov.* In the Notes that formed the plan of the Life, one seems to be reading snatches from the youth of Arkady Dolgoruky. We read of a boy's pride, his ambition, and above all of his conscious preparation for the years to come. We read of the Frenchman, we read of flogging and of self-training, through self-imposed hardship, for the accumulation of money. We read of the brothers at Sushar's and at Charmak's; Dostoevsky and his brother Michael were at the French school of M. Suchard before going to Tchermak's.

The name "Lambert" comes into the Notes; it is to appear very frequently in *A Raw Youth.* Above all, the motif of the great sinner in his boyhood is the wish to acquire money, and that is exactly the determination of Arkady. Tikhon emerges into *The Possessed* from the Notes; but he remains an understudy for Zosima. Still, he expresses exactly the literary concepts of Dostoevsky: "Tikhon says to a certain lady that she is a traitor to Russia as well as a malefactor towards her children; of how they are deprived of childish visions even from their very childhood. The study of them (by Leo Tolstoy and Turgenev), although they are exact, reveals an alien life. Pushkin alone is a real Russian." The Great Sinner to be aims consciously at intense arrogance and at becoming the antithesis of Tikhon, with his despised monastic theories of life. As one reads the Notes one gathers more specifically than from *A Raw Youth,* or perhaps from any other of the novels, the strong union that exists under the surface between the sex theory of Freud and Adler's motif of power.

In this book, for the rest, one finds all the familiar motifs of the novelist both national and individual. But here at last it is the peasant, Alexey Makarovitch, who expresses with a direct simplicity worthy of Tolstoy himself the inner meaning of Russia's so long distrusted mission. This peasant is the legal father of Arkady, whose real parent is the equivocal Versilov. That duality of nature which Dostoevsky acknowledged to be in himself has reached an astounding development in Versilov. This strange and characteristic figure seems always to be struggling to emerge from the same quagmires of evolution that were to engulf Svidrigailov, Stavroguin and so many other quasi-monsters. Versilov confesses his undisguised schizophrenia with perfect frankness: "Yes, I am really split in two mentally, and I'm horribly afraid of it. It's just as though one's second self were standing beside one; one is sensible and rational oneself, but the other self is impelled to do something perfectly senseless, and sometimes very funny; and suddenly you notice that you are longing to do that amusing thing, goodness knows why; that is you want to, as it were, against your will; though you fight against it with all your might, you want to. I once knew a doctor who suddenly began whistling in church, at his father's funeral."

And Versilov goes on to admit that he had been afraid of attending a funeral that very day, lest he should begin to whistle in church. Yet no human being could act with a more instinctive sense of rightness than this same Versilov; no human being could speak more nobly and with a deeper sincerity. No one could be more patient than he with this Arkady whom he has found again after having been cut off from him for so long. Versilov is so eager to atone to Arkady for having forsaken him that the youth is torn between the old sense of humiliation and that intense eagerness to find sympathy which pervades so many of the novels.

It is once more a question of the breaking down of barriers, just as it had been between the murderer and the prostitute in *Crime and Punishment,* between the two little girls in *Netotchka Nezvanova,* between husband and wife in *A Gentle Spirit,* between Mishkin and all sorts and conditions of men in *The Idiot.* Now it is a question of the barriers between father and son. Arkady has heard much evil of his father. But soon he comes to the conclusion that all the attacks—his supposed cowardice, heartlessness, cruelty and so on—are nothing but a tissue of lies. Versilov waits with certainty for his son's coming to him, just as Porphyry had waited for Raskolnikov's. In the dark hall, after a tense visit, the barriers are suddenly thrust aside. "We were already at the front door and I was still following him. He was just going to open the door when a gust of air put out my candle. Suddenly I gripped his hand, for it was pitch-dark. He quivered but said nothing. I bent over his hand and kissed it greedily, kissed it again and again." From that moment evil seems to have departed from the garden of their lives. But we are dealing with Dostoevsky. It is not so certain that Versilov will not kill the woman that Arkady loves. It is not so certain that he will not desert Arkady's peasant mother. No, not quite certain, but for all that he seems to the son the ideal father as well as a symbolic figure of Holy Russia. Then remorselessly the glad dream passes into a nightmare. Suddenly, to the horror of Arkady's mother, Versilov snatches up an icon and smashes it against the stove.

But it is in the duality of Arkady, and not in that of Versilov, that we come really close to the memories of Dostoevsky's youth. Arkady's childhood is unbearably unhappy, particularly at the French boarding-school, where his chief enemy, apart from the headmaster, is a certain boy named Lambert. Arkady, naturally so light-hearted and light-headed, dreams constantly of power and more particularly of the money to buy power. He will conquer his enemies, but not to trample on them but rather to enjoy the luxury of forgiveness, of forgiveness born not of kindness but of the sense of power. But the theory yields easily enough to his natural kindness of heart. The boy's clumsiness, his blunders, his wanderings from dream to dream, present the illusion of actual personal memory. And as, like a bumble-bee, he blunders through the prepared meshes of that elaborate mechanism we never lose altogether that illusion.

That fourth-form arbiter, originally the butt of the inept, has now usurped the distressing halo of Macaulay's schoolboy. With his eyes fixed on the permanence of the sixth-form mind he would inevitably laugh at many of the springs and pulleys of this mechanism. One cannot deny that it does creak audibly from time to time. The hanging scene itself is too much a challenge to Grand Guignol. The whole motif of suicide has been accepted too lightly; the will to murder has been taken too much as a matter of course. Then, the damaging secret of melodrama, with all its cat-and-mouse possibilities, is not only presented in this novel but has been unblushingly duplicated. The scamper of a nimble, but not exactly lofty, inventiveness has been raised to a frenzied gallop in which all nuances are lost. Yet from the ensemble inevitably the swarm of humanity emerges living, both individually and *en masse*.

Kant's Categorical Imperative doubtless does *not* clash with the real mandates of biology; in any case, English nineteenth-century novelists were but little concerned with clashes of that kind. But they did detect, and they did illumine, the abyss that separates *homo sapiens* as he actually is from *homo sapiens* as he pretends to be. The result is an endless gallery of hypocrites in English nineteenth-century fiction, corresponding to that endless gallery of *noceurs* in the French novel. Perhaps this accounts, at least partially, for the commonplace libels of our respective national characters. Dostoevsky, however, is but little concerned with either of these aspects of human expansion. His hypocrites are always minor characters; his sensualists smack of the alienist's clinic rather than of Boccaccio's field of love. The girl with sunken cheeks, the consumptive, the cripple, the derelict, all these crowd into those novels in which sexuality is blended disconcertingly with pity. The more familiar blend of sexuality with scorn, however, does not appear in *A Raw Youth*. And, though we have in Versilov a direct descendant of

Svidrigailov, we have no understudy of the old Karamazov who is to come. But there is the recognition here as elsewhere in the work of Dostoevsky that sin, like any other poison, has its usefulness. Incidentally, it was Dostoevsky's curious belief that a certain inescapable banality in the so-called "new" races can be accounted for by the fact that they have never sinned collectively. For all that, no novelist either before or after Dostoevsky has been more preoccupied than he by the motif of repentance and by the almost physical need of confession.

Try as he will to conceal them, the Raw Youth blurts out every little meanness of memory, every humiliation that he can never forget. He has that touchiness, that quick reflex to every sort of slight, that was Dostoevsky's own added torment through life. "If a Russian deviates," Versilov observes, "ever so little from the rut of routine laid down for him by tradition, at once he is at a loss what to do. While he is in the rut everything's clear—income, rank, position in society, a carriage, visits, a wife—but ever so little off it—and what am I? A leaf fluttering before the wind, I don't know what to do!" Perhaps there is only one person in the whole novel who has a differentiated knowledge of what to do. She is the influential Tatyana Pavlovna. With her at first we seem to be on ground made familiar to us by whole libraries of Anglo-Saxon fiction. For she appears to be a study in disagreeableness.

Now in nineteenth-century English novels the snub, which began as an art, really had ended as a science to become the life-work of the Victorian English lady. But Tatyana Pavlovna simply cannot keep up her unnatural rôle. She relapses, almost at the very first opportunity, into the Russian atmosphere of kisses and forgiveness and tears. It is the Russian atmosphere certainly, but it must never be forgotten that these people are "tough" in the very toughest sense. Even the happy-go-lucky, blundering bumble-bee of an Arkady is by no means devoid of the strong qualities of his race. The poor boy is only too willing to fight if only he can secure an opponent who will take him seriously. It is easy to see that, while apparently jeering at him, the novelist will bring him to safe anchorage at last. But the future of Versilov is anything but obvious. Will he go the way of Svidrigailov and Stavroguin at the last? In regard to this problem, however, one may recall an enigmatic note on the Great Sinner: "Out of pride and infinite haughtiness towards people he becomes meek and charitable to all because he is already higher than all."

Just as Versilov endeavours to see the Russian in himself, so Arkady, who admits, much too harshly, that he has the soul of a spider, refers this strange duality to what he believes to be the national character: "It always has been a mystery, and I have marvelled a thousand times at that faculty in man (and in the Russian, I believe, more especially) of cherishing in his soul his loftiest ideal side by side with the most abject baseness, and all quite sincerely. Whether this is breadth in the Russian which takes him so far or simply baseness—that is the question!" But it is certainly Versilov who expresses, as fully as any character in any of the novels, the wider side of Dostoevsky's nationalism: "To the Russian, Europe is as precious as Russia; every stone in her is cherished and dear. Europe is as much our fatherland as Russia. Oh, even more so. No one could love Russia more than I do, but I never reproached myself that Venice, Rome, Paris, the treasures of their arts and sciences, their whole history, are dearer to me than Russia. . . . Only Russia lives not for herself, but for an idea . . ." It is Versilov, too, who pays a tribute to Russian women that, after its fashion, may well be compared with similar tributes of Turgenev: "Russian women go off quickly, their beauty is only a passing gleam, and this is not only due to racial peculiarity, but is because they are capable of unlimited love. The Russian woman gives everything at once when she loves—the moment and her whole destiny and the present and the future: she does not know how to be thrifty, she keeps nothing hidden in reserve; and their beauty is quickly consumed upon him whom they love." It is Versilov, too, who interprets that enjoyment of sorrow which Dostoevsky has confessed to feeling. "How could I be unhappy," he remarks to Arkady, "with a melancholy like that? No one is freer and happier than a Russian wanderer in Europe, one of our thousands. I am not laughing when I say that, and there's a great deal that's serious in it. And I would not have given up my melancholy for any happiness. In that sense I've always been happy, my dear, all my life."

The peculiar humour of Dostoevsky, the existence of which M. Gide is inclined to deny, shows itself in this book as in *The Double,* as in *Poor Folk,* as even in *Crime and Punishment* itself. There is in *A Raw Youth* an echo, or rather a suggestion, of that particularly clever, grotesque comedy *Uncle's Dream.* For Arkady's patron, the poor old Prince, is indeed almost inclined to accept his own crazy romance as something that he has dreamed and nothing more. "Maybe," he exclaims to Arkady, "it is a dream, but don't let them rob me of this dream." But the tone of the novel from the first page to the last, in spite of all Arkady's grotesque blunders and blurred plans and futile hopes, is permeated by the deeply serious loathing of cruelty. The novelist had always been peculiarly sensitive to any manifestation of cruelty. As a boy of fifteen on his way to the School of Engineering at Petersburg with his father, he had witnessed from the window of an inn a scene that he never forgot. A courier of the Tsar in full uniform had pulled up before the house. Presently another troïka arrived with fresh horses. The courier took his place and the postilion started, "but at that very instant, the courier rose from his seat without saying a word, raised his solid fist and brought it down on the postilion's neck. He staggered, slipped forward, then brandished his whip and struck the horses with all his might. They rushed forward at a fantastic speed, but this did not calm the courier. It was his method and not due to any burst of anger; it was something premeditated, tested by long experience; the terrible fist rose and fell upon the neck. It went on like that until the troïka had disappeared beyond the horizon. The postilion, be it understood, who had difficulty in keeping his seat, continually flogged the horses; one might have said that the blows made him lose his senses, for he ended by striking them with such violence that they rushed on like maddened beasts." The Dostoevskys' coachman explained to the boy that almost all these couriers behaved like this. Only this one, particularly after a glass of spirits, was famous for his brutality. When he returned home he would be greeted by jokes: "Ah, the courier has twisted your neck!"

Very likely, the coachman insinuated without censoriousness, the postilion would revenge himself on his young wife. "This abominable scene," Dostoevsky tells us, could never be blotted out from his memory.

The novel is, of course, remote from actual autobiography. It would be almost as absurd to read Dostoevsky's youth into Arkady as it would be to read his maturity into Stavroguin. But the illusion of memory is wonderfully sustained. The novelist recalls so festeringly the raw hurt of youth, the scald of slights and injuries, the regret not so much always for one's faults as for having put up with too much, not having been quick enough to take vengeance on insulters. And with it all the wish to blurt everything out, in accordance with the deep psychology of the confessional-box. It is not so great a novel as several that preceded it; it is not nearly so great as the novel that followed it. But it has the full depth of Dostoevsky and it is natural to search in it for some clue to that "dark legend" which was attached so persistently, and without any real evidence, to the reputation of this already sufficiently persecuted man of genius. No such clue, however, is to be found in the confidences of Arkady, who tells his story in the first person. Nor is it to be found in *Crime and Punishment,* nor in *The Possessed* nor even in *The Brothers Kardmazov.* It is to be found, though, in the book of which Prince Mishkin is the doomed hero.

As if in a conscious parody of one of Boccaccio's joyous reunions, Nastasya proposes to a little group of people that each should confess honestly the most miserable action of his life, the one of which he is most secretly ashamed. One after the other they tell little stories, but one feels, just as Nastasya herself feels, that they have not cut down deep enough, that they have been content with the thin layers of comparative seemliness and good taste. It comes to the turn of Totsky, the man who had bought Nastasya in her inexperienced youth. He tells tranquilly what he alleges to be the basest action of his life, ignoring his purchase of Nastasya. Now in the background, there is another question of purchase, a marriage to Ganya, who has himself been bought by the old general in order to free Totsky for another marriage. The beautiful young woman knows all the truth behind the truth of this involved intrigue; she knows what she has gone through and what is being prepared for her to go through. All the rest is the miserable comedy of seemliness. But there is one person to whom she can appeal; it is Prince Mishkin. And while her "whole life was hanging in the balance" it is the Prince who must decide.

Rogozhin comes upon the stage and the tempo quickens in the typical Dostoevsky manner. The sense of outrage deepens in Nastasya's heart. She pours out her whole life, making herself out a hundred times worse than she is. "Well," she exclaims to Rogozhin, "you are a shameless fellow! I am a shameless woman, but you are worse." And then a little later: "I must either have a spree with Rogozhin or go out as a washerwoman to-morrow. For I've nothing of my own. If I go away, I shall give up everything of his, I shall leave every rag behind. And who'll take me with nothing?" The Prince's name is thrown out as a challenge by one of the party and the distraught woman turns to Mishkin. "Is that true?" she asks. And in the presence of Rogozhin he answers: "It's true." Then Nastasya asks this question: "What are you going to live on if you are so in love that you, a Prince, are ready to marry Rogozhin's woman?" The reply comes at once, not on the old set lines of redemption but in the truly Dostoevsky manner: "I am going to marry an honest woman, Nastasya Philipovna, not Rogozhin's woman." "Do you mean that I am an honest woman?" she asks. And in a world that is as remote as another planet from *Lady Windermere's Fan,* for instance, the Prince says "Yes."

Certainly this suggests, more pointedly than anything that poor Arkady or even Versilov himself could blurt out, the mental habit of Dostoevsky's excruciating inquisition. Like a veritable Inquisitor he asks always, only with varying degrees of intensity, What is the real sin deep down beneath the make-believe of transgression? Like a vivisector, he drives the lancet far below the faintly inflamed flesh to cut under the final mask. But the full outpouring of confession, the actual whirlpool of the novelist's creative torment, was yet to come. When *A Raw Youth* appeared in "Otechestvennia Zapiski," Dostoevsky was exasperated by some of the critics. He had been very anxious about his health, and the summer before, while at Ems, he had actually made entries about his health on the cover of the notebook containing the plan of this very novel. Writing to his wife in June 1875, again from Ems, he expresses the same anxiety: "I am now drinking the maximum, four glasses in the morning, and two after dinner, but you can imagine for yourself how dull I am and how upset my nerves are. Worst of all, I am worried about my work. Until now I sit and worry and doubt and I have no energy to begin. Works of art should not be written like this, written to order with someone always at the back of you with a stick; they should be written at one's own leisure and inclination. . . . But the novel, and the question when I shall write it, is driving me simply mad. I dare not be late with it, and besides we need the money. Anya, how will things turn out for us this winter? What will happen? Absolutely everyone in the literary world has turned away from me; I shall not run after them. Even the 'Journal de St. Pétersbourg,' which would have praised *The Hobbledehoy*, was probably told by someone to criticise it unfavourably, and so I read in the last number that *everything* at the end of the second part is dull and 'there is nothing outstanding in it.' " Poor Arkady, it seems, is to be forthwith "buried with all honours and with general contempt."

At Ems, during this second cure, the small things of life have become tortures: "I have a neighbour who talks and bangs about too loudly in the morning when he is going out, and upstairs there is an appallingly bad piano student, who tortures me for an hour and a half with her dreadful schoolgirl playing." It may be worth noting, in view of the fact that so many of Dostoevsky's characters, including Raskolnikov, are almost always in rags, that the author was himself quite sufficiently careful about his personal appearance, a fact rather stressed by his daughter. "I wore Sharmer's suit," he tells his wife in this letter, "for the first time yesterday and I was quite shy about it. It was amazing—I felt just like a fashion plate, I swear I did. It is perfectly made; I bought a hat, quite a different shape, and I think it suits me wonderfully well." A few days later he urges his wife to fight against the depression which he himself knows so well, to go to the theatre and to take more frequent walks. But his own boredom is deepening; he complains that his neighbours have hideous faces, that there are no distractions, that the ladies' manners are mincing, that they have a tendency to sink down on chairs and faint: "While I was in the church three fainted (probably because there was so much incense and no air); but, no doubt, they are quite able to dance through the night and eat enough dinner to satisfy two peasants. Horrible!"

One of the Russians taking the cure was Professor Ilovaysky, who was Chairman of the Society of the Lovers of Russian Letters. A reading of Tolstoy's famous novel took place, and just at the point where Anna Karenina is travelling in the railway carriage, the professor "got up and loudly proclaimed that we (the 'Lovers') didn't want gloomy novels even if they were full of talent (i.e. mine), but that we wanted light and playful novels like the works of Count Tolstoy." It is submitted that the interpolation might well have been more irritating to Tolstoy than to Dostoevsky, but the author of *A Raw Youth* decided not to seek the professor's acquaintance. In the same letter he gives good advice to Anna Grigorievna, who is in a better position to give it herself: "My darling, live more happily, go about, take walks, chase away black thoughts. Have you got a doctor?" But only a few days later there is an outburst against the physician at Ems: "That rogue Orth! He is so casual with his patients in spite of the fact that he has as many as fifty patients during his consulting hours!"

There was no question of gambling this year any more than there had been the year before; but there was the vexed question of a flat in Petersburg and the necessity of borrowing money to pay the deposit. In a letter from Petersburg of July 6th, 1875, the novelist writes: "I have less money than I expected. I shall have to borrow some from the Trishins; that worries me slightly. If I don't borrow it from the Thishins, I shall have to find the money somewhere else so as to pay a deposit for the flat; I will tell you later on why I have had to spend so much money. I met Pisemsky and Paul Annenkov on the way. They were returning to Petersburg from Baden-Baden (where Turgenev and Saltykov are at present). I could not help giving Annenkov the 50 thalers (i.e. for Turgenev), and that is what has crippled me now." The deposit, to be borrowed at interest from the merchants Trishin, was not needed, for the new villa was purchased at Staraya Russa.

The incident of a comparatively trifling debt to Turgenev—so different in significance from "the dark legend" and the extraordinary interview imagined by M. Gide—was referred to years afterwards by Anna Grigorievna: "In March 1876 a certain misunderstanding took place, which greatly upset F. M., especially as two or three days previously my husband had had an epileptic fit. A certain young man, A. F. Otto (who later on settled in Paris under the pseudonym of Onegin, and who made a valuable collection of Pushkin's books and possessions), came to see F. M. Mr. Otto said that his friend, Turgenev, had asked him to see F. M. and to receive from him the remaining money which was owing to him, i.e. to Turgenev. F. M. was surprised and said: 'Hadn't Turgenev received the 50 roubles from Annenkov, which I gave to Annenkov when we were together in a railway carriage somewhere?' F. M. told him that Turgenev had sent 50 thalers to him when he was in Wiesbaden, and that those 50 thalers had been given to P. V. Annenkov in July of last year to be handed back to Turgenev. Otto confirmed the receipt of this money, but said that Turgenev remembered having sent not 50 but 100 thalers to Wiesbaden, and he, therefore, considered that F. M. still owed him 50. He then showed him Turgenev's letter. F. M. was very agitated, for he thought he had made a mistake, and he immediately called me. 'Tell me, Anya, how much do I owe Turgenev?' my husband asked after introducing me to the visitor." The answer was "fifty roubles," and a search through the correspondence proved, to everybody's satisfaction, the accuracy of the reply. I have thought it worth while to give this petty misunderstanding, as casting at least a sidelight on the relations between the two novelists, relations which, however strained, certainly do not suggest in the slightest degree that truly horrible interview mentioned in such detail by M. Gide.

In the meantime, Dostoevsky had become agitated about the Ryazan estate, which had been left by their Aunt Kumanin to the four brothers Dostoevsky—500 dessyatins to each. Dostoevsky looked forward eagerly to the ownership of land and, under his direction, Anna Grigorievna went to inspect the estate with the chief heirs. She chose 200 dessyatins of woodland and 100 dessyatins of pasture, but the discussions over partition dragged on endlessly. "Here in Petersburg," Dostoevsky wrote to his wife, "I am always dreaming about the settlement of our future and of how we can buy an estate. Can you believe it, I have almost gone mad over the idea and I tremble for the children and their future." In June 1875 Anna Grigorievna read in a Petersburg paper the following announcement: "We have heard that our famous writer Fyodor Mikhailovich Dostoevsky is seriously ill." In actual fact, his health had improved and his seizures, of which he kept accurate notes, had become very much more infrequent.

Chapter XV

GREAT SINNERS

ALL through his life, almost indeed from childhood, Dostoevsky had been partially under the influence of Schiller, a strange influence for a Russian realist. He began to read aloud to his children before they were able to read themselves, and the first of these readings impressed itself indelibly on Mlle Dostoevsky's memory: "One autumn evening at Staraya Russa when the rain was coming down in torrents and the yellow leaves lay thickly on the ground, my father announced that he was going to read us Schiller's *Robbers*. I was then seven years old and my brother was just six. My mother came to listen to this first reading. Dostoevsky read with fervour, stopping every now and then to explain some difficult expression. We listened open-mouthed; this Germanic drama seemed very strange to our childish minds." Russian legends suited her better, and after them the stories of Pushkin, particularly his mediaeval legend, *The Poor Knight*.

When her father was away in Ems, or had no time to read aloud himself, he would urge Mme Dostoevsky to read Walter Scott and Dickens, whom he called "that great Christian" in his *Diary of a Writer*. "He, who forgot his wife's name and the face of his mistress, could remember all the English names of the characters of Dickens and Scott which had fired his youthful imagination, and spoke of them as if they were his intimate friends." Glancing back at those early days, Mlle Dostoevsky was surprised that her father never gave her any actual children's books. The only book of this kind that she ever received was *Robinson Crusoe,* and it came from her mother. Mme Dostoevsky would tell her about her own childhood in minute detail, but her father seems to have maintained an unbroken reserve about his own difficult childhood, and particularly about his father.

In 1876 he resigned his post on the "Grazhdanin," but, in spite of his preoccupation with his great novel, he plunged into *The Diary of a Writer.* In these pages all the hobby-horses are at full gallop, from the national demand for Constantinople to the moral superiority of the Russians over all other races. When he sat down to write the *Diary* he had, by his own admission, at the very least ten or fifteen subjects in his head. Inevitably, many of them had to be sacrificed, but what was perhaps his main preoccupation—the youth of his country, the family, the students—always took first place. Dostoevsky, writing in the first person, goes far beyond the enigmatic Versilov in his appreciation of the Russian woman who "has so wisely despised mockery and obstacles." The girl students seem to have accepted him as a feminist, and no one could have more patiently encouraged their aspirations for careers of their own. But he considered the rôle of a good wife and a good mother the highest of all. At all times, though, he would urge them to widen their culture; he had no patience with the narrowness of the specialist who looked down on every subject except his own. Towards children, naturally, he showed all the deep sympathy that is revealed in his novels. Asked by one of his correspondents to give him a list of books suitable for his little daughter, he replied: "Walter Scott, Schiller, Goethe, Don Quixote, Gil Blas, Prescott, then Pushkin, Turgenev, Goncharov, and myself, Dostoevsky, after a very careful selection."

That list, so typical of Dostoevsky, endorses amply his daughter's view of her father as an instructor of childhood. It also illustrates an eclecticism which, however, excluded Zola. That same summer at Ems, while haunted by the probability of finding work impossible, he subscribed to a lending library: "I have taken Zola to read, because during the last few years I have neglected European literature terribly, and just imagine, I can hardly read it, it is such filth. And they shout about Zola in Russia as if he were a celebrity, a beacon of realism!" The *Diary* undoubtedly delayed the writing of *The Brothers Karamazov,* and only *A Gentle Spirit* was published between that book and *A Raw Youth.* But this journalism, with its almost too frank propaganda, undoubtedly increased the spell of Dostoevsky's personal contact with his compatriots. At the literary soirées of Petersburg his prestige spread from the intellectuals to the men of action: "A whole society of patriots gathered round my father, foremost among whom were Constantin Pobedonostsev and General Tcherniaev." It was this Pobedonostsev who was chosen by Dostoevsky as the guardian of his children in the event of his dying suddenly. This powerful Minister, so trusted by the Emperor Alexander III, "accepted the responsibilities, and, in spite of his preoccupations with affairs of State, watched over us until my brother's majority, refusing to touch the money due to him as guardian. He had, however, never had any children of his own, and knew little about education, so he had not much influence upon us."

General Tcherniaev was as ardent a Slavophil as any in Russia; it was largely through his example, in collecting volunteers against the Turks, that Alexander II was induced to declare war to free the Slav peoples from Turkish dominance. When the war was over and he was living in Petersburg with his family he became a daily visitor in the Dostoevskys' house: "Whenever I went into my father's study I found the General seated in his usual place on the sofa, discussing the future confederation of the Slav peoples. My father took the deepest interest in this question. A Slav Benevolent Society had just been founded in Petersburg under the presidency of a great Russian patriot, Prince Alexander Vassiletchikov. My father was offered the vice-presidency, and he accepted it eagerly. He attached so much importance to his functions that he would deprive himself of sleep in order to attend the meetings of the society, which took place in the afternoon. Dostoevsky had so accustomed himself to going to bed very late, that he was unable to sleep until five o'clock in the morning; but he always insisted on being called at eleven on the days of the meetings."

But those days were not yet, and during that summer of 1876 the novelist was once more under the discipline of Dr. Orth at Ems: "As for my life here, the food is bad and I cannot say it is very quiet for me; the lodgers are terribly thoughtless, they are noisy on the stairs, they bang doors and shout loudly. I don't know what Orth will say; he is only anxious to get rid of his patients as quickly as possible, he never examines them thoroughly except at the first visit, and even then he only examines them for the sake of decency, so as not to alarm them at the outset by his carelessness." It is in this letter that he, one of the most tortuous psychologists that ever made a direct appeal to a large public, alludes, without the slightest affectation, to his innate simplicity: "Don't neglect Lily, and if possible, begin to teach her how to read a little. I think Lily has your character; she will be kind and good and honest, and at the same time *generous,* whereas Fedya has my character and my simple-heartedness. You know that is the only thing I can boast of, although I know you have probably often laughed to yourself about my simple-heartedness. Isn't that so, Anya?"

The letters follow each other through the summer days in much the same key. The topics remain curiously the same: the annoyances of the inane chatter of chance acquaintances, the torture of noise, the boredom of pretentious visitors, anxiety about the family at home, anxiety about expenses, about the capacity for work when the grip of Dr. Orth is relaxed. As a variation from the familiar themes, just as familiar in the novelist's private life as are those national shibboleths of the *Diary,* we have an occasional faint hint of jealousy. Long ago there had been an old admirer of Mme Dostoevsky whom she had met again by chance: "I was never, never jealous of you and V., and you know I won't be jealous, and yet you write 'Guess who it was and be jealous.'" Only a week or two later he protests against the question, "How can you love such an ugly old woman as I am?" with considerable emphasis: "The trouble is that, nowadays, you so seldom go out to see people, otherwise you would soon be amazed at your conquests; but, Anya, though you are the queen and mistress of my heart, I would sacrifice everything, even my attacks of jealousy, if you would only go out more and amuse yourself."

Dostoevsky himself is denied the very suggestion of amusement: "Would you believe it, I have absolutely no time! I get up at six, dress, and at seven I drink the waters. I return at nine, breakfast and rest until ten (or take exercise). From ten I write, half an hour for preparation and then I write until twelve, but from twelve to one, again exercise—this is all as the doctor ordered. Dinner at one, it is impossible to begin work again immediately after dinner and, above all that, time goes in copying out my work (that is why, Anya, you mustn't be cross if I only write short letters in future). I take the waters again at four and home at six. Then I have to sit down to copy out my work, but at seven again I have to get up and go for a long walk. Tea at eight and bed at ten.—So actually I have only two hours for my writing and one and a half hours for copying —it's terrible, terrible! What *can* I write? It isn't like writing in the night at home."

Years before, he had related a horrible dream in which his little daughter Lily, as she was called at home, was an orphan in the hands of a woman who beat and tortured her. The dream of Michael or his father would reappear; this, as already noted, was always regarded as of ill omen. His wife, however, did not take that sort of thing seriously. Once he said to her, "This morning I had a wonderful dream." And when she burst out laughing he expostulated: "Please don't laugh, I attribute great significance to dreams." Dreams, indeed, have a significance in the correspondence almost equal to their significance in the novels. What is still more extraordinary is the fact that the day-dream of which Anna Grigorievna was the core, remained undimmed through the years. "You can judge for yourself," he exclaims in this year 1876 in a letter from Ems, "with what delight I think of you when we are separated from each other. And I repeat, although I have been in love with you about four times for several days on end at different times, I don't think I have ever been in love with you as I am now. I think of you and have you in my thoughts every minute, and I go over in my mind all we have talked about." He is anxious about his wife's health, about the baths which she is taking, about the change of air which is so necessary. Above all, she must not work as hard as she has done in the past. There must be no more shorthand or copying. She must get her health back in Russia and then return to Petersburg to resume life under more easy conditions. But in the very same letter he exclaims: "If only we had earned more money—but we did not even do that, and if there is any reward perhaps it is the hope for next year, but that after all is only a castle in the air."

The most prurient would become discouraged in seeking for any explanation of the "dark legend" thoughout this correspondence. But during the last years a certain amativeness, here and there at long intervals, perhaps rather akin to what Strindberg used to call Madonna-worship, makes its appearance. In regard to it, incidentally, there has already been a demand for the professional psycho-analyst to get busy over this dead man, exactly as his aid was demanded in the case of Edgar Allan Poe. It has also been suggested that towards the end Dostoevsky was inclined to alcoholism, and as proof of this it is said that on one occasion he burst into his wife's drawing-room to upbraid a tea-party for indulging in tea! The correspondence throws no light whatever on this alleged failing beyond a statement that he took light wine but abstained from vodka. As time passed, he undoubtedly became more and more under pressure from casual correspondence. He speaks of this in a letter written the following March to a Mlle Gerassimov: "You must know that I am almost overwhelmed with work. Besides the work for the periodically appearing *Diary*, I have to get through a quantity of letters. I receive daily several letters of the same kind as yours, which cannot possibly be disposed of in a few lines. Moreover, I have lately suffered from three attacks of epilepsy, and those of such violence and quick recurrence as I have not had for years. After each attack, I was bodily and mentally so shattered that for two and three days I could not work or write, or even read. Now you know that, you will forgive my long silence."

Some two months later, in the spring of 1877, he is apologising once more for not having answered a stranger's letter. This correspondent had asked for his advice on embarking on a literary career, stating at the same time that he would be content to occupy a position of the second rank. Dostoevsky, the unpractical, demonstrates for once his own practical good sense: "I should like to add this: my own youthful impulse hindered me in no wise from taking a practical grasp of life; it is true I was a writer, not an engineer; nevertheless, during my whole course at the College of Engineering, from the lowest to the highest class, I was one of the best students; later I took a post for a while, although I knew that sooner or later I should abandon that career. But I saw nothing in the career itself which could thwart that to which I aspired; I was even more convinced than before that the future belonged to me, and that alone should control it."

There was no cure at Ems during this year, and the complaints about the novelist's relations are not conspicuous. But in the summer he called on his wife's people, the Snitkins, in Petersburg and came into conflict with Marie Nikolaevna, his wife's cousin. This lady was complaining about certain packets that had been left with her by Anna Grigorievna: "Imagine how pleasant that was for me to hear! She puts on airs, talks grandly and feels she is important and indispensable. I expect she will be rude to me and make me lose my temper. I am quite ill enough as it is without all that. The suspense of waiting for the day of publication is having a very bad effect on me. But for my part I shall try to avoid the wretch without making myself miserable and I shall be patient." The real point was first of all the delay in the appearance of the *Diary* and, still more important, his belief that its sales were falling. His health, too, had made the novelist increasingly touchy.

A few days later, as might have been expected, he took his cousin some copies of the *Diary*, as though nothing had happened. But again and again his nerves were on edge and he accuses Anna Grigorievna of distrust. Oddly enough, Mlle Dostoevsky herself acknowledges that her mother was not without a certain amount of suspiciousness in her character. Before the publication of his famous book the novelist would attend the evening receptions of Countess Alexis Tolstoy, the widow of the poet, to read some of the chapters aloud: "He got into the habit of going to see Countess Tolstoy during his afternoon walk, to talk over the news of the day with her. My mother, who was of a rather jealous disposition, made no objection to these visits, for at this time the Countess was past the age of seduction." The novelist's presence proved a great attraction: " 'When Countess Sophie invited us to her evenings, we went if we had no other invitations more interesting; but when,' she added, 'Dostoevsky has promised to come, we forgot all other engagements and hastened to her house,' said an old lady of the great Russian world (now a refugee in Switzerland) to me the other day." But, just as he had been long ago in Mme Kovalevsky's old home, the now famous novelist became mute when the drawing-rooms of Petersburg began to fill up, and he would merely answer "Yes" or "No" to direct questions.

He was just as much an attraction at the literary soirées given by the students. It had been his habit to read aloud the Marmeladov outbursts from *Crime and Punishment*. But as fashionable audiences now thronged these gatherings, he substituted for this the picture of the *staretz* Zosima receiving the women peasant pilgrims: "He put so much feeling into the simple story of the poor mother that all the women in his audience were deeply moved." It was when the future Empress of Russia heard this story, so soon after the loss of her own little son, that she expressed the wish to meet Fyodor Dostoevsky.

In the June of 1878, Dostoevsky relates that visit paid with Soloviev to the Optina Pustin Monastery. According to Anna Grigorievna, he had a conversation on this occasion with the Elder Ambrosius; the topic was "how we grieve and weep over the loss of our little boy, who died a short time ago." It seems to have been a rough journey to the monastery:

"We spent the nights in the villages and were rattled about in a terrible carriage. We spent two days and nights in the Optina Pustin Monastery. Then we returned with the same horses and again travelled for two days; altogether it took us exactly *seven days,* including the day we started."

This letter is from Moscow, and he goes on to tell his wife that there may be some little difficulty in finding Katkov, the publisher, in his office. About a week later, he reports failure to find Katkov and also difficulty in getting into touch with certain Moscow booksellers: "All these people seem to be good folk and splendid payers, only they are short of money. Gentleness conquers them, but bluntness repels them. Soloviev, of course, is quite another story because he is rich." Katkov, too, was of course quite another story, and the very next day, November 8th, 1879, the novelist reports a most cordial reception from that eminent publisher: "During my visit his daughters came in, also his son and Prince Shakhovskoy, his eldest daughter's husband. They came in to say good-night, but it was fairly obvious they wanted to see me and because of this they sat there for half an hour. They were all very nice, amiable and attentive—especially Prince Shakhovskoy and the daughter (whom I had met in Ems), who has grown extremely pretty." As the author was leaving, the publisher mentioned the not unimportant subject of money. In his hurry, the visitor asked for an advance of a thousand roubles, the rest to be paid in about three weeks from date. "I have no idea now how it will all work out in actual fact. I am sorry, for I really wanted to ask for *three* thousand this time and not two, but as he hesitated I only asked for two."

Katkov had been amiability itself but had not invited the author to dinner, and so he hesitated about paying his respects to him again. However, he thought better of it, and this time he was shown into the drawing-room to be greeted by his hostess, Sophia Petrovna. Afterwards, in Katkov's study, he met the Governor-General, Prince Dolgoruky. One remembers the Raw Youth who had always to explain that he was *not* Prince Dolgoruky: "Bowing and remembering the dignity of his rank with Katkov (rather comical!), he began to shake hands with all the guests and he came up to me first. At this Katkov hastened to tell him who I was, and Dolgoruky deigned to say: 'Of course, su-uch a ce-leb-ri-ty, hum, hm-hm,' just as if it were forty years ago, in the good old days."

After staying for a short time the novelist rose to say good-bye and the publisher saw him to the door: "I did not go back to Sophia Petrovna again, but went out by another way, through the dining-room, and incidentally, I noticed that the table was laid for no more than twenty or perhaps eighteen people. And as no fewer than twelve of Katkov's own family sit down to his table every day I concluded that he was not giving a party, but was only having his nearest relations to dinner." He then went to pay a visit to Professor N. A. Lyubimov, who, it seemed, had begged his chief to let him read the manuscript of the new novel. The publisher, however, had refused and had insisted on reading it himself. Lyubimov promised Dostoevsky to hurry him with the reading: "After that, he begged me to stay to dinner, 'to take pot luck.' I agreed. Now I am wondering whether they always dine like that or if it was a special occasion. (Two ladies and a Professor Arkhipov were dining there besides myself.) Hors-d'œuvre, wine, five courses, one of them boiled fresh sturgeon cooked in the Moscow way." It sounds a very nice dinner, but that is not the important point: "Lyubimov confirmed that there had not been a dinner-party at Katkov's."

Dostoevsky seems to have been just as easily exasperated by subordinates in a Moscow publishing house as by clerks in a Russian consul's office abroad, "All the clerks in Katkov's office are terribly haughty and off-hand with everyone. I feel that Shulman puts on airs so as to show what power he has." So the year passed, and in the summer of 1879 he is back at Ems, pursuing his cure with the greatest zeal: "I have an appetite, but my nerves are in a dreadful state. Orth assures me that it is the effect of the Kränschen waters. I sleep very badly at night, I cannot drop off to sleep for a long time and I sweat about three times at night. I have a terrible spasmodic cough for half an hour or more on end, and before falling asleep or on waking up it is worse than it was in the winter." He went to see Orth about the cough, only to be told that it was a good sign because, despite the emphysema, the waters cleanse the lungs and make them capable of taking in more air, but the extra quantity irritates them. "Perhaps there is a grain of truth in what he says, and no matter how stupid he seems to be as a doctor, his very long experience here must have given him some knowledge."

In that summer of 1879 he is able to make from Ems this important announcement: "To-day, the 7th August, I was at last able to post a very thick package to Lyubimov, i.e. the novel for August—53 half-sheets." The novelist notes that the registered post for this portion of his greatest book cost him only 2 marks 25 pfennigs instead of the expected 5 marks. "I think I am pleased with what I have sent off [i.e. with the work]. I think it will be very good." The Great Sinner, in actual fact, has emerged into four separate manifestations of sin. All four figures are, in quite different fashions, menacingly alive. The deep psychology of the book has at no stage infringed upon its essential realism, nor has the tortuous evasions of the human mind ever permitted the slurring over of external detail. In no Russian book, perhaps, is it clearer that neither Russian dreams nor Russian tears may be confused with the Germanic. Russian mysticism, born in Byzantium, has no kinship with the dark forests of Wotan. And, just as the *Seagull* of Chekhov differs from the *Wild Duck* of Ibsen, there is a gulf between Slavonic and Teutonic mysticism. Not only does this book convey, for all its chaotic manner, the actual illusion of life as experienced by humanity; it also conveys through its atmosphere of chaos the illusion of space and time. The actual stage extends from the house of old Karamazov with its neighbourhood to the monastery of the *staretz* Zosima with its neighbourhood. There are but few excursions beyond these confines, and yet the suggestion of ample space is unerringly conveyed. There is a seeming chaos of space with but one illumination; it comes from the monastery. The chaos of humanity which circles round the sensualists is illumined by Zosima, who is linked to the world of the Karamazovs by the youngest of the family, Alyosha. The seeming chaos of time conveys the illusion of long duration, though, as far as possible, the Greek unities of time and space have been observed.

The principal actors rush forward in a tumult of speed. Each one of them emerges quite free from the background of any previous novel. Old Karamazov stands out by himself, of himself, for himself. He is as complete as Falstaff in an outer sense and, in an inner sense, as Oedipus. His eldest son, Mitia, like Paris in the *Iliad,* gallops stallion-like to his doom. His creator who, all through the novels, employs the word "Schilleresque" as an affectionate gibe, has allowed the adjective to be applied to him. But his character has that essentially Russian tang, at once derisive and passionate, sceptical and all-embracing, vindictive and forgiving, which can never harmonise with the loftiness of that too facetiously derided poet. One has to go back not to Schiller but to the great Greek poets for the sense of doom that pervades that turbulent scene in which the family meets at the monastery in the presence of Zosima, to discuss old Karamazov's debt to his eldest son. Pointing first to his second son and then to the older brother, their father exclaims: "Most pious and holy elder, that is my son, flesh of my flesh, the dearest of my flesh! He is my most dutiful Karl Moor so to speak, while this son who has just come in, Dmitri, against whom I am seeking justice from you, is the undutiful Franz Moor—they are both out of Schiller's *Robbers,* and so I am the reigning Count von Moor! Judge and saviour! We need not only your prayers but your prophecies!"

The din of buffoonery deepens, and then suddenly Father Zosima rose from his seat and "distinctly and deliberately bowed down at Dmitri's feet till his forehead touched the floor." The meaning of this disconcerting action came afterwards to Alyosha in a dream when the *staretz* replied to his question: "Do not ask me. I had foreseen in him something terrible, I had read the whole of his destiny in his glance. Oh! that look overwhelmed me. Once or twice in my life I had met with that expression in the faces of certain men: it presaged crime, and the prophecy, alas! has been verified. Crime was in Mitia." Old Karamazov's eldest son knew well that crime was in him, just as his younger brother, Ivan, was to become conscious of an impending evil which was in himself. It is Ivan and not Mitia who is to project from his tormented unconsciousness a satanic apparition, but it is not the Mephistopheles of Goethe. Still less is it a mere revival of Goliadkin in *The Double*. Nor is the sinless Alyosha a mere revival of the Prince in *The Idiot*. This youngest son of old Karamazov is fresh from the monastery, but is for all that a man amongst men, a companion rather than a redeemer. Still more remote from the previous novels is Smerdyakov, the illegitimate son of old Karamazov. From this pitiable figure Dostoevsky, the novelist of pity, appears to have withheld the faintest nuance of compassion. It is never in the nature of this great writer to sentimentalise over those who are stricken by their own sins, but, on the other hand, he has always lit up the long tunnel of atonement even for such as Raskolnikov.

Only in Smerdyakov we are allowed to see the very dregs of the lust which had flung him into life. And yet it is this Smerdyakov who attempts to use the brain of the Karamazovs. This belongs to the second son, Ivan, whose subtle dream of The Grand Inquisitor, though it stands entirely apart from the whole action of the book, none the less reveals the corrupted energy of the whole sunken family. Not even the sinless Alyosha can hope to atone for such a clan. Grushenka, the woman who has aroused the fierce passions both of old Karamazov and his son Mitia, is quite distinct and remote from the self-tormented Nastasya in *The Idiot.* Nor is the proud Katya, swayed between the two brothers Mitia and Ivan, in any sense a duplicate of Aglaya, though, like the *jeune fille* of *The Idiot,* she is brought face to face with her lawless rival. Inevitably, duality is not wholly absent from this amazing book. There is, for instance, the *odi et amo* attitude of Ivan towards Katya, but it comes in only occasional outbursts. And, for the most part, the characters all hurl themselves forward with much of that simplicity which is so often, and perhaps quite wrongly, attributed to Count Leo Tolstoy. Simplicity of this kind leads to direct action, and direct action cuts like a knife through all the incursions of reflection in this long novel, which is so much shorter than its creator intended it to be.

Snatches of personal memory pervade the narrative from the beginning right up to the time when the public prosecutor analyses, for the benefit of Mitia in the dock, the feelings of a man drawing nearer and nearer to the scaffold. How well Dostoevsky understood at first hand what actually happened in such a case! There are, too, in this book as in all the novels, not only anecdotes but anecdotes wrapped up in anecdotes. Not one of them is merely discoursive. Least of all is the famous "Grand Inquisitor" of Ivan Karamazov merely discoursive. In brief, it may be claimed that in no other work of Dostoevsky, perhaps indeed in no other work of fiction, has art emerged more triumphantly from the meshes of mass incoherence and intense individuality out of collective passivity.

Even the obvious mechanism—the withheld letter, the package sewn up under a jacket—is less cynically displayed than, for example, in *A Raw Youth*. The sequence of incidents, passing swiftly into episodes, is infinitely more artistically inevitable than in any of the preceding novels with the possible exception of *Crime and Punishment*. The actual case is presented with the precision and worrying conscientiousness of a police-court reporter. Here are the bald facts, as elaborated in the provincial court where a famous Petersburg advocate is appearing for the defence of Mitia, who is on trial for parricide. The circumstantial evidence is overwhelming. Old Karamazov has a package of three thousand roubles in an envelope on which is written in his own hand: "For my angel Grushenka, if she wishes to come." Now three thousand roubles is exactly the sum of which Mitia considers himself to have been robbed by his father. He is madly in love with Grushenka and has raved openly against his father, whom, on one occasion, he has violently assaulted. Then, as though all this was not enough, he has robbed his fiancée Katya of exactly three thousand roubles with which she had entrusted him.

Half of this sum, fifteen hundred roubles, is sewn up in a little bag under his jacket, while he waits in the garden outside his father's villa. In the little house at the back, the old servant Gregory and his wife are sleeping. In the next room to them is the epileptic Smerdyakov, who is supposed to have fallen down the cellar steps after a seizure. Mitia has armed himself, without quite knowing why, with a brass pestle. While he is still lying in wait the old servant, Gregory, makes a rush at him. Mitia fells him with the pestle, leaving him there in the garden, as he believes, stone dead. These five people, including old Karamazov, are the only human beings about the house, for Ivan Karamazov had gone away that morning. Every scrap of evidence, all the small details, every outburst taken down in the protocol from Mitia's own lips, tend to convict the prisoner. But Katya, the fiancée whom he has forsaken and robbed, is generous to him in the witness-box, explaining that he has not robbed her at all but that the money had been given to him freely. It is really the very first piece of favourable evidence, and this is how the prisoner accepts it: "Katya, why have you ruined me? . . . Now I am condemned!"

That is just one instance in this book out of innumerable instances of Dostoevsky's manner, as distinct from that of the familiar amateur criminologists of English fiction. No rule-of-thumb logic can explain Mitia, who is, after his fashion, simple with the simplicity of human nature into which the little logicians, only too often, inject the virus of their own precision. Certainly Mitia will say this or that, will even write this or that, when exasperated by alcohol into exaggerating his sense of wrong. For such a man there is no barrier between impulse and action. He will avenge insult almost before he understands it meaning. Yet, while flying for his life, he will waste five minutes of precious time in tending the man whom he believes that he has killed. He gives way as a matter of course to tears, but it never crosses his mind to shrink from bullets. He will act honourably at one moment from instinct, and dishonourably the next from passion. He is a magnificent animal, courageous and magnanimous; he is also a Karamazov. But he is quick in his own way to detect the reality of his doom, over which all these learned people are fumbling so pretentiously.

At last there is yet another witness wholly in Mitia's favour, for Grushenka, though she means well, has not been convincing. Ivan Karamazov states that the servant Smerdyakov, who had hanged himself the day before, had confessed the murder to him before he died and had handed him the three thousand roubles of which he had robbed his master. Ivan produced the three thousand roubles in court and stated that the murder had been committed at his own instigation. Then he broke down and became incoherent. Asked for some sort of proof of his statement, asked for a witness, Ivan answers: "He has a tail, your excellency, and that would be irregular! *Le diable n'existe point!* Don't pay attention!" The reference is to the dialogue between Ivan and the devil, which seems to me incomparably inferior to Ivan's impression of the Grand Inquisitor. Yet a critic has maintained that this scene between Ivan and the devil is stronger than that between Faust and Mephistopheles. I do not think that this view can be seriously maintained. Faust is distinct and separate from Mephistopheles, whereas Ivan is facing a projection from his own unconsciousness. However that may be, his evidence in the court was not taken seriously. He was seized by the police and dragged out while Katya collapsed in hysterics. Only too surely had Mitia divined that this woman would prove his undoing.

Forthwith Katya produces a document which, up

to now, she has suppressed; it is a drunken letter in which Mitia threatens definitely to murder his father, who, in actual fact, was murdered so soon afterwards. It was through this letter that she had been able to convince the conscience-stricken Ivan that Mitia, and not Smerdyakov, was the actual parricide. Then, while she is relapsing into hysterics, her rival Grushenka wails out: "Mitia, your serpent has destroyed you!" This document, needless to say, has entirely obliterated the effect of Ivan's unsupported and seemingly insane evidence. But considerable stress is laid on the evidene of the old servant Gregory, who, with the exception of the accused, is apparently the only human being in a position to tell the real story of the crime. Now Mitia himself has acknowledged the objective truth of Gregory's evidence, except on one point. The old servant had stated that he saw the door leading into the garden from the house open, while Mitia insisted that it was shut. The speech for the defence had naturally to emphasise this all-important door. For if it had been opened, the inference was that Mitia had entered his father's house. Counsel for the defence could neither ignore nor dispute this inference. So he prepares to fire the second barrel of his legal virtuosity. Even supposing the very worst of the worst, could this case be called one of parricide? Could the dead buffoon of lust be accepted in any real sense as a father? Had he not practically deserted all his sons from childhood? And so on and so forth; the thesis was simple enough.

Even counsel for the defence considered Ivan as a broken reed whose wish to save his brother, at the eleventh hour, was deserving of but little serious consideration. The jury, too, despised the evidence of Ivan as a mere improvisation of despair. But they were wrong. It was no improvisation but the result of five concentrated interviews, two before the crime and three after it, between Smerdyakov and Ivan, who had set himself the task of peeling layer after layer of his illegitimate brother's hatred. Smerdyakov is almost ill with hatred. He knows that Ivan is alone with his father in that house, and that as long as Ivan is there the dreadful thing, at which he has begun to hint almost openly, will not take place. But why should not Ivan go to Tchermashnia, a village only a few miles away, where old Karamazov had been urging his second son to transact a piece of business for him? Things will become simpler if Ivan is out of the way, even if Mitia and Grushenka arrive at the house together. Nobody else will be in a position to interfere. The servants will not be available, for old Gregory is to be given a special cure for his lumbago by his wife. The stuff contains alcohol, and the two of them will drink the remainder of the bottle and pass into a long sleep. Smerdyakov himself is an epileptic; he may have a fit that night. If he should have a fit that night nobody could blame him for what had happened. Least of all can the terrible Mitia blame him: "For even if Agrafena Alexandrovna comes to see his father while I am ill, his honour can't blame a sick man for not telling him. He'd be ashamed to." Yet, under the present conditions, if anything happened, Smerdyakov would be taken for the assassin's accomplice because he had confided to Mitia certain signals that were to be used by Ivan's father.

Smerdyakov knows all about that envelope with the three thousand roubles, "To my angel Grushenka, if she will come," and even about the additional words written three days later, "for my little chicken." Cunningly Smerdyakov insinuates that if old Karamazov should marry his little chicken not a rouble would come to any one of his sons: "But if your father were to die now, there'd be some forty thousand for sure, even for Dmitri Fyodorovitch whom he hates so, for he's made no will. . . . Dmitri Fyodorovitch knows all that very well." The danger is terrible and Ivan exclaims with a shudder: "Then why on earth do you advise me to go to Tchermashnia? What did you mean by that? If I go away, you see what will happen here." But as Ivan leaves the house the next morning, he exclaims suddenly: "You see . . . I am going to Tchermashnia." Smerdyakov eyes him significantly and replies, "It's a true saying, then, that 'it's always worth while speaking to a clever man.' " In actual fact Ivan changes his mind and goes to Moscow, as though this change could affect, one way or the other, that devilish unspoken compact between himself and this despised epileptic who is preparing to sham a fit this very night.

When the crime has taken place, Ivan is tortured by a sense of guilt until Mitia's drunken letter, shown him by Katya, convinces him that, after all, his brother is guilty. But again and again he flutters round Smerdyakov like a moth round a candle. At last he forces the servant to tell the truth: "Aren't you tired of it?" Smerdyakov exclaims with his new familiarity. "Here we are face to face; what's the use of going on keeping up a farce to each other? Are you still trying to throw it all on me, to my face? *You* murdered him; you are the real murderer, I was only your instrument, your faithful servant, and it was following your words I did it." But Ivan is not convinced until from a long white stocking Smerdyakov produces that roll of banknotes which, after all, was to make so slight an impression on the jury. Smerdyakov, for his part, finds it almost impossible to understand that this "clever man" had not grasped the truth from the very first.

This "clever man" was not only the victim of an apparition in the shape of the devil, but was the author of a curiously subtle impression of Western scepticism which he reads to Alyosha in the hours of comparative tranquillity before the crime. This interpreter of Ivan's dream, the Grand Inquisitor, has been visited by Jesus, who stands silently in front of him while He is accused of failure to understand those to whom he had brought freedom. It was a gift, the Grand Inquisitor urges, that they were unfit for and incapable of understanding. It had been necessary to correct the works of Jesus. "And we," he exclaims to the silent one, "who, for their happiness, have assumed the weight of their sins, we shall stand before Thee saying: 'Judge us, if Thou canst, and if Thou darest!' I do not fear Thee. I have gone into the desert, I also; I also, I have lived on locusts and roots; I also have blessed the liberty that Thou gavest to man, and I have dreamed of being counted among the strong. But I soon abandoned this dream, and I renounced Thy madness to go and join the groups of those who corrected Thy work. I have left the proud to go and make the happiness of the humble."

Still Christos maintains His silence. When the words die away at last He kisses the Grand Inquisitor, still in silence. Then the corrector of His work who has decreed that He shall be burnt on the morrow exclaims: "Go! and come never again!" Ivan,

Julius Meier-Graeffe reminds us, took the outline of the Grand Inquisitor from Schiller. He claims that the fanaticism of the Grand Inquisitor is from the Inquisitor in *Don Carlos,* but he goes on to indicate much that is wholly beyond the range of the German poet to whom Dostoevsky was so curiously faithful: "The Saviour appears in place of the feeble king who completely breaks down in the final scene of *Don Carlos.* This exchange of personages permits the inner action, which Schiller omitted, to be worked out with a masterliness which has no counerpart in the domain of Philip and his son." In sober truth nothing, probably in the whole world of letters, is less "Schilleresque" than the strange figure of Ivan's Grand Inquisitor.

Dostoevsky has been reproached with garrulity, but it would be difficult to find a scene in modern literature more significant, through silence, than that of Ivan's dream. In the same way, it is the unspoken during those five interviews between Ivan and Smerdyakov that pervades the whole atmosphere of crime and fear. But this terrible book is by no means without the relief of humour. Mme Hohlakov, for example, urging Mitia to seek his fortunes in the gold-fields when he is absolutely frantic for a loan of three thousand roubles, is almost Dickensian. But her daughter, the fifteen-year-old cripple Lise, mildly attracted by Alyosha and quite uselessly fascinated by Ivan, is, regretably perhaps, wholly remote from the English writer. Alyosha, although tempted by Grushenka, finds no difficulty in parrying Lise. He is almost solely preoccupied by the affairs of his elder brothers, but he is at no time remote from the world. He does not avoid life, but somehow or other the filth of life appears to avoid him. And behind Alyosha, like a veritable Greek chorus in this Russian drama of passion, is a large circle of youth that comes willingly under the influence of "Mr. Karamazov."

The interest of the book would seem to have played itself out with the verdict of the jury which has spelt out Siberia for Mitia and his severance from both of the women who have distracted him —the young girl who had thrown herself upon his mercy, to save her father from dishonour, and the woman who had maddened him and his father alike with her animal beauty. One thinks that the drama is over, but the curtain rises again on a scene that is extraordinarily true to human nature, when it is left quite to itself and not interfered with by the clever stage-hand. Katya, who has destroyed Mitia, visits him in the prison hospital. Alyosha is a witness of his brother's reception of the woman who has sent him to Siberia in order to defend the man with whom she is, presumably, in love: "He leaped impulsively to his feet, and a scared look came into his face. He turned pale, but a timid, pleading smile appeared on his lips at once, and with an irresistible impulse he held out both hands to Katya. Seeing it, she flew impetuously to him. She seized him by the hands, and almost by force made him sit down on the bed. She sat down beside him, and still keeping his hands pressed them violently. Several times they both strove to speak, but stopped short and, again speechless with a strange smile, their eyes fastened on one another. So passed two minutes." It is Mitia who asks for forgiveness. " 'That's what I loved you for, that you are generous at heart!' broke from Katya. 'My forgiveness is no good to you, nor yours to me; whether you forgive me or not, you will always be a sore place in my heart, and I in yours—so it must be. . . .' She stopped to take breath. 'What have I come for?' she began again with nervous haste: 'to embrace your feet, to press your hands like this, till it hurts—you remember how in Moscow I used to squeeze them—to tell you again that you are my god, my joy, to tell you that I love you madly,' she moaned in anguish, and suddenly pressed his hand greedily to her lips."

After a little he asks her directly if she ever believed that he was a murderer. "I did not believe it even then. I've never believed it. I hated you, and for a moment I persuaded myself. While I was giving evidence I persuaded myself and believed it, but when I'd finished speaking I left off believing it at once. Don't doubt that! I have forgotten that I came here to punish myself." She spoke now with quite a new expression and a different tone. Then her rival appears, but there is no reconciliation between the two women. Venomous and vindictive, Grushenka exclaims: "We are full of hatred, my girl, you and I! We are both full of hatred! As though we could forgive one another! Save him, and I'll worship you all my life." Grushenka is alluding to the planned escape of Mitia, and the book, so far as it was actually finished, leaves us with the hope, or rather the promise, of Mitia's escape.

Dostoevsky seems to have had in his mind a cycle of five books for the work evolved out of the Life of his Great Sinner. But in its actual form it gives, in an intensive sense, as the *Comédie Humaine* does in an extensive sense, the full panorama of life as it sweeps by. There is, just as in Nature, a pathetic fallacy in art. You may assuredly read yourself in one or other of the figures of this panorama, but you must be infinitely careful not to read yourself into Dostoevsky. More than one by no means inept enthusiast for the Russian has been unable to resist this trap of officious sympathy. Undoubtedly, all sorts of saints and sinners might see themselves mirrored in the novels, from St. Francis of Assisi to, let us say, Landru of Paris. And the extraordinary intensity of the novelist betrays itself even in the *nouvelle*—in *A Gentle Spirit* for instance—almost as unmistakably as in the greatest scenes of this his last and greatest novel.

In all the works alike, with scarcely a single exception, the main preoccupation is the idea of sin. It is submitted that this preoccupation in itself goes very far to explain the origin of the dark legend which attempted to befoul his name. How close the motif of *The Possessed* is to *The Brothers Karamazov* is plain to any reader of the Notebooks and, as already indicated, *A Raw Youth* itself might be added to the background of the last novel—so far as the motif of sin is concerned. In his introduction to the unpublished chapter of *The Possessed* V. Komarovich writes: "It should be plain that Dostoevsky's interest in this conception had risen not from personal recollections, and was not maintained by them, but by the artist's desire to find some adequate way of expressing in the plot his religious conception of the world." For the very worst sinner, it was the novelist's belief, redemption was possible, and because of this he shrank in his novels from no manifestation of sin.

Chapter XVI

APOTHEOSIS

IN THE meantime, the old matter of that inheritance is added once more to the novelist's troubles. His wife has decided to visit the estate, and her husband is nervous and worried over her having to stay "six days in the country where there is no food, where you have to live in a stuffy peasant's hut with the children and knaves of hearts." He goes on to remind her that she will be travelling third class with the children: "Those knaves of hearts have such hearts and such minds that your air of humility and poverty (in the third class) will arouse their scorn for you. You will stop with those knaves in the same inns and perhaps in the same huts in the village, there you may have to endure a thousand impudent familiarities from them." By the knaves of hearts he refers to the other claimants to the estate; he applies to them also the terms "rogues, swindlers, and knaves." Three days later, however, he is more satisfied about Anna Grigorievna's expedition, but he suggests travelling second class: "Questions are simply buzzing in my head. Still, I place my trust in God and in you too, my capable though harebrained little wife."

That is the last letter from Ems, and the next missive to his wife is dated May 23rd, 1880, from Moscow. In it he speaks of his sorrow over the death of the Empress. This meant the postponement of the Pushkin celebrations, participation in which had been the object of his visit to the old capital.

He was received amiably by a host of people, including the very influential Mme Novikov, who was already becoming an international figure. Both Professor Lyubimov, the associate editor of the "Russky Viestnik," and Katkov were most friendly. Dostoevsky found himself in the unaccustomed position of almost being able to auction his journalistic products. Besides this, the literary youth of Moscow were most eager to make his acquaintance. It was the beginning of a triumph which very soon was to rise to a veritable crescendo. But only the month before in Petersburg, in a letter to a certain Mlle N. M. he had written: "I swear to you that though I have received much recognition, possibly more than I deserve, still the critics, the literary newspaper critics, who certainly have often (no, rather, very seldom) praised me, nevertheless have always spoken of me so lightly and superficially that I am obliged to assume that all those things which my heart brought forth with pain and tribulation, and which came directly from my soul, have simply passed unperceived. From this you can divine what a pleasant impression must have been made upon me by the delicate and searching comments on my work which I read in your letter to your lady-mother." In this letter there is an allusion to Vladimir Soloviev's interesting claim for humanity: "I am firmly convinced that mankind *knows much more* than it has hitherto expressed either in science or art." The novelist was conscious of much in himself that had never found expression and never would find expression. But what interests him most of all is his admirer's confession to a certain duality: "It is precisely on this ground that I cannot but regard you as a twin soul, for your inward duality corresponds most exactly to my own. It causes at once great torment and great delight."

It was just at this period that Count Tolstoy abandoned artistic work to absorb himself in religious and philosophical speculations. Dostoevsky alludes to this so-called "conversion" in the letter to his wife dated May 27th, 1880, when he found himself rather unwillingly a guest of Moscow: "Grigorovitch told me to-day that Turgenev, who has just returned from visiting Leo Tolstoy, is ill, and that Tolstoy is deranged and has perhaps gone mad." Tolstoy was, of course, in no way mad, but he definitely refused to take any part in the Pushkin celebrations, which he labelled unfairly "a farce." On June 8th, 1880, Dostoevsky described to his wife the marvellous reception given to his speech on Pushkin. "As soon as Theodor Mikhailovitch," writes Strakhov, the same Strakhov who was to send more than one defamatory letter to Tolstoy after Dostoevsky's death, "began to speak, the hall trembled with applause, and then became absolutely still. True, his speech was read from a manuscript, but it constituted less a written oration than a living, a direct, a sincere utterance from the heart. And to it we listened as though until that moment Pushkin had never even been mentioned. The inspiration, the naturalness which ever distinguished Dostoevsky's style, he imparted in full measure to his reading; and though I will not say more concerning the subject-matter of the oration than that it communicated to that reading an added impressiveness, I may add the remark that to this day I can hear floating over the heads of the great, silent multitude the tense, sympathetically uttered words: 'Humble thyself, thou man of pride! Set thy hand to labour, thou man of leisure.' "

The applause that followed the conclusion of the speech was nothing short of rapture. People leaped on to the platform. A young man is said to have swooned at Dostoevsky's feet. The speech was made under the auspices of the Society of the Lovers of Russian Letters, and Yuriev, the Chairman, rang his bell to announce that the Society had, then and there, elected the novelist an honorary member. Aksakov, who was to follow with his own speech, declared that everything had been said, but he was compelled to read it. He then turned to Fyodor Dostoevsky: "This day you have delivered a speech which entails upon Turgenev, as the representative of the Westerners, and upon myself, as the representative (if I may say so?) of the Slavophils, the duty of expressing to you our joint sympathy and our joint gratitude." It was indeed a strange appeal; it brought the author of *Smoke* within range of the Idea born in the convict prison of Omsk. It was particularly strange, perhaps, as an item in the celebrations to Pushkin. For Pushkin himself, like Lermontov, had been killed in a duel. Turgenev had been more than once on the verge of a duel with Leo Tolstoy. Dostoevsky appears to have clung to his hereditary noblesse largely because it gave him a right to demand satisfaction from anyone who insulted him. In novel after novel the deepest wound is that felt by a man who has failed to meet his enemy in a duel. And yet here he was, in an atmosphere of absolute fraternity, even with his old enemy Turgenev: "When I finished—I can't describe to you the roar, the frenzy of delight; people in the audience who were strangers to each other, wept, sobbed, embraced *and swore to one another to be better, and henceforth not to hate but to love.*"

Two old men, perfect strangers to the novelist, stopped him and exclaimed: "We have been enemies for twenty years, we have not spoken to each other, and now we have embraced and are friends. You have reconciled us. You are our saint, our prophet."

Society women, students, Secretaries of State, all rushed up to the platform to embrace the speaker. "Turgenev, about whom I had put in a good word in my speech, rushed up to me to embrace me with tears in his eyes." Mme E. E. Delidov has recorded that moment: "Everyone remembers that wave of the hand and the kiss sent by Turgenev to Dostoevsky at the moment when he [Dostoevsky] spoke in his speech of Liza in *The Nest of Gentlefolk*. Everyone knew their unfriendly relationship and this was one of the best moments of these amazing celebrations." It is submitted that it was not only the best moment of the Pushkin celebrations but a moment which would seem to make that interview, described by M. Gide, almost absolutely incredible.

It is no wonder that the Russian women were peculiarly enthusiastic at this historic meeting, for the novelist, in his *Diary*, had become an unwearied supporter of their movement: "To every obstacle, to every jeer, the Russian woman has opposed supreme contempt. Proudly she has averred her desire to share in the work of the State, and to set about the same, not only with disinterestedness, but also with self-denial. In short, whereas, during the last few decades, the male citizen of Russia has yielded to excesses of greed and cynicism and materialism, the Russian woman has rested proudly true to the pure worship, the pure service, of her ideal. Lastly, in her hunger for the higher education she has displayed a measure of patience and responsibility which has set before her fellows an example of splendid heroism." It is natural enough, then, that in this apotheosis of Dostoevsky's triumph—in itself a fulfilment of Mme de Staël's prophecy—they came thronging on to the platform to crown him with a magnificent wreath of laurel, "In the name of the Russian women, about whom you have said so much good." It was indeed the apotheosis of the novelist's personal career, and it was after this speech that he allowed himself to exclaim, with one of the very few touches of vanity since the mortification following the success of *Poor Folk,* but at the same time with truth: "My name alone is worth a million roubles."

It was a veritable crescendo for the weary man of letters, but the inevitable de-crescendo was not long in coming. Writing to Frau E. A. Stachenschneider from Staraya Russa, on July 17th of that year, Dostoevsky speaks of having returned home on June 11th to resume work on the Karamazovs: "After I had sent off the MS., I applied myself to the reading of all the newspaper articles that dealt with my speech at Moscow (I had been so busy till then that I had had no time for them), and I decided to write a rejoinder to Granovsky; it was to be not so much an answer to him as a manifesto of our faith for all Russia: for the significant and moving crisis in the life of our society which declared itself at Moscow, during the Pushkin celebrations, was deliberately misrepresented by the press, and thrust of set purpose into the background."

Then, a little later on in that summer, Turgenev expressed to V. V. Stassov his antipathy to Dostoevsky's speech, which to him appeared false and mystical. He objected to such phrases as the "Russian

All-Man" and the "Russian All-Woman Tatyana." The enthusiasm of the audience seemed to him, at this later date, quite incomprehensible: "Turgenev was most upset and very annoyed at this amazing enthusiasm, which affected not only the whole of the Russian crowd, but also the whole of the Russian intelligentsia." It was the old prejudice, undoubtedly, but it was merely the prejudice against the peculiar nationalism of the rival novelist. Turgenev was opposed to Dostoevsky's whole conception of historic evolution. It was not for the author of *Smoke* to stress the gleams of beauty which Dostoevsky caught always, not only in the convict prison but in Russia herself, in spite of the degradation of the masses: "I repeat that the Russian masses ought not to be judged by the abominations which frequently they perpetrate, but by the many noble and radiant things which they produce amid their degradation. For the ideals of the people are clean, strong, and holy." Even at Omsk, Dostoevsky detected potential humanity: "What a wealth of young manhood here lies buried to no purpose! What a wealth of vigour lies annulled within these walls! Yet truly it may be said that once these same convicts were splendid men—perhaps the best, the most virile, the most gifted, of all whom we possess: whereas their powers and faculties lie ruined—they lie ruined abnormally, irrevocably, and illegally." It was upon this particular fragment and not upon *The House of the Dead* as a whole that Nietzsche fastened, when claiming Dostoevsky as akin to himself. That there was no genuine kinship but, on the contrary, actual hostility I have tried to show all through this book.

Nor had the author of *Smoke*, from first to last, anything remotely to do with the evolution of the superman. On the contrary, he was preoccupied with curiously intelligent but will-less heroes, working hopelessly upon that same inchoate mass which Dostoevsky was to protect so lovingly. Yet the clash between the two writers was inevitable; they were hopelessly incompatible. Turgenev was ironical, though, except in the case of Dostoevsky, intensely sympathetic to what he recognised as talent even when he disliked the particular kind of talent. He helped Zola and did his best for Tolstoy whose work was the antithesis of his own. He was sophisticated and at the same time a man of the most unassuming simplicity. Aristocratic in tone, he showed himself repeatedly, both in his work and in his life, singularly devoid of social prejudice. He has been unjustly viewed in many countries. Only the other day he was introduced, in a little English sketch, as an absurd figure in an absurd scene *fourteen years after his death*. In that scene he was presented as clashing with Tolstoy almost as much as he used to clash with Dostoevsky. But one must never forget the letter which he addressed to the author of *War and Peace* from his death-bed. "My good and dear Friend, It is a long time since I have written to you, because I have been and I am, to speak frankly, on my death-bed. I cannot get well, there is no use in thinking of it. I write to you before everything else to tell you how happy I have been to be your contemporary, and to express to you my last and immediate prayer. My friend, return to literature! Reflect that this gift has come to you from the Source of all things."

If Turgenev was indeed hopelessly incompatible to Dostoevsky, it may be claimed that, by reason of his deep and sustained duality, the author of

Crime and Punishment clashed with himself. Emotional not sentimental; realistic not pornographic; compassionate not effusive; irritable not rancorous; sensitive not plaintive; enduring not plodding; frail not yielding; exasperated not spiteful; dreamy but intensely observant and attentive to detail; no sort of label would ever fit the creator of *The Brothers Karamazov*. He was undoubtedly a man of strong passions, but he was in no sense of the word a Karamazov. Convoluted and tortuous in his mentality, he yet always preserved something at least of that childlike openness which he claimed to have in common with his small son. Such as he was, his life and work cannot be put into separate tight-fitting compartments any more than can his qualities. Examine the correspondence closely, read between the lines, and you will not find yourself in a world by any means remote from that of the novels. In ordinary daily life he remained, to no small degree, the psychologist and the psychopathist of his creative work. It is no wonder that M. Bérard des Glajaux, President of the Paris Assize Court of Appeal, quotes with approval a French judge who maintained that the book by which he had profited most in his study of criminology was *Crime and Punishment*.

In the case of Catherine Kornilov, in 1876, Dostoevsky intervened on the side of mercy. The woman had been condemned by a Russian jury for having thrown her little step-daughter out of a fourth-storey window. She had been enceinte at the time, and in an article, entitled "A Simple but Complicated Affair," Dostoevsky analysed the tragedy as he saw it. After visiting the woman in prison he wrote to a friend: "I have seen her in the prison hospital.

Five days ago she became a mother. I confess to you that I was extraordinarily struck by the result of the interview. In my article I had *almost* divined everything literally." Asked why she had committed the crime, she anwered gently: "I don't know myself. It was as though a will outside of myself impelled me." And the novelist drew from her yet another curious fact: "When I had dressed myself, I had no wish to go to the police-station; I went out like that into the street, and I don't know how I found myself at the station." The wardens informed Dostoevsky that at first the prisoner had been "rough, insolent with everybody. She was almost out of her mind." The birth of her daughter, according to the wardress, had produced a great change: "She has become so simple, so intelligent, so gentle." Through Dostoevsky's efforts a second trial was held, and, though the President of the Court warned the jury to be on their guard against "certain talented *littérateurs,*" a verdict of "not guilty" was returned.

Dostoevsky's equivocal simplicity of disposition was peculiarly baffling. There was nothing of "the Great Man" about him in the domestic annals of Mme Dostoevsky. He did not confine psychology, though, to the problems of others. On one occasion, he was savagely attacked by an out-of-work whom he had never seen in his life. The case was brought into the police court and the novelist pleaded for the man on the ground that he had been driven to the act by despair. Such a plea seemed to many at the time, and, indeed, seems to many to-day, incomprehensible. It is certainly no wonder that all the adjectives of description flounder helplessly over the personality of this ex-convict of Omsk.

But in spite of that de-crescendo, the official verdict of the Lovers of Russian Letters had an enduring significance for Dostoevsky. It may be urged certainly that it came very late in the day, but such procrastination in literary judgments is by no means confined to nineteenth-century Russia. It was the late Lord Fisher who warned us that we might be in danger of losing the Empire because it was Buggins' turn. In literary matters, Buggins had his turn only too often in nineteenth-century England. His brothers all over Europe were almost equally busy, barring conscientiously the difficult path of genius. But now, at long last, they could no longer bar it effectually on the creator of *The Brothers Karamazov*. Thirty-six years had elapsed since he abandoned the translation of *Eugénie Grandet* for the creation of *Poor Folk*. He had wished passionately then to join the *Littérateurs*, "to become one with, to become one of those men!" His fame then had been seemingly a mirage, but now, when it mattered comparatively so very little, it was real enough. Undoubtedly he could claim equality at least with the authors of *War and Peace* and *Smoke,* the book that he abhorred! This abhorrence shows in itself that the chasm between Dostoevsky and Turgenev was mainly political, just as the chasm between Dostoevsky and Bielinski had been long ago.

There was no serious argument against the power of *The Brothers Karamazov,* but it is not until November 8th, 1880, that the author dispatches to N. A. Lyubimov, the associate editor of the "Russky Viestnik," the final instalment of the great novel as it was to appear. It is in this letter that he writes: "Let me not say good-bye to you! Indeed, I intend to live another twenty years and to go on writing." Almost to the very last gasp, the novelist is harassed by the torment of the rouble. On January 26th, 1881, he writes once more to N. A. Lyubimov: "I now need money badly. Kindly inform Michael Nikiforovich of this. Could you please instruct the editorial office to send me that amount?" The amount was another four thousand roubles for the last novel.

Only the day before, on Sunday the 25th of January, there was a family dinner at the Dostoevskys' home in Petersburg. The novelist's sister, Vera, was a guest: "It began gaily with jokes and reminiscences of the games and amusements of Dostoevsky's childhood. But my aunt was anxious to get to business, and she began to discuss the eternal question of the Kumanin estate which had poisoned the lives of all the Dostoevskys. My father frowned; my mother tried to turn the conversation by questioning her sister-in-law about her children. It was no use; my aunt Vera was the least intelligent of the whole family. Well coached by her cleverer and more cunning sisters, she was afraid of forgetting their instructions, and continued to talk of her business, with growing excitement." Sobs followed. The harassed novelist, at his wits' end for money, was reproached for cruelty when he refused to sacrifice his own family to his sisters. While Mme Dostoevsky escorted the sobbing visitor to the door, the author of *The Brothers Karamazov* retired to his own room.

As from the grave, the figure of the Grandmother in *The Gambler* had come back to him. It was strange, for it was she, with her close associations with Pauline, who had brought Dostoevsky to the one sanctuary of his stricken life—his second marriage. She had brought him the diamond of his dream—Anna Grigorievna. And now, through this same Grandmother, the family had closed in upon him once more, the family which even on the honeymoon in Dresden had seemed to stand perpetually between his bride and a home of her own. From the time of his father's death, all his memories may well have hovered round Mme Kumanin. She had given him a small allowance in the days of *Eugénie Grandet*. She had come to the rescue, too, in the days of the "Epoch," and ever since her death, while he and Anna Grigorievna were abroad, her property had been the cause of wrangles worthy of Dostoevsky's fiction. His head drooped over his hands as he leaned on the writing-table. He could feel a moisture on his hands. He examined them. They were covered with blood, so was his mouth, so was his moustache. Mme Dostoevsky sent at once for the family doctor, and in the meantime the novelist joked with the children over the illustrations of a comic paper. The doctor attributed the hemorrhage—the first that Dostoevsky had ever had —to catarrh of the respiratory organs, and ordered complete rest and quietude: "My father lay down obediently on his Turkish sofa, never to rise again. . . ."

The next day a specialist was summoned. He gave it as his opinion that the night would decide the case. "Alas! when my father woke in the morning after a very restless night, my mother realised that his hours were numbered. My father, too, realised it. As always in the crises of his life, he turned to the Gospel. He begged his wife to open his old prison Bible and to read the first lines on which her eyes should fall." Checking her tears, Mme Dostoevsky read aloud: "But John forbade Him, saying: I have need to be baptised of Thee, and comest Thou to me? And Jesus answering said unto him, Hold me not back; for thus it becometh us to fulfil all righteousness." After reflecting for a moment, Dostoevsky said to his wife with all his old direct simplicity: "Did you hear? Hold me not back. My hour has come. I must die." To his little daughter and son he said: "Even if you should be so unhappy as to commit a crime in the course of your life, never despair of God. You are His children; humble yourselves before Him as before your father, implore His pardon, and He will rejoice over your repentance, as the father rejoiced over that of the Prodigal Son."

He asked for a priest and received the last sacrament. To the last moment he retained consciousness. In his daughter's words: "He saw death approaching without fear. He knew that he had not buried his talent, and that all his life he had been God's faithful servant."

The funeral that followed brought a swarming concourse of people to pay homage to the man who, all through his life, had stood for the national vision of Russia. It was a spontaneous tribute to the dead man, who perhaps best of all had understood the heart of the Russian people. It was not merely official, and something of the very atmosphere of the novels penetrated the popular tribute to Fyodor Dostoevsky. That is not strange. What is strange is the fact that Russians of to-day have accepted Dostoevsky, the champion of the old order, of the old faith, of the old Eastern dream of a renewed Byzantium. For all that, the Dostoevsky family, for which he had toiled so unceasingly to the end, was ruined by the Revolution. After the great writer's death his heirs not only came into their share of the Kumanin property but reaped the rewards of his genius. Edition after edition of his works followed in quick succession, and every edition brought them 75,000 roubles. But the confiscation that followed the Revolution spelt out ruin, and the widow and son of this man of genius died of privation in Russia in 1920.

"The other members of the family," says Serge Persky, writing in 1924, "are living partly in Russia, partly abroad in profound misery. A collection made quite recently in Switzerland made it possible to send some food and clothes to the grandson of Dostoevsky, the sole male descendant of this writer of genius." Mlle Dostoevsky herself became a writer, rather in the manner of her father, in the city that changed its name to Leningrad. It is indeed a sombre ending, but the dreams of the great writer were always tinged with the sombreness of reality, and his works at least have persistently refused to die.

This brave daughter of brave parents was anxious to celebrate Dostoevsky's centenary in her native country. As this was impossible, she published, in 1921, her invaluable biography, just a hundred years after his birth. His life is so much an integral part of his work that one can almost think of him as having been born in *Poor Folk,* lived in the lodgings of the early *nouvelles,* paid a dreadful visit to *The House of the Dead,* occupied a cellar in *Letters from the Underworld,* moved from hotel to hotel abroad in *The Gambler,* investigated crime through different lodging-houses in *Crime and Punishment,* appeared in drawing-rooms in *The Idiot,* been hunted from pillar to post in *The Possessed*, emerged into a fleeting affluence in *A Raw Youth*, to reach finally his apotheosis in the villa of old Karamazov.

His political aspirations were transparent in their direct simplicity, though time has already proved Chestov wrong in saying that all Dostoevsky's prophecies were wide of the mark. Apart from the truly prophetic ring of *The Possessed*, one must not forget the prophecy that there would come a day when Western Europe would turn for sanctuary to Russia. Still, in the sum of things, Dostoevsky was no more a prophet than he was a philosopher. His personality from first to last seems to evade occasionally even the strong searchlight of Chestov, so penetratingly serious under the mask of mockery. Yes, even that searchlight flickers momentarily over his equivocal compatriot. For instance, he appears to claim from Dostoevsky always the expression of self rather than the exposition of character, the eternal subjective instead of that objectivity of which Dostoevsky was just as capable as Zola himself. It is from this special point of view that this critic has found both Zosima and Alyosha pale, whereas, it is submitted, Dostoevsky, as an artist, left them pale deliberately against the dark and terrible background of the brothers Dmitri and Ivan Karamazov. Admittedly, Dostoevsky was no philosopher, yet he read unerringly not the answers but the questions of the human heart, over which the very wisest have fumbled through the centuries.

But what was the inner core of the man himself, that core for which he was always seeking in his imaginative investigations of others? Anna Grigorievna, who gave him the sanctuary of his second marriage, has made no pretence of revealing that.

For her he remained a natural force, admittedly alien from the common herd. She saw that, though he was stronger than the herd in one way, yet in another way he was the most stricken of all. Because of this, she shielded him as best she could from the jars of his outer life, without penetrating the concealed torment within. Doubtless she suspected its existence, but she never associated it with that happy jog-trot of domesticity right under her own eyes, but rather with those too scaldingly realistic scenes, one of which, when read aloud, made her almost faint.

His faithful and courageous daughter, so objective in things outside of that inner core, was undoubtedly anxious to protect her father's memory from what one may call Strakhov eyes, the sort of eyes eager to see in front of them the vengeance of their owners' hearts. Soon after the great writer's death, this critic considered it his duty to write to Tolstoy: "I cannot consider Dostoevsky either a good or a happy man. He was wicked, envious, vicious, and he spent the whole of his life in emotions and irritations which would have made him pitiable, even ridiculous, had he not been so wicked and so intelligent; in Switzerland he treated his servant, in my presence, so abominably that the latter cried out, offended: 'I too am a human being.' . . . Naturally, he more often offended people in order not to be offended by them, but the most terrible thing about it was that he enjoyed it and never acknowledged his villainies to the end." This in itself, apart altogether from the "dark legend," may well account for Tolstoy's change of attitude towards Dostoevsky shortly after his death. It may well account, too, for Turgenev's comment on his dead rival: "the most evil Christian I have ever met in my life."

But, it must be submitted, the whole tone of that letter is vindictive. It is hard to attribute it to the same person who acknowledged the power of Dostoevsky's speech on Pushkin. Obviously, in view of Dostoevsky's known loathing of cruelty, expressed in book after book, the scene described must have been hideously exaggerated or else it must have taken place after one of the novelist's terrible seizures when he became as remote from himself as was Hyde from Jekyll. But, it must be acknowledged, this extraordinary duality extended, even when the novelist was perfectly himself, to his physical appearance. The French critic de Vogüé was not in the least inclined to view him with Strakhov eyes, and he has left impressions of the man both when agitated (but not under the influence of epilepsy) and when perfectly impassive: "His face was that of a Russian peasant—of a real moujik of Moscow, with an animated expression, now gloomy, now mild. His forehead was large, wrinkled and bumpy, his temples hollow as if beaten with a hammer; and all these drawn, convulsed features were drooping over a melancholy mouth. Never have I seen on a human face such an expression of accumulated suffering."

The Frenchman maintained that the crises of Dostoevsky's soul could be read on his body even more clearly than in his Memoirs of the convict prison: "His eyelids, his lips, each muscle of his face, twitched with nervous spasms. Whenever he became excited or angry in dispute over ideas, one could have sworn that one had seen that face before —either on the benches of the criminal court or among those vagabonds whose road leads to the prison gates. At all other moments his face was full of that sad meekness which is characteristic of the old saints painted on the Slavonic ikons. Everything in this man was of the people, with the inexpressible mixture of coarseness, subtlety and sweetness which the Russian peasants so often possess; and a something indefinably troubling, resulting perhaps from the expression of concentrated thought on that mask of a proletarian. At first he often repelled —before his strange personal magnetism began to have effect."

In reality, de Vogüé was as unable as any other human being to arrive at a synthesis of the two Dostoevskys. It is equally certain, among all these uncertainties, that the great novelist himself never arrived at any such synthesis, and that, to the very last, he remained an enigma to himself. And though it is perfectly true that Freud was unable to account for Dostoevsky, it may be equally true that it is only through Freud that a real approach to the great Russian writer is possible. Millions might have led the tortuous and tormented life of Dostoevsky, without a single one of them being able to create his novels. But it is almost impossible to imagine Dostoevsky as the writer of those novels without having led the life that was his. His contradictions, so stoutly defended by that difficult and subtle thinker who revels in the irony of his own simplicity—Léon Chestov—strike at the very roots of his work. He is "vertical," as Janko Lavrin points out, in his imaginative work, but he is excessively "horizontal" in all his political propaganda, so that though the innovators have accepted him as a reality his political dreams have long ago been discarded.

It is those other dreams, both in life and in fiction, that have persistently survived. Before Freud he realised their significance. But what would he have thought if he had realised that one day the famous Viennese psychopathist would claim him as a prey to the Oedipus complex? Freud did actually maintain that Dostoevsky was pursued by remorse for having wished to kill his father. But where is the evidence? In his letter to the doctor, from which I have quoted, there is nothing remotely suggestive of any such unconscious antagonism. In the letter to his brother Michael about his father there is the suggestion of pity rather than of hostility. His father's murder, though, was a terrible shock to him, and, as already noted, was the cause in all probability of his first seizure. It is true that in *A Raw Youth*, as well as in *The Brothers Karamazov*, father and son are rivals in their passion for the same woman. But it is equally true that in *First Love* Turgenev, in a frankly autobiographical work, introduces exactly the same motif. Yet no one in his right mind would fasten that already sufficiently vulgarised complex on to the author of *Fathers and Sons*.

The now familiar terms, complex, libido, regression, fixation and so on, do not appear in Dostoevsky's vocabulary, but the ideas are fully interpreted. Both in his life and in his work he translated the full meaning of the word "introvert" long before Jung. But, both in his letters and in his books, Dostoevsky has given overwhelming proofs of having the extravert's full capacities when required. Whenever he chooses, the Russian can reproduce, with far deeper acidity of registration, the photographic results of Emile Zola's notebook industry.

Long before Adler, Dostoevsky was to stress the craving for power as the real motif in life, as distinct from that of sex. No one has illustrated the inferiority complex more poignantly than the author of *A Raw Youth,* in which, all unconsciously perhaps, the novelist arrived at a real synthesis between Freud's motif of sex and Adler's motif of power, though the germ of this thesis can be detected in many of the earlier works.

Many unoriginal writers have preserved themselves through carefulness and, it must be added in justice, through a certain kinship with the great mass of their fellows. Dostoevsky was original, and separated from the great mass half willingly, half unwillingly. He would have destroyed himself through carelessness had not someone cared for him and brought solace and healing to this over-sensitive creative writer who, at different periods of his life, came very close to the actual state of persecution mania. All through his life, both actual and literary, he was interested in dreams. Undoubtedly, his best dream was that of the diamond lurking in a heap of rubbish, for it brought him the one human being who was able to save him both from and for himself.

Dostoevsky was, after his fashion, a psychiatrist not by right of science but by right of suffering. Of all the novelists on earth, he was perhaps the nearest to being actually a psychopathist because he was so very near to becoming a psychopath. In spite of *The Diary of a Writer,* he had no claim to any special vision of statecraft, but he was a man who realised instinctively the instinctive orientation of his fellow-countrymen. Above all, he was a creator of living characters rather than a preacher. When he did preach it was only to assuage that spiritual thirst of Russians which was his own. He studied his compatriots not as an aloof student of manners and customs, not as a censor and castigator, but, like Gogol before him, as one of themselves. Perhaps *au fond* he delivered no message of finality but only a repeated question. But this question included all the lesser ones that emerged from his novels, his "propaganda," and his correspondence. It seems to have been as much in the heart of Chatov as it was in the heart of Kirilov. Euripides had asked it thousands of years before: Do the gods indeed rule over us or are we the sport of chance?

Indubitably, the great mass of his fellow-countrymen reacted to this supposedly isolated man of genius as to no other writer. In the history of his country, throughout the uncertain flux of time, there would appear to be at least two certainties. One of these is the repetition of destruction; the other is the racial courage of the Russians. The first Dostoevsky detected only too surely in his demons of *The Possessed*. Of Russian courage he was always fully conscious. He interpreted it in his heroes, from the sinless Mishkin to the monstrous Stavroguin. He interpreted it in his heroines, from Sonya to Nastasya. He found it in the palace of the Romanovs; he found it in the convict prison of Omsk. It is peculiarly fitting, then, that his memory and his surviving genius should be cherished even by those for whom his political tenets have become anathema.

CHRONOLOGY

1821. Born in Moscow.
1837. Enters School of Engineering.
1843. Leaves School with rank of Sub-Lieutenant.
1844. Leaves the Army.
1846. Publishes *Poor Folk*.
1849. Arrested.
" Reprieved from the scaffold and sentenced to Siberia.
1850-54. Serves his sentence in the prison at Omsk.
1854. Enrolled as private in the 7th Siberian Regiment of the Line.
1856. Becomes a non-commissioned officer.
" Promoted to be Ensign in the same battalion.
1857. Marries Madame Issayev.
1858. Rights of Hereditary Nobility restored. Leaves the Army.
" Returns to St. Petersburg.
1861. Publishes *Injury and Insult*.
1861-62. Publishes *The House of the Dead*.
1862. Visits the Continent for the first time.
1863. Abroad again.
1864. Death of his wife.
" Death of his brother Michael.
" Death of his friend and collaborator on the "Vremya" and "Epoch," Apollon Grigoryev.
1865. Autumn in Wiesbaden.
1866. Employs Anna Grigorievna Snitkin as his stenographer. Publishes *Crime and Punishment*.

1867. Marriage to A. G. Snitkin.
1867-71. Life on the Continent.
1868. Publishes *The Idiot.*
1870. Publishes *The Eternal Husband.*
1871. Publishes *The Possessed.*
" Returns to St. Petersburg.
1873. Publishes beginning of *The Diary of a Writer.*
1874. Arrested for infraction of Censorship regulations.
1876-77. Continues *The Diary of a Writer.*
1876. Summer at Ems.
" Publishes *A Raw Youth.*
1879-80. Commencement of *The Brothers Karamazov* in the "Russky Viestnik."
1880. Famous speech on Pushkin at the meeting of the Society of Lovers of Russian Letters.
1881. January 28th: at 8.38 p.m., death.
January 31st: public burial in the cemetery of the Alexander Nevsky Monastery at St. Petersburg.

HIS WORKS

Poor Folk
The Landlady, etc.
The Double, etc.
Mr. Prokharchin, etc.
Netotchka Nezvanova
The Friend of the Family
The Little Hero
Uncle's Dream, etc.
Injury and Insult
The House of the Dead
Letters from the Underworld
Crime and Punishment
The Gambler
The Idiot
The Eternal Husband
The Possessed
The Diary of a Writer
A Raw Youth
A Gentle Spirit, etc.
The Brothers Karamazov

AUTHOR'S NOTE

IN ADDITION to the Vizetelly translations and those by Constance Garnett, the author is indebted to the following works:

Correspondance de Dostoievsky. Traduit de russe par J. W. Bienstock. (Paris: Société du Mercure de France.)
Dostoievsky. By Dmitri Merejkowski. (Constable.)
La Psychologie des Romanciers russes du XIX Siècle. Par Ossip Lourié. (Paris: Alcun.)
Journal d'un Ecrivain. Traduit du russe par J. W. Bienstock et J. A. Nau. (Paris: Bibliothèque Charpentier.)
The Sisters Rajevsky. By Serge Kovalevsky. (Unwin.)
The Diary of Dostoyevsky's Wife. Edited by René Fülöp-Miller and Dr. Fr. Eckstein. Translated from the German edition by Madge Pemberton. (Gollancz.)
Fyodor Dostoyevsky: A Study. By Aimée Dostoyevsky. (Heinemann.)
The Letters of Dostoyevsky to his Wife. Translated from the Russian by Elizabeth Hill and Doris Mudie. (Constable.)
Dostoievsky: His Life and Literary Activity. By Evgenii Soloviev. Translated from the Russian by C. J. Hogarth. (Unwin.)
Les Révélations de la Mort Dostoïevsky—Tolstoi. Par Léon Chestov. (Paris: Plon-Nourrit.)
Dostoevsky. The Man and his Work. By Julius Meier-Graefe. Translated by Herbert H. Marks. (Routledge.)
La Vie et l'Œuvre de Dostoïevsky. Par Serge Persky. (Paris: Payot.)

AUTHOR'S NOTE

Dostoevsky and his Creation: A Psycho-critical Study. By Janko Lavrin. (Collins.)

Letters of Fyodor Michailovitch Dostoevsky to his Family and Friends. Translated from the German by Ethel Colburn Mayne. (Chatto and Windus.)

Dostoevsky. By André Gide. Translated from the French. (London: Dent).

F. M. Dostoevsky: Stavrogin's Confession, etc. Translated by S. S. Koteliansky and Virginia Woolf. (Hogarth Press.)

Dostoevsky: A Study. By Janko Lavrin. (Methuen.)

New Dostoevsky Letters. Translated by S. S. Koteliansky. (The Mandrake Press.)

INDEX

[A]
Achilles, 32
Adler, 20, 247, 310, 311
Aeschylus, 205
Aksakov, 237, 294
Alexander II, 71, 266
Alexander III, 214, 237, 265
Ambrosius, *Staretz*, 233, 272
Anna Karenina, 106, 210
Aeneid, 180
Aphrodite, 33
[B]
Baden-Baden, 78, 132, 142, 143, 145, 146, 149
Bakunin, Michael, 207
Balzac, 3, 18, 21, 205, 245
Bergson, Henri, 118
Berlin, 131
Bible, The, 35, 42, 61
Bielinsky, 24, 28, 29, 30, 34, 40, 129, 164, 183, 208
Boccaccio, 250
Bovary, Mme., 207
Bosphorus, The, 172
Brown, Martha, 232
Brückner, Dr. A., 98
Byron, 22, 216
Byzantium, 117, 304
[C]
Caligula, 50
Carlyle, Thomas, 33, 129
Catherine Kornilov, The Case of, 299
Cesarevna, The, 213
Cézanne, Paul, 120
Chateaubriand, 20
Chekov, 276

Chestov, Léon, 87, 88, 89, 186, 309
Comédie Humaine, La, 128, 157, 205, 289
Constantine, Emperor, 172
Constantine, Grand Duke, 213
Constantinople, 264
Copenhagen, 98
Corinne, 1, 2, 3
Corneille, 3, 22
Crime and Punishment, 21, 33, 61, 90, 98, 101 et seq., 149 et seq., 170, 185, 193 et seq., 235, 253, 255, 272, 280, 299, 305

[D]
Danilevsky, 166
Darovoye, 6
Daudet, Alphonse, 241, 242
Dead Souls, 1, 115
Decembrists, 52
Delacroix, 115
Denmark, 76
Diary of a Writer, The, 165, 229, 235, 263, 311
Dickens, Charles, 26, 171, 204, 212, 241, 242, 245, 263
Diodorus, 10
Don Quixote, 264
Dostoevsky, Aimée, (daughter) 4, 14, 81, 105, 218, 229, 231 et seq., 263 et seq., 271, 272, 305
Dostoevsky, Alexandra, (sister) 185
Dostoevsky, Alexey (infant son) 233

Dostoevsky, André Mihaïl, (brother) 11, 14, 15
Dostoevsky, Anna Grigorievna, (second wife, née Snitkin) 4, 91 et seq., 120 et seq., 135 et seq., 149 et seq., 181 et seq., 227 et seq., 259 et seq., 303 et seq.
Dostoevsky, Barbara, (sister) 14, 15
Dostoevsky, Emilia, (Michael's widow) 92, 154
Dostoevsky, Maria D., (widow of A. I. Issayev, first wife) 67, 70 et seq., 81 et seq., 232
Dostoevsky, Michael, (brother) 12, 15 et seq., 25, 41, 42, 45, 48 et seq., 54, 62, 76, 90 et seq., 183, 208, 234, 243
Dostoevsky, Mikhail Dr., (father) 4 et seq., 12 et seq.
Dostoevsky, Nicolaï, (brother) 14, 96, 185
Dostoevsky, Sofia, (niece) 154, 165 et seq., 178
Dostoevsky, Sonya, (infant daughter) 152, 175, 233
Dostoevsky, Vera, (sister) 35, 302
Dostoevsky, Varya, (sister) 35
Double, The, 3, 31, 89, 101, 115, 253, 278
Dresden, 95, 131 et seq., 155, 166 et seq., 184, 241
Durov, Sergey F., 38, 40, 47, 49, 64 et seq.

[E]

Egypt, 32
El Greco, 115
Eliot, George, 241, 242
Elle et Lui, 77
Ems, 238, 239, 257, 258, 266 et seq.
Engineering, School of, 11, 15, 17, 51, 68, 243

Epanchin, Adelaida, 163
Epanchin, Aglaya, 159, 162
"Epoch", 81, 90, 93, 127, 219, 303
Eternal Husband, The, 170 et seq., 246
Euclid, 164
Eugénie Grandet, 18, 68, 87, 243, 301, 303
Euripides, 33, 312

[F]

Falstaff, 85, 277
Fathers and Sons, 183, 186, 310
Faust, 98
Faust, 282
Feeble Soul, A, 222
Feuillet, Octave, 157
Fisher, Lord, 301
Flaubert, 20, 22, 33, 37, 50, 207
Flavius, 10
Florence, 154, 164, et seq.
Fourier, 38
France, 180
France, Anatole, 68
Franco-German War, 180
Frankfort, 182
Frederick the Great, 33
French Revolution, The, 38
Freud, 12, 20, 32, 125, 192, 247, 309 et seq.

[G]

Gambler, The, 28, 76 et seq., 127, 137 et seq., 151, 170, 245, 246, 302, 305
Gautier, Théophile, 50
Geneva, 76, 150, 152, 153
Gentle Spirit, A, 170, 248, 265, 290
Germans, The, 105 et seq., 133, 134, 217
Germany, 76

INDEX

Ghosts, 80
Gide, André, 26, 36, 67, 107, 198 et seq.. 242, 253, 260, 261, 295
Gil Blas, 265
Goethe, 1, 33, 264
Gogol, 1, 2, 40, 44, 115, 312
Goliadkin, 31, 32, 115, 119
Goncharov, 131, 144, 169, 179, 265
Grave, General de, 66
"Grazhdanin", 235, 237, 264
Grigorovitch, D. V., 2, 11, 23, 27, 68, 293
Grigoryev, Apollon, 97, 219, 226
Griswold, Rufus, 129
Gros, 115

[H]

Hamlet, 99
Hegel, 10, 69
Heine, 33
Herodotus, 10
Herzen, Alexander, 30, 84
Hindus, Maurice, 106
Homais, M., 20
Homburg, 137 et seq., 177
Homer, 22
House of the Dead, The, 53 et seq., 87, 89, 118, 123, 149, 150, 164, 204, 212, 244, 297, 305
Hugo, Victor, 22, 156, 163, 245
Huxley, Thomas, 85

[I]

Ibsen, 245, 276
Idiot, The, 21, 48, 85, 120, 153 et seq., 166, 185, 231, 232, 278, 279, 305
Illiad, The, 277
Illium, 33
Ilmen, Lake, 225

Injury and Insult, 80, 115, 215, 220
Issai Fomitch, (convict) 59, 60
Issayev, Captain A. I., 67
Issayev, Paul, 70, 71, 92, 95, 96, 138, 153, 185, 214, 228 et seq.
Ivanova, Mme., 62

[J]

Jerebajtnikov, Lieut., 58
Jung, 20, 310

[K]

Kant, 10, 88, 223, 250
Karamazov, The Brothers, 21, 28 et seq., 88, 114, 137, 164, 170, 178, 207 et seq., 246, 255, 265, 275 et seq., 290, 301
Karamzin, 5
Kachpirev, (editor) 169
Katkov, (publisher) 131, 135, 144, 147, 151, 168, 206, 210, 273 et seq., 292
Komarovich, V., 206
Koran, 10
Kovalevsky, Sophie, 39, 45, 125 et seq., 202, 272
Kraevsky, (publisher) 25, 31, 51
Krivzov, Major, 53, 58, 66
Kumanin, Mme., (aunt) 87, 127, 235, 261
Kusnezk, 70, 75
Kutuzov, 1

[L]

Landlady, The, 31, 166, 170
Lavrin, Janko, 31, 192, 230, 309
Lermontov, 294
Lesage, 1
Letters from the Underworld, 87 et seq., 164, 305

Levin, 106
Lisa, 89
Little Hero, The, 42, 195, 244
Lombroso, 102
London, 76, 150
Luther, 33
Luzhin, 114
Lyubimov, Professor N. A., 274, 292, 301

[M]

Macaulay, 249
Macbeth, 102
Maĭkov, Apollon N., 49, 62, 130 et seq., 150, 152, 163, 164, 168, 235
Marei, 8, 9, 142, 243
Marmeladov, 104, 112
Marmeladov, Sonya, 3, 36, 104 et seq., 116, 157, 198, 312
Martyanov, P. K., 64, 65
Maupassant, 122
Meier-Graefe, Julius, 87, 102, 115, 180, 200
Mephistopheles, 278, 282
Merejkovsky, 42
Meschersky, (publisher) 236
Milan, 154
Milyukov, A. P., 48
Miserables, Les, 105
Miskin, Prince, 48, 155 et seq., 202, 257, 312
Moscow, 8, 90, 197, 273, 291, 293, 296
Mother Russia, 106
Munich, 67

[N]

Nabokov, Commandant, 49
Naples, 86
Napoleon, 1, 81
Nastasya, 158, 231, 255, 279, 312
Necker, 1
Nekrassov, 2, 24, 34, 241 et seq.

Nero, 50
Netchaiev, Case of, 176, 189
Netotchka Nezvanova, 31, 38, 85, 248
Nicolas I, 214
Nietzsche, 33, 88 et seq.. 187
Novikov, Madame, 292

[O]

Oblomov, 131, 145
Odoevsky, Prince, 25
Oeidipus, 277
Ogarev, 30
Omsk, 51, 61 et seq., 87, 91, 212, 219, 244, 294, 297, 312
Optina Pustin, Monastery of, 232, 233, 273
Orth, Dr., 239, 260, 266, 275
Ostrovsky, 2
Otchestvennia, Zapiski, 18, 240, 257

[P]

Panaiev, 25
Panaiev-Golovachev, Mme., 27
Paradise Lost, 180
Pariš, 76, 167, 180, 256
Père, Goriot, Le, 157
Perov, Vasily G., (painter) 233
Persky, Serge, 305
Petersburg, 11, 19, 23, 51, 54 et seq., 127 et seq., 175, 184, 210, 227 et seq., 265, 266, 292, 302
"Petersburg Almanac", 34
Petrachevsky, 4, 38, 46, 70, 207
Petropavlovsky, Fortress of, 40, 195, 209, 244
Pissaren, 10
Plato, 88, 90
Plestcheev, 47
Pliny, 10
Plutarch, 10
Pobedonostsev, Constantin P., 15, 237, 265

Poe, Edgar Allan, 68, 128, 269
Poland, 210
Polyakov, 211
Poor Folk, 12, 23 et seq., 67, 68, 75, 105, 121, 123, 243, 296
Porphyry Petrovitch, 103, 104, 109, 110 et seq., 248
Possessed, The, 21, 82, 100, 170 et seq., 225, 235, 246, 290, 306, 312
Pushkin, 2, 22 et seq., 106, 156, 216, 225, 263, 265, 291 et seq.

[R]
Racine, 22
Raskolnikov, Rodion, 3, 32, 36, 87 et seq., 99 et seq., 150, 158, 175, 176, 193, 198, 200, 248
Raw Youth, A., 236 et seq., 246 et seq., 280, 290, 306, 311
Rembrandt, 115
Resurrection, 105
Retz, Gilles de, 36
Revel, 41
Revisor, 1
Richter, Jean Paul, 33
Riesenkampf, 17
Rogozhin, Parfen, 158, 160, 161, 162, 256
Rome, 76, 86, 253
Rozanov, Vasily, 78, 232
"Russky Viestnik", 13, 98, 99, 153, 165, 178 et seq., 292

[S]
Sade, Marquis de, 118, 192, 200
Saint Francis of Assisi, 290
Sainte-Beuve, 21
Salavin, 32
Sand, George, 11, 38, 77
Saveliev, M., 11
Saxon-les-Bains, 150

Schiller, 1, 22, 263, 264, 277, 287
Schopenhauer, 33, 99
Scott, Walter, 9, 263, 264
Semipalatinsk, 61 et seq.
Semyonovski Square, 45, 62, 79, 120, 244
Shakespeare, 43, 99, 207, 222
Siberia, 8, 17, 29, 50 et seq., 110 et seq., 171, 217
Siminov, Dr., 238
Slavs, The, 217
Smekalov, (Official in Siberia) 58
Smoke, 2, 26, 28, 131 et seq., 297, 301
Society of the Lovers of Russian Letters, 259, 294, 301
Soloviev, E., 4, 7, 9, 27, 30, 43, 117
Soloviev, Vladimir, 233 et seq., 292
Sophocles, 192, 245
Sovremennik, 34
Spiridonov, (Military Governor) 66
Staël, Madame de, 1, 2, 3, 156, 296
Staraya Russa, 224 et seq., 260, 263, 296
Stavroguin, 36, 180 et seq., 252, 255, 312
Stelovsky, (publisher) 98, 120, 123, 209, 227
Stendhal, 33
Stepanchikovo Village, 80
Stepanov, Captain, 63
Strakhov, Nicolas, 29, 79, 85, 155, 166, 179 et seq., 293, 307
Strindberg, 269
Suchard, M., 9, 243
Suslova, A. P. (Pauline), 76 et seq., 123 et seq., 230 et seq.

INDEX

Svidrigailov, 36, 112 et seq., 201, 252
Switzerland, 166, 194, 238

[T]

Tacitus, 1, 10
Talleyrand, 203
Tarass Bulba, 1
Tchermak, 9, 243
Tchermashnia, 6, 14
Tcherniaev, General, 265
Thucydides, 10
Tiberius, 50
Tobolsk, 52
Todleben, 73
Tolstoy, Count Leo, 2, 20, 35, 42, 100, 105, 128, 179 et seq., 216, 245 et seq., 279 et seq.
Tolstoy, Countess Leo, 219
Trojan War, 33
Troy, Helen of, 33
Tula, 7
Turgenev, Ivan, 2, 18, 28 et seq., 100, 128, 129, 154, 169 et seq., 180, 216, 242 et seq., 293 et seq., 310
Tver, 76
Twins, The, 31

[U]

Uncle's Dream, 80, 253
Ural, 52

[V]

Van Gogh, 115
Venice, 167, 253
Vergunov, 75
Versilov, 32, 247 et seq.
Vevey, 153, 154
Vienna, 167
Vogüé, Vicomte de, 308, 309
Vrangel, Baron Alexander, 62 et seq., 98, 173
"Vremya", 76 et seq., 219

[W]

War and Peace, 106, 107, 210, 216, 298, 301
Weissmann, (dealer) 144, 227
Wiesbaden, 77 et seq., 123, 183, 231, 261

[Z]

Zagoski, O., 18
Zarathustra, 87, 99
"Zarya", 166, 168
Zola, Emile, 156, 195, 265, 298, 306, 310
Zosima, *Staretz*, 19, 206, 232 et seq., 272 et seq., 306

[W]

Wallace, Mackenzie, 214